Insect Photoperiodism

INSECT

ACADEMIC PRESS

PHOTOPERIODISM

Stanley D. Beck

DEPARTMENT OF ENTOMOLOGY
UNIVERSITY OF WISCONSIN
MADISON, WISCONSIN

NEW YORK And LONDON   *1968*

ACADEMIC PRESS INC.
111 Fifth Avenue, New York, New York 10003

United Kingdom Edition published by
ACADEMIC PRESS INC. (LONDON) LTD.
Berkeley Square House, London W.1

LIBRARY OF CONGRESS CATALOG CARD NUMBER: 68-16514

PRINTED IN THE UNITED STATES OF AMERICA

Preface

Biological rhythms, biological clocks, and the biological effects of daylength constitute the subject matter of photoperiodism. As a field of scientific inquiry, photoperiodism has shown a meteoric growth during the past decade. There are several reasons for the increasing interest in this area of biology. The natural rhythm of daylight and darkness provides a link between the organism and its environment. And through this link, environmental information is communicated to the living system. The daily photoperiod supplies the temporal signals needed for the synchronization of internal functions and some of the information required for coping with the exigencies of the outside world. The ability to detect photoperiodic stimuli and to respond to them in adaptive ways has enabled organisms to exploit environments and ecological niches that would otherwise remain inaccessible. The responses of organisms to photoperiod have been found to play essential roles in phenomena as diverse as geographical distribution and the programming of developmental patterns. Modern interest in biological periodism ranges from investigations of the effects of space travel on the human system to studies of the temporal organization of single cells.

A large body of published research has accumulated on the different aspects of the general subject of photoperiodism and on the specific photoperiodic responses of major plant and animal groups. Because of their great biological importance and their widespread use as experimental animals, insects have figured prominently in research on photoperiodism. Photoperiodism has been found to be of significance in many aspects of insect biology, and there has been a need for a gathering-together of available information so that the current state of the field might be assessed and some of the unifying principles developed.

This work has been organized in such a way that basic terms and concepts are introduced and developed in the early chapters; the later chapters are devoted to the more complex aspects of photoperiodism. This method of presentation was adopted so that the volume might be a useful reference for the student and nonspecialist, as well as a technical monograph addressed to the specialist in photoperiodism. Although every effort has been made to consider all aspects of insect photoperiodism, there has been no attempt to cite every known publication touching on the subject. The several aspects of insect photoperiodism are reviewed in detail, but with emphasis on the concepts that serve to place the subject in a meaningful relationship to the whole of modern biology.

October, 1967

STANLEY D. BECK

Contents

viii

1 □ Introduction to Photoperiodism

From its earliest molecular origins, life on earth has evolved in the presence of a daily cycle of daylight and darkness. This environmental rhythm of recurring alternation of illumination and darkness is the earth's natural *photoperiod*. Photoperiod has played an extremely important role in biological history; virtually every major group of organisms has evolved the ability to utilize the daily cycle and seasonal progressions of daylength as sources of environmental information. The geographical distribution, seasonal biology, growth, form, metabolism, and behavior of animal organisms are profoundly influenced by the diel rhythm of photoperiod. The effects of photoperiod on the organisms have to do not only with bioclimatic adaptations, but also with the temporal organization of the internal processes that characterize the living system. The diverse ways by which organisms are influenced by photoperiod are the subject matter of the biological field known as *photoperiodism*.

Biological phenomena such as photosynthesis and phototaxis are reactions to light energy, and cease immediately upon a cessation of illumination. A day-to-day rhythmicity is apparent in such reactions, because the environmental photoperiod provides a rhythmic input of light energy. The nocturnal or diurnal habits of some animals could conceivably involve only such direct responses to the presence or absence of light energy. Photoperiodism has been found to involve much more than this, however. In nearly all cases, photoperiodic responses of insects and other animals have been shown to be based on the effects of the environmental photoperiodic rhythm on internal biological rhythmic processes. It is apparent, therefore, that photoperiodism is primarily

1

an aspect of the more general subject of biological periodism, and only secondarily the responses of organisms to photostimuli *per se.* The evidence in support of this generalization will be considered in subsequent chapters, but its importance as a principle should not be overlooked in even a preliminary consideration of the subject.

Time concepts are involved in the subject of photoperiodism. Rhythmic processes that are integral parts of the functional organization of the animal (*endogenous rhythms*) are influenced in respect to their time relationships by the *exogenous rhythm* of the environmental cycle of daylight and darkness. The influence of the photoperiod is most frequently in the form of time-dependent stimuli—the beginning of daylight and the beginning of night—rather than in the form of a continuing input of light energy. And this characteristic distinguishes photoperiodic responses from the more direct responses of the organism to environmental factors such as temperature, moisture, and light.

In much of the published literature on photoperiodism, the term "photoperiod" is used ambiguously, in that it is used to denote the entire cycle of illumination and darkness and also to denote only the lighted portion of the cycle. In order to avoid such ambiguity, we will use the term *photoperiod* only in the sense of defining a cycle consisting of a period of illumination followed by a period of relative darkness. The daylight portion of the photoperiod will be referred to as the *photophase*, and the dark portion will be termed the *scotophase*. The term *daylength* is generally synonymous with photophase, but will be used in this volume only in reference to the photophases of natural 24-hour (*diel*) photoperiods.

Photoperiod as a Geophysical Pattern

The basic diel period of 24 hours is caused, of course, by the simple fact that the earth rotates at the rate of one revolution per 24 hours. If the earth's polar axis were precisely perpendicular to the plane of the earth's orbit about the sun, the photoperiod would consist of 12 hours of daylight and 12 hours of night everywhere on earth and throughout the entire year. But the earth's axis is at an angle of 23.5°, and this results in seasonal changes of daylength. These seasonal changes form a photoperiodic pattern over the surface of the globe, so that the daylength at any given geographical point is determined by the latitude of that point and the date of observation.

Daylength, in the strict sense, is measured as the number of hours and minutes elapsing between sunrise and sunset. Daylength values for different northern latitudes and different times of the year are presented in Table I. These daylengths were compiled for the first year after leap year, but only very small errors will attend their use in other years. The daylengths are based on the times of appearance (sunrise) and disappearance (sunset) of the upper limb of the sun at an unobstructed sea level horizon. Except possibly at very high latitudes (well above 70°) at times near the solstices, the observation point's altitude above sea level

TABLE I

Daylengths (Sunrise to Sunset) and
Twilight Periods for Northern Hemisphere Latitudes[a]

Lat. (°N)	Daylength (hr)(min)		Twilights		Daylength (hr)(min)		Twilights	
			Civil (hr)(min)	Nautical (hr)(min)			Civil (hr)(min)	Nautical (hr)(min)
	January 1				January 15			
0	12	8	0 22	0 48	12	8	0 22	0 48
10	11	34	0 23	0 49	11	36	0 23	0 48
20	10	58	0 24	0 51	11	32	0 24	0 51
30	10	16	0 26	0 56	10	25	0 26	0 55
35	9	52	0 28	1 00	10	2	0 28	0 59
40	9	24	0 31	1 5	9	37	0 30	1 3
45	8	52	0 34	1 11	9	08	0 33	1 9
50	8	12	0 38	1 19	8	31	0 37	1 17
55	7	19	0 45	1 32	7	44	0 43	1 30
60	6	04	0 57	1 53	6	40	0 53	1 48
65	3	53	1 24	2 36	4	54	1 14	2 21
70	0	00	— —	— —	0	0	— —	— —
	February 1				February 15			
0	12	7	0 22	0 47	12	7	0 21	0 45
10	11	43	0 22	0 47	11	49	0 22	0 47
20	11	17	0 23	0 49	11	31	0 23	0 49
30	10	46	0 25	0 54	11	10	0 25	0 53
35	10	30	0 26	0 56	10	58	0 26	0 56
40	10	10	0 28	1 1	10	45	0 28	0 59
45	9	48	0 31	1 6	10	29	0 30	1 5
50	9	20	0 35	1 14	10	11	0 33	1 11
55	8	46	0 40	1 24	9	48	0 37	1 20
60	8	0	0 47	1 38	9	17	0 44	1 32
65	6	52	0 59	2 2	8	35	0 53	1 51
70	4	56	1 26	2 44	7	30	1 9	2 20

[a]Compiled from U.S. Naval Observatory data.

(Continued)

3

TABLE I *(Continued)*

Lat. (°N)	Daylength (hr)(min)	Twilights Civil (hr)(min)		Nautical (hr)(min)		Daylength (hr)(min)		Twilights Civil (hr)(min)		Nautical (hr)(min)	
		March 1						March 15			
0	12 7	0	21	0	45	12	6	0	21	0	45
10	11 55	0	22	0	46	12	4	0	21	0	45
20	11 44	0	22	0	48	12	1	0	22	0	48
30	11 31	0	24	0	51	11	58	0	24	0	51
35	11 24	0	25	0	55	11	56	0	26	0	54
40	11 15	0	27	0	59	11	55	0	27	0	58
45	11 6	0	29	1	3	11	53	0	29	1	3
50	10 54	0	33	1	10	11	51	0	32	1	10
55	10 41	0	37	1	18	11	47	0	36	1	19
60	10 22	0	42	1	30	11	44	0	41	1	30
65	9 57	0	50	1	47	11	39	0	49	1	49
70	9 21	1	2	2	13	11	33	1	1	2	15
		April 1						April 15			
0	12 7	0	21	0	45	12	7	0	21	0	45
10	12 13	0	22	0	46	12	20	0	22	0	47
20	12 22	0	22	0	48	12	35	0	23	0	49
30	12 30	0	24	0	52	12	51	0	25	0	54
35	12 36	0	25	0	56	13	2	0	26	0	57
40	12 42	0	27	1	0	13	13	0	28	1	1
45	12 50	0	29	1	5	13	26	0	31	1	7
50	12 59	0	33	1	13	13	42	0	34	1	16
55	13 8	0	38	1	22	14	2	0	38	1	28
60	13 23	0	43	1	36	14	28	0	46	1	47
65	13 38	0	54	2	2	15	3	0	58	2	57
70	14 10	1	7	2	47	16	0	1	20	—	—
		May 1						May 15			
0	12 6	0	22	0	47	12	7	0	22	0	47
10	12 30	0	22	0	47	12	35	0	22	0	48
20	12 54	0	23	0	50	13	4	0	24	0	52
30	13 21	0	25	0	56	13	39	0	26	0	57
35	13 37	0	27	1	0	13	59	0	28	1	2
40	13 56	0	29	1	6	14	21	0	31	1	8
45	14 18	0	33	1	13	14	49	0	34	1	17
50	14 45	0	37	1	24	15	22	0	39	1	31
55	15 19	0	43	1	43	16	15	0	48	1	53
60	16 4	0	54	2	20	17	4	1	3	—	—
65	17 11	1	17	—	—	18	37	—	—	—	—
70	19 6	—	—	—	—	22	12	—	—	—	—

TABLE I *(Continued)*

Lat. (°N)	Daylength (hr)(min)	Twilights Civil (hr)(min)		Nautical (hr)(min)		Daylength (hr)(min)	Twilights Civil (hr)(min)		Nautical (hr)(min)	
		June 1					June 15			
0	12 7	0 22		0 49		12 7	0 23		0 49	
10	12 40	0 23		0 50		12 43	0 23		0 50	
20	13 16	0 24		0 53		13 21	0 24		0 54	
30	13 57	0 27		1 0		14 05	0 27		1 0	
35	14 14	0 28		1 9		14 30	0 29		1 6	
40	14 50	0 32		1 12		15 1	0 33		1 14	
45	15 22	0 37		1 24		15 36	0 38		1 27	
50	16 04	0 43		1 43		16 21	0 44		1 50	
55	16 59	0 55		— —		17 21	0 59		— —	
60	18 17	1 24		— —		18 50	1 44		— —	
65	20 48	— —		— —		24 0	— —		— —	
70	24 0	— —		— —		24 0	— —		— —	
		July 1					July 15			
0	12 7	0 22		0 49		12 8	0 22		0 48	
10	12 42	0 23		0 50		12 40	0 22		0 49	
20	13 19	0 24		0 54		13 14	0 24		0 52	
30	14 3	0 27		1 1		13 53	0 27		0 59	
35	14 29	0 29		1 6		14 16	0 29		1 5	
40	14 58	0 33		1 15		14 43	0 32		1 12	
45	15 33	0 37		1 27		15 15	0 36		1 22	
50	16 17	0 45		1 49		15 55	0 42		1 40	
55	17 17	0 57		— —		16 47	0 52		2 24	
60	18 43	1 39		— —		18 1	1 17		— —	
65	22 6	— —		— —		20 14	— —		— —	
70	24 0	— —		— —		24 0	— —		— —	
		August 1					August 15			
0	12 7	0 22		0 47		12 7	0 21		0 46	
10	12 34	0 22		0 48		12 27	0 22		0 47	
20	13 3	0 24		0 51		12 49	0 23		0 50	
30	13 36	0 26		0 57		13 14	0 25		0 55	
35	13 56	0 28		1 2		13 29	0 27		0 59	
40	14 18	0 31		1 8		13 46	0 29		1 4	
45	14 44	0 34		1 17		14 6	0 32		1 11	
50	15 17	0 39		1 30		14 30	0 36		1 21	
55	15 59	0 47		1 55		15 1	0 42		1 37	
60	16 57	1 0		— —		15 41	0 51		2 7	
65	18 25	— —		— —		16 40	1 10		— —	
70	21 36	— —		— —		18 15	— —		— —	

(Continued)

TABLE I *(Continued)*

Lat. (°N)	Daylength (hr)(min)		Twilights				Daylength (hr)(min)		Twilights			
			Civil (hr)(min)		Nautical (hr)(min)				Civil (hr)(min)		Nautical (hr)(min)	
			September 1						September 15			
0	12	7	0	21	0	45	12	7	0	21	0	45
10	12	18	0	21	0	46	12	11	0	21	0	46
20	12	31	0	22	0	48	12	17	0	22	0	48
30	12	45	0	24	0	52	12	23	0	24	0	52
35	12	53	0	26	0	56	12	27	0	25	0	55
40	13	3	0	27	1	0	12	31	0	27	1	0
45	13	13	0	30	1	6	12	36	0	30	1	5
50	13	29	0	34	1	13	12	42	0	33	1	12
55	13	44	0	38	1	25	12	50	0	37	1	21
60	14	5	0	44	1	43	13	0	0	42	1	35
65	14	35	0	55	2	14	13	14	0	51	1	56
70	15	21	1	14	—	—	13	35	1	4	2	34
			October 1						October 15			
0	12	7	0	21	0	45	12	6	0	21	0	45
10	12	1	0	21	0	46	11	46	0	21	0	45
20	11	57	0	22	0	47	11	44	0	22	0	47
30	11	51	0	24	0	51	11	30	0	24	0	52
35	11	48	0	25	0	55	11	22	0	25	0	55
40	11	44	0	27	0	59	11	14	0	27	0	58
45	11	41	0	29	1	3	11	4	0	29	1	3
50	11	38	0	32	1	10	10	51	0	33	1	10
55	11	31	0	36	1	18	10	37	0	37	1	19
60	11	24	0	41	1	30	10	19	0	42	1	30
65	11	11	0	50	1	49	9	53	0	51	1	47
70	11	0	1	0	2	13	9	15	1	2	2	13
			November 1						November 15			
0	12	7	0	21	0	46	12	7	0	22	0	48
10	11	47	0	21	0	46	11	40	0	22	0	48
20	11	25	0	22	0	48	11	11	0	23	0	50
30	10	59	0	25	0	53	10	39	0	25	0	54
35	10	45	0	26	0	56	10	19	0	27	0	58
40	10	29	0	28	1	0	9	57	0	29	1	2
45	10	11	0	30	1	5	9	32	0	32	1	7
50	9	48	0	34	1	12	9	1	0	36	1	15
55	9	20	0	39	1	21	8	21	0	41	1	25
60	8	43	0	45	1	35	7	29	0	49	1	41
65	7	50	0	56	1	54	6	9	1	4	2	8
70	6	27	1	14	2	28	3	39	1	40	3	3

TABLE I *(Continued)*

Lat. (°N)	Daylength (hr)(min)	Twilights			Daylength (hr)(min)	Twilights		
		Civil (hr)(min)		Nautical (hr)(min)		Civil (hr)(min)		Nautical (hr)(min)
		December 1				December 15		
0	12 8	0 22		0 48	12 7	0 23		0 49
10	11 38	0 22		0 48	11 33	0 23		0 49
20	11 0	0 24		0 51	10 56	0 24		0 52
30	10 22	0 26		0 55	10 13	0 26		0 56
35	9 59	0 28		0 59	9 49	0 28		1 0
40	9 34	0 30		1 3	9 21	0 31		1 5
45	9 2	0 33		1 10	8 47	0 34		1 11
50	8 25	0 38		1 18	8 7	0 38		1 20
55	7 37	0 43		1 30	7 12	0 45		1 34
60	6 29	0 54		1 48	5 55	0 58		1 54
65	5 6	1 2		2 11	3 35	1 28		2 41
70	0 0	— —		— —	0 0	— —		— —

will introduce no appreciable errors. The errors introduced by both time within the leap-year cycle and the altitude of the observer may be considered of negligible biological significance.

From the standpoint of photoperiodism, daylengths can seldom be taken as strictly sunrise to sunset times, because organisms may respond to the weaker light intensities of twilight. The importance of twilight will vary among species, depending upon their individual light-intensity response thresholds. Twilights are divided into three types, depending upon the angle of the upper limb of the sun below the horizon. *Civil twilight* is defined as the time required for the upper limb of the sun to traverse an arc from the horizon to a point lying 6° below the horizon. *Nautical twilight* is the time required for the sun's upper limb to travel from the horizon to a point 12° below the horizon. *Astronomical twilight* involves an 18° angle between sun and horizon. Astronomical twilight is of little or no pertinence to photoperiodism, because the light intensities are extremely low—well below any known response level. Both civil and nautical twilights may be of importance, however, and these twilight values are also given in Table I. It should be noted that the twilight times listed are for but one of the two daily twilight periods. If daylength is to be corrected for both morning and evening twilights, the total twilight correction would be twice the figure shown in the table.

The duration of the twilight periods varies with both latitude and season, because the time required for the sun to reach a defined point

7

below the horizon depends on the angle of the sun's path relative to the horizon. Although twilight is defined in terms of the sun's angle below the horizon, its photoperiodic importance is in terms of the attending change of light intensity. Assuming that one knows the approximate light-intensity response thresholds associated with the photoperiodic responses of a given experimental animal, the problem is then to determine what portion of the twilight periods should be added to the astronomical daylength in order to obtain the biological daylength. Nielsen (1961) proposed that the period of civil twilight be designated as a time unit called a *crep* (derived from *crepusculum*). The number of minutes constituting a crep would, of course, vary with both latitude and season. The use of such a twilight time unit provides the biologist with a basis for calculating twilight corrections to daylength. Light intensity measurements at the moment of sunset have shown that an unobstructed horizontal plane will be illuminated by an incident light intensity of 395 lux. The presence of clouds, shade, or adjacent reflective surfaces will introduce measurement errors. Under such ideally defined conditions, the light intensity will have fallen to 3.55 lux at the end of civil twilight. One crep unit can be defined as the time required to effect this change in illumination. To express twilight times in terms of creps, one needs to know the duration of civil twilight and the local times of sunrise and sunset. Creps may then be calculated by the formulas:

$$\text{evening creps} = \frac{\text{time of day} - \text{time of sunset}}{\text{duration of civil twilight}}$$

$$\text{morning creps} = \frac{\text{time of sunrise} - \text{time of day}}{\text{duration of civil twilight}}$$

If, for example, sunset time is 1800 (6 P.M.), and twilight is 30 minutes, the time of day represented by 1900 (7 P.M.) will be 2.0 creps.

The relationship between creps and twilight illumination (log lux) is shown in Fig. 1. This curve was plotted from the extensive twilight illumination data published by Nielsen (1963). The plotted data deal with twilight light intensities for latitudes between 25° and 40° N; for latitudes of 45° and higher, corrections must be applied to the illumination values at 2 or more creps. These corrections are listed in Table II, as applicable to twilights occurring during the months of May, June, July, and August.

In the above paragraphs, light intensity was expressed in terms of an arbitrary unit, the *lux*. One lux is the illuminance of a surface receiving one lumen per square meter. A lux is equivalent to 0.093 *foot-candles*

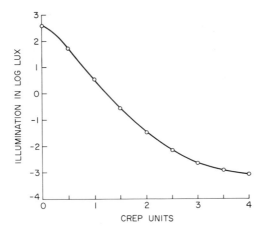

Fig. 1. Relationship between creps and illumination intensity (log lux). [Based on data of Nielsen (1963).]

(ft-c). Both lux and foot-candles are units of measurement that are based on the spectral sensitivity of the human eye, rather than on units of physical energy. The only point of direct interchangeability between light expressed as lux and light energy expressed as ergs per unit surface is at a wavelength of 555 mμ, at which point 1 lux = 4 ergs/cm^2/second. There are obvious disadvantages to the use of luminosity units based on human vision, and more meaningful results would be obtained if the visual spectra of experimental organisms were known and were

TABLE II

Seasonal and Latitude Corrections for Twilight
Illumination Values (Log Lux; All Corrections Additive)[a]

Latitude	Creps	May	June	July	August
45°N	2	0.12	0.17	0.11	—
45°N	3	0.20	0.23	0.18	—
50°N	2	0.12	0.27	0.23	—
50°N	3	0.20	0.41	0.33	0.11
54°N	2	0.29	0.44	0.26	—
54°N	3	0.39	0.79	0.59	0.20
58°N	2	0.41	0.95	0.67	0.18
58°N	3	0.73	—	—	0.30
60°N	2	0.58	—	—	0.25
60°N	3	1.12	—	—	0.41

[a]From Nielsen (1963).

usable. In addition to lux, a few other related units of illumination are sometimes used, although their applicability to photoperiodism is doubtful. A *phot* is equal to 10,000 lux, and a *milliphot* is equal to 10 lux.

The question of how much twilight correction should be added to the sunrise-to-sunset daylength cannot be answered by any generality. Several complicating factors require consideration. The most obvious factor is the light-intensity response threshold of the reacting organism, as mentioned earlier. The second factor, too frequently ignored, is that photoperiodism involves responses to changes in illumination, with such changes acting as sign stimuli. It is, therefore, possible to evoke photoperiodic responses under experimental conditions by alternating brightly lighted periods with dimly lighted periods. Under such conditions, the organism may respond to the dimly lighted phase as if it were darkness. Similarly, dim light may function as the photophase if alternated with darkness (Buck, 1937; Mori, 1944; Brown *et al.*, 1954; Cloudsley-Thompson, 1960a; Aschoff, 1960). The third modifying factor is that of temperature. The environmental temperatures may be sufficiently low during twilight that the biological effects of light are nullified. Organisms may also display thermoperiodism, and the twilight temperature changes may constitute stimuli that override the photoperiodic stimuli.

The question of whether or not moonlight may influence the photoperiodic responses of insects and other organisms has not been fully answered. In general, the intensity of moonlight is considered to be below the response thresholds involved in photoperiodism, as moonlight seldom exceeds an intensity of 0.2 lux. Starlight values are usually about 0.001 lux. Although moonlight may not play a part in photoperiodism, lunar periodism is frequently of biological importance, as will be discussed in a later section (Chapter 3).

Photoperiod is a geophysical rhythm of considerable precision, and there is voluminous evidence of its biological importance. There are other geophysical rhythms that may also have significant effects on living systems — lunar days and cycles, marine tidal rhythms, atmospheric pressure rhythms, rhythmic changes in geomagnetic fields, and rhythmic patterns of radiation (see Brown, 1965 for a recent review). In the present volume, however, these factors will be considered only where they have been shown to have a modifying influence on photoperiodic responses.

Introduction to Insect Photoperiodism

Insects have exploited extensively the geophysical patterns of photo-period in their evolution of ecological, physiological, morphological, and behavioral adaptations. The function of photoperiod in these biological adaptations is to provide environmental information in the form of temporally spaced signals (dawn and dusk), to which the insects respond in diverse adaptive ways.

Some aspects of insect photoperiodism are easily observed, as for example, the motor activity patterns that divide insects into diurnal, nocturnal, and crepuscular species. In such cases, one or the other of the daily photoperiodic signals serves to evoke the motor activity or to induce daily temporal adjustments in the expression of an endogenous motor activity rhythm. In either case, the end result is a synchronization of insect activity with the daily photoperiod. There would appear to be no seasonal effects in this type of photoperiodic response, other than a simple day-to-day adjustment of activity to match the day-to-day changes in daylength. Motor activity rhythms that are influenced by photoperiod include locomotion, feeding, adult emergence, mating, and oviposition. Even in such apparently simple responses to photoperiod, there are some fundamental biological problems that have proved to be very difficult. These problems are concerned with the identity of the receptor-effector system involved in photoperiodism, the nature of the endogenous motor activity rhythm, and the mechanisms by which endogenous functions are regulated by photoperiodic signals.

The seasonal biology of many temperate zone insect species is timed so as to allow the yearly production of two or more generations under favorable climatic conditions, but only one generation in areas where the summer season is short and the climate is relatively rigorous. In either case, the species overwinters in a state of hibernation known as *diapause*, but whether diapause occurs in a particular generation or is delayed until a subsequent generation is determined by the daylengths under which the insect population has been maintained. Photoperiodic induction of diapause has been studied in a number of species, and has been shown to be a genetically controlled response to photoperiods experienced as much as one generation prior to the growth stage at which diapause is actually manifested. The characteristics of diapause induction clearly indicate that the photoperiodic effects are not attributable to single daily dawn or dusk signals, but to the time elapsing between such signals. In other words, absolute daylength, nightlength, or the

11

seasonal rate of change appear to play the major role in this type of photoperiodism.

A number of instances of polymorphism have been shown to be controlled through the insect's photoperiodic responses. These include differences in body form, pigmentation, and even mode of reproduction. The latter type of polymorphism can be exemplified by a number of aphid species. Such aphids reproduce by parthenogenesis during the spring and summer, with many generations being produced. In the late summer and early autumn, sexually reproducing forms are developed. The development of the sexual generation has been shown to be caused by the effect of the relatively short daylengths of late summer and autumn on the aphid population. In response to daylength, the aphids switch from continued production to parthenogenetically reproducing females over to the development of a generation which reproduces sexually and produces eggs which overwinter in a state of diapause. As in the case of photoperiodically induced diapause, polymorphism is a response to actual daylength—the time elapsing between dawn and dusk (or vice versa) is the environmental factor evoking the response.

In northern latitudes, the summertime growing season is relatively short, but the summer daylengths are quite long. Conversely in more southern areas, the growing season is very long, but daylengths never reach the extremes attained in the northern areas. A given insect species of wide geographical distribution would encounter relationships between climate and daylength that varied systematically over its north-to-south range. Ecological adaptations that were of good survival value in a southern area, such as Missouri, would be of no use in a northern Wisconsin locality. One might expect, then, that photoperiodic responses of different geographical populations of a given species might vary according to latitude. Such has been found to be the case with virtually every species investigated. Photoperiodism plays an obviously major role in the insects' ecological adaptations to climate and phenological synchronization of insects with their food sources—other plant and animal species.

The responsiveness of insects to photoperiod in terms of specific effects on behavior, growth and form, reproduction, diapause, and distribution would seem to imply the existence of basic physiological functions associated with photoperiodism. Some rhythmic physiological processes have been identified, and endocrine functions have been found to be involved in some instances. In general, however, there is only fragmentary understanding of the physiological aspects of insect photoperiodism.

The ability of the insect to respond in different ways to different day-lengths (diapause, polymorphism, etc.) would appear to necessitate the existence of some method of biological measurement of time. The need to postulate the operation of a time-measuring system has given rise to the concept of the "biological clock." There is much current research being devoted to the study of biological time measurement. This is not the hope of finding a discrete organ or system that can be labeled "biological clock." It is, rather, toward the goal of determining the nature of the internal integration of numerous rhythmic functions, from which the time-measuring capability emerges.

This brief survey of limited aspects of insect photoperiodism is meant only to introduce the reader to some of the principal problems and concepts associated with the subject. The modern development and current status of these several aspects will be considered in greater detail in the chapters that follow.

2 □ Behavioral Photoperiodism

Daily patterns of behavior are apparent in the activities of most insect species. Locomotion, feeding, mating, and oviposition are behavioral phenomena that may occur at species-typical times of the day. Many are typically active during daylight hours (*diurnal* species); others tend to be active at night (*nocturnal*); while still others are active mainly during evening or morning twilight (*crepuscular*). These different activity habits have long been known, and have been considered to be governed by daily cycles of temperature, humidity, and light intensity. A nocturnal insect might be thought to be active only at night because its motor activity was inhibited by daylight; if kept in continuous darkness, its activity would be expected to be more or less continuous. Early experiments under controlled conditions, however, demonstrated that daily activity rhythms were at least partially endogenous, with photoperiod playing a regulating role.

F. E. Lutz (1932) studied the nocturnal locomotor activity of both nymphs and adults of the common house cricket, *Acheta domesticus*, and the field cricket, *Acheta assimilis*, under conditions of constant temperature and controlled photoperiod. The insects became active shortly after the onset of darkness (scotophase), continued to move about actively for from 4 to 6 hours, and were then relatively quiescent until the following day. When the crickets were held in constant darkness, they continued to display an activity rhythm in which a few hours of activity would occur once every 24 hours. If, after a period of a few days of darkness, the insects were exposed to a reversed photoperiod, the activity rhythm adjusted to the new light-dark schedule so that the time of maximum activity began shortly after the beginning of the scotophase, even though this now occurred at civil noon. From these results, Lutz concluded that the activity rhythm represented an endogenous periodicity that was subject to regulation by the environmental photoperiod. Lutz's original findings have been confirmed and extended by modern studies.

Some of the basic characteristics of the relationships between an endogenous behavioral rhythm and the exogenous photoperiod are illustrated in Fig. 2. In this figure, the hours of illumination and darkness (the photoperiod) are represented by white and black bars along a horizontal time axis. The periods of maximum motor activity of the insect are shown as shaded blocks. In Fig. 2A the photoperiod is 12 hours of light (L) followed by 12 hours of darkness (D), and the photoperiod is abbreviated as 12L:12D. The insect activity is seen to begin shortly after dark in each cycle. Because the beginning of the insect's activity is maintained in a constant time relationship to the photoperiod,

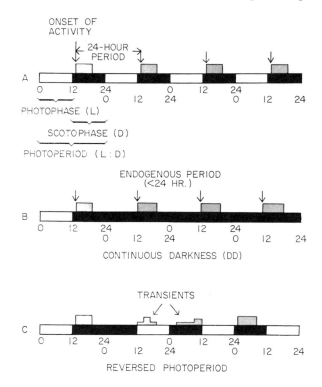

Fig. 2. Some characteristics of photoperiodically regulated behavioral rhythms.

16

the activity rhythm is said to be *photoperiodically entrained*. The role of the photoperiod in such entrainment is that of providing the time signals needed for daily adjustment *(phase setting)* of the endogenous behavioral rhythm. If, however, the photoperiodic conditions are changed so that the insects are held in continuous light (LL) or in continuous darkness (DD), as in Fig. 2B, the endogenous rhythm is no longer entrained, but is *free running*. Free-running rhythms usually display periodicities that are only approximately 24 hours. The *period* of a rhythm is the time elapsing from the beginning of one cycle to the beginning of the next. The period of the free-running endogenous rhythm depicted in Fig. 2B is slightly less than 24 hours; many free-running rhythms have longer periods. This characteristic has been found in a wide variety of behavioral and physiological rhythms among plant and animal species, and is described by the term *circadian* (meaning approximately daily), coined by Franz Halberg (Halberg *et al.*, 1959). The reentrainment of the behavioral rhythm to a reversed photoperiod (Fig. 2C) may not be accomplished in one cycle of the rhythm, but may result in the appearance of intermediate responses during a transition period of from one to several cycles. These transitional responses are generally known as *transients* (Pittendrigh *et al.*, 1958). These several characteristics of biological rhythms will be examined in greater detail in subsequent sections of this chapter.

Under natural field conditions, insect activity is influenced by many factors in addition to photoperiod, and some of these factors may modify or totally suppress normally periodic behavior. Temperature, humidity, light intensity, as well as physiological factors such as age and reproductive state of the insect may strongly influence the manifestation of behavioral patterns. Young adults of the emperor dragonfly, *Anax imperator*, for example, tend to fly mainly during a few hours following dawn in preference to other times of the day. Older, reproducing dragonflies do not display a dawn flight habit, but tend to fly during midday (Corbet, 1957, 1960). Age differences in daily patterns of flight, feeding, and oviposition have been reported in a number of biting Diptera (Nielsen and Nielsen, 1962; Haddow and Gillett, 1958). The circadian activity rhythm of females of the cockroach *Leucophaea maderae* was observed to vary with the insect's reproductive state (Leuthold, 1966). During the time that mature eggs were present in the lower reproductive tract, locomotor activity rhythms were greatly suppressed. Other physiological stresses may also lead to a modification or reversal of activity patterns; the ground beetle *Feronia madida*, for example, is normally nocturnal, but may adopt a diurnal habit under starvation conditions (Williams, 1959).

Daily cycles of temperature and humidity almost invariably accompany photoperiodic cycles under field conditions. For this reason, it is not possible to determine the role of photoperiod in the biology of an insect through field studies alone. In a number of instances, the effects of photoperiod on rhythmic functions have been duplicated by thermoperiod under laboratory conditions. An extreme example of entrainment of behavioral rhythms by an exogenous rhythmic factor has been reported for a species of bird. The circadian locomotor rhythm of the common sparrow, *Passer domesticus*, could be entrained by sound; tape recordings of bird songs were used as the entraining factor (Menaker and Eskin, 1966). Although sound has not been shown to entrain insect activity rhythms, the standardization of environmental as well as biological factors is essential to any meaningful investigation of photoperiodism. Conversely, the investigator must be cautious about making premature extrapolations from laboratory to field situations, under the naive assumption that the variable studied in the laboratory is the only factor influencing the insect in its natural environment.

With these basic characteristics of behavioral rhythms in mind, let us examine what is currently known about different specific types of photoperiodically regulated rhythmic behavior.

METHODS FOR STUDY OF PERIODIC BEHAVIOR

Daily rhythms of locomotor activity, such as running, swimming, and flying, have been studied by a number of techniques. The simplest method is that of direct observation, in which the experimenter observes and records activity on a continuous or intermittent basis. This technique was used in early studies of locomotor activity among cockroaches and beetles of the forest (Park and Keller, 1932); in studies of mayfly nymph activity (Harker, 1953); and in studies of ground beetle behavioral rhythms (Greenslade, 1963). Direct observation has distinct disadvantages, however; observer-errors because of fatigue and the necessity of illuminating the insects during the scotophase are the principal shortcomings. The use of dim red light to enable the experimenter to observe activity during the scotophase is based on the general concept that insects are insensitive to red light. It should be realized, however, that the visual spectra of some species (e.g. *Calliphora*) may include wavelengths as high as 630 mμ (Dethier, 1963). Photoperiodic responses have also been reported with light of wavelengths up to 675 mμ, although most species fail to respond to wavelengths above 550 mμ. The possible involvement of spines and other nonoptical sensoria in the reception of infrared frequencies might also have important bearing on photo-periodic responses (Callahan, 1965a).

Field studies of flight and running activities have frequently involved the use of trapping methods. Pit traps have been used in studies of ground beetle activity (Williams, 1959), and flight traps in the case of several species of mosquitoes, mayflies, caddis flies, moths, and beetles (Corbet, 1960). Nuorteva (1965) employed baited traps in a study of muscid fly activity; trapped flies were collected and counted at 3-hour intervals. Bait traps do not permit a clear separation of flight activity from feeding activity, however. A number of studies of the flight and biting activities of mosquitoes have utilized the observers as bait, with each observer recording the numbers alighting and probing on a fellow observer (Haddow, 1964).

Automated recording of insect activity involves instrumentation (*actograph*) that will meet two requirements: (1) the detection of move-ment and its transduction into a recording system, and (2) the recording of activity signals on a time scale (*actogram*). Techniques have been developed in which insect activities are detected by either mechanical or electrical means. In his studies of cricket activity, Lutz (1932) utilized a very sensitive treadle switch located in a narrow runway between two compartments of the cricket cage. When an insect stepped on the switch, an electromagnet caused a deviation in the tracing of a recording pen on a moving paper strip. A second pen was used to record hourly time signals. The intensity and duration of locomotor activity could then be determined from counts of the recorded signals. Another type of acto-graph that has been used by several investigators is based on the insect being confined in a small light-weight cage that is delicately balanced on knife edges. Movements of the insect are transduced as movements of the balanced cage to open and close a mercury dip switch. The making and breaking contacts are recorded on either a kymograph or strip chart recorder. This system has been used in studies of periodic behavior of crickets (Cloudsley-Thompson, 1958; Nowosielski and Patton, 1963) and cockroaches (Harker, 1956; Cloudsley-Thompson, 1960b). Light-weight activity wheels, comparable to those used with higher animals, have proved useful in studies of relatively heavy insects, such as the larger cockroach species. The running activity of the insect causes the wheel to turn, activating a microswitch, an event which is recorded on a strip chart recorder (Roberts, 1960).

19

The locomotor activity of very small insects, such as *Drosophila* adults, has also been recorded automatically (Roberts, 1956). A grid of fine wires was laid over the inside walls of the insect cage; alternate wires were attached to a common terminal. When the flies walked or landed on the grid, a short circuit was produced. This effect was fed through a high-gain amplifier and recorded on a strip chart. A method for measuring flight activity of small moths was developed by Edwards (1960), which was based on detecting and recording changes in the electrostatic charge on the flying insect. The actograph apparatus

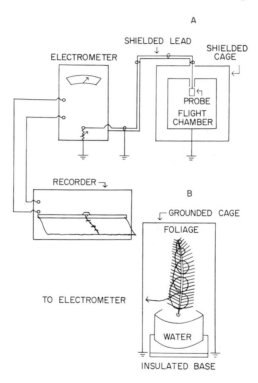

Fig. 3. Electroactograph for recording insect flight (A) and movement (B). [Redrawn from Edwards (1960, 1964a).]

(Fig. 3A) consisted of a shielded wooden cage and an electrostatic probe connected to an electrometer, which was connected to an amplifier. A strip chart recorder was used to record signals from the amplifier. Flight activity among insects as small as adult *Drosophila* could be recorded by this system. The crawling and feeding activity of lepidopterous larvae was recorded by means of a modification of the flight electroactograph (Edwards, 1964a). This was accomplished through the use of sensitive transducers to detect the insect-caused disturbances in the electromagnetic field around the food plant (Fig. 3B). Schechter and co-workers (1963) developed an activity-monitoring system in which movements of the cockroach *Leucophaea maderae* were detected by a capacitance-sensing device and were recorded via amplifier and chart recorder. A similar system was used in the study of locomotor rhythms in ants (McCluskey, 1958), except that the capacitance sensor operated a relay and the number of detected movements was recorded by a digital computer.

Ovipositional activity rhythms have been studied by means of making periodic counts of eggs deposited on suitable surfaces (Gillett, 1961). An automated system was devised for a study of ovipositional behavior of the pink bollworm, *Pectinophora gossypiella* (Minis, 1965). This system involved caged moths that were provided with a moving paper surface on which to deposit eggs; calibration of the paper in terms of its rate of movement permitted calculation of the time of egg deposition.

Control of Photoperiod

Methods for the control of experimental photoperiods are usually relatively simple. Commercially available clock switches of the 24-hour and 7-day types are generally satisfactory for programming the photoperiodic schedule to be followed. Such switches produce abrupt changes, in that the lights are switched on and off without any simulation of twilight. For most experimental work, however, gradual changes of light intensity are quite unnecessary, and the use of abrupt switches simplifies the problem of standardizing phase duration.

Light intensity during the photophase should be relatively low. In most studies, light intensities between 2 and 20 lux have proved to be adequate. High intensities should be avoided in cases where the experimental insects are in relatively exposed situations, such as on synthetic diets in glass vials. Higher than necessary intensities of light may have the effect of inhibiting growth and altering behavioral patterns. Under experimental conditions of continuous illumination, the light should be of minimum effective intensity. Because of the problem of controlling the temperatures within the experimental arrangement, fluorescent lighting of the "daylight" type is usually preferable to incandescent bulbs. With the use of fluorescent lights, light intensity may be controlled by the use of partial masking or the installation of light baffles, but this type of light source does not perform well with a rheostat for intensity control. Incandescent bulbs, on the other hand, may be used with a rheostat for intensity control, but it must be remembered that as the intensity of light output is decreased, the spectrum of emitted light shifts toward the red and infrared.

Control of the scotophase is also important. Precautions should be taken to maintain light tightness during the period of darkness. Almost imperceptible light leaks have been known to destroy the effectiveness of the scotophase, particularly in experiments on behavioral rhythms. In view of the phase-setting effects of very short flashes of light (to be discussed in a subsequent chapter), interruptions of the scotophase must be avoided.

Experimental containers and cages used in photoperiodic research have varied from room-sized growth chambers to very small portable units, such as those described by Dutky *et al.* (1962), Cothran and Gyrisco (1966), and Sparks (1966). The type of set-up used will depend on the nature of study being conducted and on the requirements of the insect involved. It should be remembered, however, that environmental conditions of light intensity, temperature, and humidity are usually more easily controlled in small units than in large ones.

Photoperiodic Entrainment of Locomotor Rhythms

Examples of daily activity rhythms in relation to a 24-hour photoperiod are shown in Fig. 4. The ordinate values of "relative activity" are indicative of the frequency of recorded activity within the experimental group at the different times indicated on the abscissa. Such data do not measure the intensity of activity exhibited by the individual insects, except as it affects the total activity of the group. Figure 4A is based on the experimental results of J. E. Harker (1956) with the running activity of the American cockroach, *Periplaneta americana*. A well-defined nocturnal activity is apparent, with the greatest activity occurring during several hours after the beginning of the scotophase. During the latter part of the scotophase and all of the photophase, the insects were relatively inactive. It can be observed that the activity of the insects began to increase prior to the beginning of the scotophase, as if the actual onset of darkness did not directly stimulate locomotion. The activity rhythm appeared to "anticipate" the change from light to dark, an effect suggesting that the time of activity onset on a given day was determined by the photoperiod experienced by the insect on the previous day.

The daily flight activity of *Drosophila robusta* (Fig. 4B) is based on the experimental data of Roberts (1956). Most of the daily flight activity occurred during the last three hours of the photophase, and flight ceased abruptly when the lights went out. Under natural conditions of

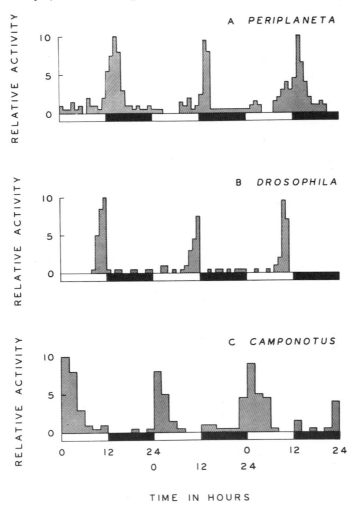

Fig. 4. Locomotor activity rhythms in three different insects, illustrating typical photoperiodic entrainment. [Sources indicated in text.]

the slowly changing light intensities of twilight, this flight activity pattern would be typically crepuscular.

The diurnal locomotor activity of male ants *(Camponotus clarithorax)* under controlled photoperiodic conditions is shown in Fig. 4C [based on the work of McCluskey (1965)]. The ants showed a well-defined peak of activity at the beginning of the photophase, and little activity was recorded at any other time of the day. The frequency of activity increased before the onset of light, again suggesting that the phase-setting stimulus was associated with the photoperiod of the previous day. Under conditions of constant darkness in the cases of *Periplaneta* and *Camponotus* and constant dim light in the case of *Drosophila*, the activity rhythms were demonstrated to be endogenous and to display a circadian rhythmicity (Harker, 1956; McCluskey, 1965; Roberts, 1956).

The activity rhythms depicted in Fig. 4 show some day-to-day variability in both the time of beginning and the duration of activity. This effect might suggest that the time relations of the rhythm are only approximate. However, such data are from the study of experimental popula-

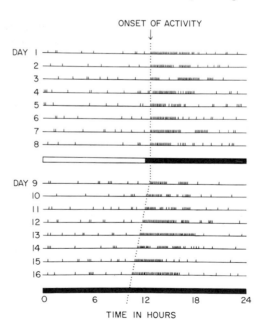

Fig. 5. *Typical actogram of a nocturnal insect under the influence of a photoperiod (days 1–8) and continuous darkness (days 9–16).*

tions of insects, and much of the variability may be attributed to individual variations within the population. Studies of the activity rhythms displayed by individual insects have shown that the timing of the rhythm is surprisingly exact. This important point is shown in Fig. 5, which is a typical actograph tracing of a single insect over a period of 16 days. Each vertical mark on the time line is the record of a single switch closure caused by the turning of an activity wheel. The onset of locomotor activity, other than sporadic movements, occurred at almost exactly the same time each day as long as the insect was exposed to the phase-setting influence of a photoperiod. The period of the entrained rhythm was 24.0 hours. When transferred to continuous darkness at Day 9, the free-running (unentrained) activity rhythm showed a circadian periodicity of about 23 hours and 40 minutes. Such actograph records usually show that the duration of the active period may be quite variable. The onset of intense activity is usually very regular and predictable from day to day. For this reason, most research on activity rhythms has dealt with the time of commencement of activity rather than with its duration or termination.

In the examples discussed thus far, the activity rhythms have been simple and regular; that is, with but one peak of activity per 24-hour cycle. Many behavioral rhythms have been reported to be bimodal or even trimodal, in which two or three periods of activity occur during each 24-hour cycle. A study of the nocturnal flight activity of a number of moth species (Edwards, 1962) revealed both species and sex differences in the forms and modalities of the flight patterns. Females of the Mediterranean flour moth, *Anagasta (=Ephestia) kühniella*, flew most actively during the hour before sunset and for a short time following sunset. Males of the species, however, displayed two daily periods of flight: one immediately following sunset, and a second major peak of flight activity during the two hours immediately preceding sunrise. Females of the silver-spotted tiger moth, *Halisidota argentata*, were found to engage in active flight during 2 hours following sunset, intermittently thereafter but with a noticeable increase around midnight, and then a cessation of flight occurred prior to dawn. Males of the species displayed a well-defined trimodal flight pattern, with peaks of flight activity occurring after sunset, about midnight, and preceding sunrise. These flight rhythms are shown in Fig. 6, which is based on the data of Edwards (1962). Of the moths that Edwards investigated, a predawn burst of flight activity was characteristic of the males of several species, but such behavior was not observed among the females. A bimodal flight

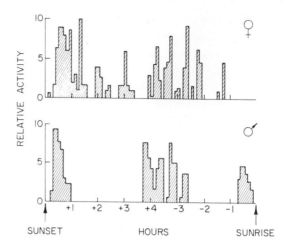

Fig. 6. Photoperiodic entrainment of flight activity rhythms in the silver-spotted tiger moth, Halisidota argentata. [Redrawn from Edwards (1962).]

pattern has also been described among aphids (*Aphis fabae* and *Rhopalosiphum maidis*), in which there is both a morning and an early evening period of general flight activity (Johnson and Taylor, 1957; Johnson *et al.* 1957; Davis, 1966). The possible role of photoperiod in aphid flight rhythms has not been demonstrated, although the observations of Davis (1966) are consistent with such a hypothesis.

When bimodal (or trimodal) activity rhythms are observed in insect populations or in confined experimental groups, there may be a question as to the nature of the observed rhythms. Two interpretations seem possible: (1) two temporally displaced types of individuals are present, each of which displays only one period of activity per photoperiodic or circadian cycle; or (2) each individual of the population may display a daily rhythm with two or more periods of activity. The choice between these two interpretations requires experimentation in which the activities of individual insects are recorded. Such experimentation has been run in several cases, and the results have shown that bimodality of activity rhythms may be found in individual as well as population responses. Many daily rhythms have been found to manifest more than one activity peak during each cycle, and we will encounter the phenomenon among physiological rhythms (Chapter 5) as well as behavioral rhythms. From a consideration of bimodal activity rhythms in higher animals, birds in particular, J. Aschoff (1966) recently concluded that the basic circadian

26

rhythm of locomotor activity is a bimodal rhythm. Whether or not more than one active period is manifested during each circadian cycle was found to depend on both daylength and the light intensity during the photophase.

When living in their normal environments, insects are subjected to daily temperature cycles, and there is conclusive evidence that such thermoperiods may have phase-setting effects on circadian rhythms. That is, a circadian rhythm such as locomotor activity may be entrained by thermoperiod as well as photoperiod. The circadian flight rhythm of a number of muscid flies was found to be entrained by thermoperiod under the continuous illumination of the arctic summer season at 69° N (Nuorteva, 1965). Similarly, diel activity rhythms in the mosquitoes *Aedes impiger* and *Aedes nigripes* were found to be regulated by thermoperiod during the summer months at a latitude of 71° N (Corbet, 1966). Although the stress of arctic conditions has led to some modification of photoperiodic responses (Downes, 1965), thermoperiod may entrain the activity rhythms of temperate zone insects as well. Such has been demonstrated in the case of the grain beetle *Ptinus tectus* (Bentley *et al.*, 1941), the cockroaches *Leucophaea maderae* and *Periplaneta americana* (Roberts, 1962), and in a number of other species. Thermoperiods and temperature stimuli have also been shown to exert phase-setting influences on a number of developmental and physiological rhythms, as will be discussed in subsequent chapters.

Photoperiodic Entrainment of Feeding Rhythms

Locomotor activity is usually accompanied by other behavioral manifestations, such as feeding, mate seeking, and oviposition. These different activities may, therefore, display a diel rhythmicity. The feeding activities of relatively sessile forms, such as lepidopterous larvae, appear to form a reasonably simple rhythmic behavior. On the other hand, the flight and feeding patterns of host-seeking mosquitoes and other blood-sucking Diptera are extremely complex.

Cockroaches tend to feed mainly at night, which is also the time of their greatest locomotor activity. The possibility of the locomotor rhythm being influenced by a physiological hunger cycle was investigated by Harker (1956). Food was made available to the cockroaches (*Periplaneta americana*) only during the middle of the photophase. This had the effect of increasing the insects' activity during the hours that food was present, but it did not exert a phase-setting influence on the general activity rhythm. The cockroaches continued to display maximum locomotor behavior shortly after the beginning of the scotophase. They did not learn to anticipate the introduction of food during the photophase. This is in sharp contrast to the ability of worker honeybees (*Apis mellifera*) to adjust their foraging activity in accord with previous experience and to display a learned circadian rhythm of feeding.

Training experiments with honeybees demonstrated that these insects possess a "time sense" (Forel, 1910; Beling, 1929; Kalmus, 1934; von Frisch, 1950; Lindauer, 1960). Bees were trained to expect a feeding of sugar-water at a designated place and at a specific time of day. The bees would appear at the feeding site at the correct time day after day, even when the entire experiment was run under constant conditions of temperature, illumination, and humidity. The bees could not be trained to seek food at intervals other than 24 hours, however, which suggests that an endogenous 24-hour periodism may be involved in their sense of time. The geographical displacement experiments of Renner (1956, 1960) showed that the internal timing mechanism was only partially responsive to environmental signals such as photoperiod.

A daily pattern of feeding was observed in adults and nymphs of the house cricket, *Acheta domesticus* (Nowosielski and Patton, 1963). These insects did little feeding during the early part of the photophase, but fed intensively during the eighth to tenth hours of a 12-hour photophase. Feeding then declined until after the beginning of the scotophase; the crickets tended to feed throughout the scotophase. An obviously circadian rhythm of feeding among nymphs of the milkweed bug, *Oncopeltus fasciatus*, has been reported (Beck et al., 1958), but the role of photoperiod was not determined. Other fragmentary evidence supports the concept that the feeding activity of phytophagous insects constitutes a photoperiodically regulated circadian rhythm. In general, the feeding activity rhythm probably is closely linked to the insect's locomotor activity, rather than constituting an independent rhythmic function (Harker, 1958), although important exceptions may occur.

Daily rhythms of general activity, presumed to be mainly feeding, have been studied among several species of defoliating caterpillars (Edwards, 1964b, 1965). Activity patterns were found to be quite complex, with developmental stage-dependent changes and also with interactions between temperature and photoperiod. Second and third instar larvae of the silver-spotted tiger moth, *Halisidota argentata*, were most active shortly after the beginning of the scotophase and showed an occasional burst of activity after the onset of light, when maintained under a natural photoperiod and a constant temperature of 23°C

28

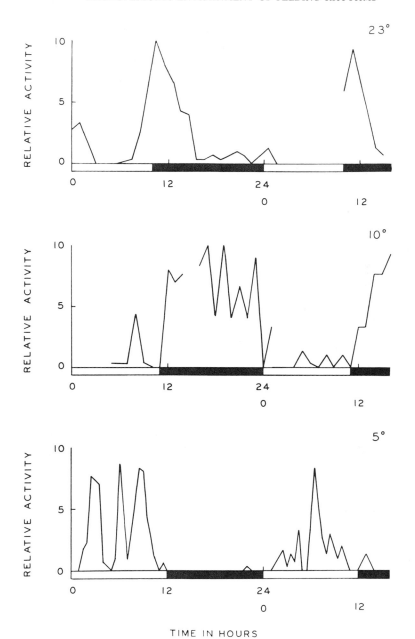

Fig. 7. *Effect of temperature on photoperiodic entrainment of larval activity rhythms in Halisidota argentata.* [*Redrawn from Edwards (1964b).*]

(Fig. 7). At lower temperatures, however, this pattern was different. When held at 10°C, activity was mainly nocturnal. When held at 5°C, the behavior pattern was reversed and the larvae were most active during the photophase. Last instar (eighth) larvae showed a rather irregular activity rhythm, with a tendency toward a nocturnal pattern. Shortly before cocoon spinning and pupation, however, the diel rhythm of activity disappeared. Young (second and third instar) larvae of the silver-spotted tiger moth were also responsive to thermoperiods, which had a phase-setting effect on their activity rhythms.

Feeding and general activity rhythms of larvae of the phantom hemlock looper, *Nepytia phantasmaria*, were typically nocturnal under conditions of a natural photoperiod and a constant 10°C temperature. This species differed from the silver-spotted tiger moth in that the larvae were completely inactive at 5°C and the circadian activity rhythm broke down when the larvae were held at 23°C. Similarly, larvae of the Douglas fir tussock moth, *Orgyia pseudotsugata*, failed to display rhythmic activity at 23°C, but when maintained at 10°C the young larvae adopted a diurnal activity rhythm. Young larvae of this species tend to drop out of their host tree via a silken thread. This activity was observed to show two daily maxima; one in the early part of the photophase and a second a few hours before the beginning of the scotophase.

The feeding behavior of mosquitoes and other blood-sucking forms has been the subject of much study. Little work has been done on feeding rhythms of these forms under controlled laboratory conditions, however, and there is some confusion as to the probable role of photoperiod in their feeding behavior. Because most mosquitoes require a great deal of space for normal flight activity, and behave poorly in confinement, most studies of their flight and feeding have been carried out in the field. Studies of tropical forest-inhabiting mosquitoes have shown that different species normally feed at different heights in the forest canopy (Haddow, 1961; Haddow *et al.*, 1960). Although the species were found to be biting at different times, their feeding behavior formed a bimodal crepuscular pattern in most cases (Haddow, 1945, 1954, 1956, 1964; Gillett, 1961; Haddow and Gillett, 1958).

Aedes aegypti displays a diurnal biting rhythm, with the most active feeding periods occurring during the morning and just prior to sunset (Teesdale, 1955; Gillett, 1961). *Aedes ingrami* showed a presunset peak of feeding activity, but the other species studied by Haddow (1964) were found to be distinctly crepuscular (*Aedes africanus, Mansonia fuscopennata,* and *Mansonia aurites*). During the rapidly declining light intensities of

30

twilight, *A. africanus* became most active shortly after crep 1.0; *M. fuscopennata* and *M. aurites* showed maximum biting activity at about 1.5 creps. Moonlight did not affect the biting cycles of these species. A predawn period of feeding was also observed as characteristic of the two *Mansonia* mosquitoes. Haddow (1964) studied this activity in *M. fuscopennata*, and found that predawn feeding activity occurred at higher light intensities than did the post-sunset activity. This effect could not be accounted for on the basis of temperature differences between the two times of day. As was pointed out by Corbet (1965, 1966b), the effect might be explained on the basis that biting activity is a two-or-more step response to light intensities of a narrow range. The initial stimulation by light of the appropriate intensity would occur after sunset and again before sunrise. The overt behavior of feeding would occur only after some time following the initial releasing stimulation. Such a two-step process would have the effect of moving the feeding time still later after sunset, but would move the morning activity closer to sunrise.

Crepuscular behavior is difficult to deal with from a photoperiodic standpoint, because the behavior is so frequently associated with a narrow and specific range of light intensities. Because these light intensities occur on a daily basis, their occurrence forms a bimodal exogenous rhythm. The question is whether the insect's behavioral pattern is the manifestation of an endogenous rhythm or a simple daily response to light of the appropriate intensity. It is important to remember, however, that most behavioral patterns require releasing stimuli from the environment. Light intensity may well be such a releaser for mosquito biting behavior, although other exogenous stimuli—perhaps host-borne—may also be involved. Circadian periodicity and photoperiodic entrainment may play a role in determining the responsiveness of the insect to the releasing stimulus. At one time of the day, then, the mosquitoes might respond readily, whereas at a different time much stronger stimuli might be required to evoke feeding. Although it is possible to induce hungry mosquitoes to feed at almost any time, under natural conditions they display a tendency to feed at only certain times. The predilection for feeding at specific times of the day may be controlled indirectly by underlying circadian physiological functions that regulate the insects' response thresholds. Such an interaction between an endogenous rhythm and exogenous environmental stimuli has not been demonstrated in mosquitoes, but it may be illustrated by the results of a study of the flight behavior of the European chafer, *Amphimallon majalis* (Evans and Gyrisco, 1958). The adult beetles of this species hide in the soil during the day, but emerge and fly actively during twilight. Emergence from the soil was found to be controlled by light intensity, but flight could not be induced at unnatural times of the day by experimental changes in light intensity. The flight behavior was apparently controlled via an endogenous circadian rhythm, whereas emergence from hiding was a nonrhythmic response to light intensity. In short, the tendency for flight formed a circadian behavioral rhythm, but its actual occurrence could occur only when the light intensity was appropriate for beetle emergence from hiding and for the evocation of flight.

PHOTOPERIODIC ENTRAINMENT OF OVIPOSITION

It has been suggested that the rhythm of biting activity in mosquitoes is closely linked to their ovipositional rhythm (Haddow, 1954; Gillett and Haddow, 1957; Haddow and Gillett, 1958). A comparison of feeding and ovipositional rhythms of *Taeniorhynchus fuscopennatus* is shown in Fig. 8, which is based on the data of Haddow and Gillett (1958). That the ovipositional behavior of *Aedes aegypti* is a photoperiodically en-

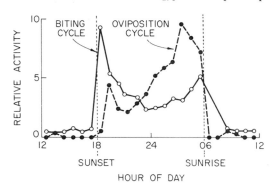

Fig. 8. *Biting and ovipositional activity rhythms in the mosquito* Taeniorhynchus fuscopennatus. [*Adapted from Haddow and Gillett (1958).*]

trained rhythm was demonstrated by Haddow and Gillett (1957). Under natural conditions, oviposition occurred mainly between 2 and 3 P.M. Under a controlled laboratory photoperiod, daily ovipositional activity was concentrated in the first hour of the scotophase, even when the photoperiod had been experimentally modified or reversed (Gillett *et al.*, 1959). Two other *Aedes* species (*A. apicoargenteus* and *A. africanus*) were also shown to oviposit on a rhythmic basis (Haddow *et al.*, 1960).

Aedes apicoargenteus deposited eggs throughout the photophase, but *A. africanus* tended to restrict its ovipositional activity to the first few hours of the scotophase. Somewhat different results were obtained by Logen and Harwood (1965) working with the ovipositional behavior of *Culex tarsalis.* Oviposition in this species showed a bimodal pattern, in which egglaying occurred in the first few hours following the onset of the photophase and again after the beginning of the scotophase. This bimodal pattern was observed with daylengths of 8, 12, or 16 hours. Under conditions of continuous illumination, however, oviposition was largely suppressed, and what little egg deposition occurred was randomly distributed throughout the day. No evidence of a circadian periodicity was obtained, and these authors concluded that ovipositional behavior was controlled only by light intensity changes.

Laboratory study of the reproductive behavior of the Mexican fruit fly, *Anastrepha ludens,* showed that oviposition occurred principally during the late photophase (Flitters, 1964). Experimental reversal of the photoperiod caused the ovipositional activity to undergo a corresponding shift, so that egg deposition continued to take place in the latter half of the photophase. The flies' ovipositional rhythm continued

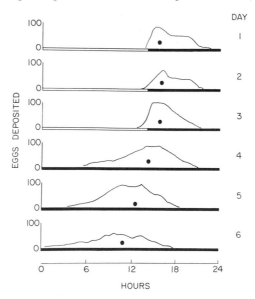

Fig. 9. *Photoperiodic entrainment of an endogenous circadian rhythm of ovipositional behavior in the pink bollworm, Pectinophora gossypiella. The filled circles indicate the time of the mode of each day's egg deposition. [Adapted from Minis (1965).]*

33

under conditions of continuous darkness in the presence of a thermo-period. Such results clearly suggest that the ovipositional activity of this tephritid fly is an endogenous rhythm that is normally entrained by exogenous photoperiod and thermoperiod.

Moths of the genus *Crambus* have been shown to oviposit mainly during the early scotophase. This ovipositional activity has been demonstrated to be both endogenous and circadian (Crawford, 1966; Banerjee and Decker, 1966a,b). Detailed study of the ovipositional rhythm of another moth, the pink bollworm (*Pectinophora gossypiella*), was made by D. Minis (1965). In this species, ovipositional activity started at or slightly before the beginning of darkness, reached a peak intensity in about 2.5 hours, and continued until about the seventh hour of the scotophase. Under experimental conditions of constant temperature and continuous darkness, the ovipositional rhythm continued on a circadian basis, with a free-running periodicity of 22 hours and 40 minutes (Fig. 9). Experimental changes in the photoperiod resulted in corresponding phase setting in the activity rhythm, demonstrating photoperiodic entrainment.

Although extensive experimental data on the role of photoperiod in ovipositional activities are not available, the existing evidence clearly indicates that photoperiod plays a phase-setting role in the ovipositional rhythm of diverse insect forms.

PHOTOPERIODIC ENTRAINMENT OF MATING BEHAVIOR

Although many insects have been observed to mate more readily at one time of the day than at others, relatively little experimental work has been done on the effect of photoperiod on mating behavior. The complex emergence, swarming, and mating behavior of nematocerous Diptera will be discussed in the following chapter; the present discussion will deal with the few instances where an uncomplicated effect of photoperiod on sexual activity has been investigated.

In his study of the Mexican fruit fly, Flitters (1964) observed that the flies mated during the late afternoon and early evening. When the photoperiod was experimentally reversed, the daily mating behavior was also reversed so that the flies continued to mate during the latter part of the photophase. The existence of a photoperiodically entrained copulatory rhythm was strongly suggested by these results.

Sexual excitability of males is frequently easier to observe and measure than is actual copulation. Such sexual excitability has been studied in a number of insect species, and there is good evidence for its being photoperiodically entrained. McCluskey (1958, 1963, 1965) studied the mating flight activity of a number of species of ants. Males of the harvester ant, *Veromessor andrei,* entered a period of mating flight activity at the beginning of the daily photophase. *Iridomyrmex humilis,* the Argentine ant, displayed such flight activity toward the end of the photophase, corresponding to a presunset field behavior. Males of the fire ant, *Solenopsis saevissima,* showed mating flight behavior during the middle and latter half of the photophase. *Camponotus clarithorax* males tended to fly early in the photophase, corresponding to a dawn flight under field conditions. The flight behavior of these several species of ants was found to be an endogenous circadian rhythm under constant conditions. Mating flights by the males of the honeybee have also been reported to follow a circadian rhythmicity (Taber, 1964).

A most significant contribution to this area of interest has come from recent studies of rhythmicity in the sexual excitability of male moths as mediated by sex pheromones (Allen *et al.,* 1962; Shorey, 1964). In a detailed study, males of the alfalfa looper, *Autographa californica;* tobacco budworm, *Heliothis virescens;* beet armyworm, *Spodoptera exigua;* and cabbage looper, *Trichoplusia ni,* were demonstrated to display circadian rhythms of responsiveness to the sex pheromones of the respective female moths (Shorey and Gaston, 1965). The rhythm of male responsiveness was shown to be entrained by photoperiod, with maximum responsiveness occurring in the early scotophase. Experimental alterations in the laboratory photoperiod caused corresponding phase adjustments in the male response rhythm. The receptivity of the females of *T. ni* was also found to be rhythmic, with the greatest sexual receptivity occurring in mid-scotophase. Like the male response rhythm, the female receptivity rhythm was shown to be endogenous and readily entrained by the environmental photoperiod (Shorey, 1966).

SURVEY OF PHOTOPERIODIC ENTRAINMENT OF BEHAVIORAL RHYTHMS

Table III is a compilation of insect species and their behavioral rhythms that are known to be entrained by photoperiod. An effort has been made to include only those instances in which experimental manipulation of the photoperiod has resulted in a reasonably adequate demonstration of photoperiodic entrainment. This listing is not exhaustive, and there may be published reports of verified entrainment that have been overlooked. A relatively small number of insect species have been examined experimentally for the characteristics of photoperiodism, and

35

many insect orders are not represented in the compilation. As more species are brought under experimental scrutiny, the list of known activity rhythms will undoubtedly lengthen proportionally. It seems likely that virtually every species could be shown to possess circadian rhythmicity as part of its behavioral repertoire.

With a couple of minor exceptions, no non-insects are listed in Table III. A great many marine arthropods have been shown to display endogenous circadian behavior, and such behavior may be entrained by the exogenous rhythms of both daylength and the tidal cycle. Because tidal rhythms are not involved in insect responses (with the exceptions discussed in Chapter 3) to photoperiod, this aspect of biological periodism has been omitted.

TABLE III

Insects and Related Arthropods in Which
Photoperiodically Entrained Behavioral Rhythms Have Been Demonstrated

Insect	Behavior	Time of active phase	References
Crustacea — Isopoda, Oniscidae			
Oniscus asellus	General locomotion	Scotophase	Cloudsley-Thompson (1952)
Arachnida — Acarina, Tetranychidae			
Tetranychus urticae	Oviposition	Photophase	Polick *et al.* (1965)
Insecta — EPHEMEROPTERA Ephemeridae			
Ecdyonurus torrentis (nymphs) Heptageniidae	General locomotion	Photophase	Harker (1953)
Heptagenia lateralis (nymphs) Baetidae	General locomotion	Photophase	Harker (1953)
Baetis rhodani (nymphs)	General locomotion	Photophase	Harker (1953)
ORTHOPTERA Blattidae			
Leucophaea maderae	General locomotion	Early scotophase	Roberts (1960)
Byrsotria fumigata	General locomotion	Early scotophase	Roberts (1960)
Blatta orientalis	General locomotion	Early scotophase	Harker (1954)
Blaberus giganteus	General locomotion	Early scotophase	Cloudsley-Thompson (1960b)

36

TABLE III *(Continued)*

Insect	Behavior	Time of active phase	References
Periplaneta americana Gryllidae	General locomotion	Early scotophase	Harker (1954, 1955)
Acheta domesticus	General locomotion	Early scotophase	Lutz(1932)
Acheta assimilis	General locomotion	Early scotophase	Lutz (1932)
Acheta domesticus	Feeding	Late photophase and photophase	Nowosielski and Patton (1963)
Acheta domesticus	Mating	Late photophase and early scotophase	Nowosielski and Patton (1963)
Gryllus campestris	General locomotion	Late photophase	Cloudsley-Thompson (1960b)
Gryllacrididae *Stenopelmatus* sp.	General locomotion	Scotophase	Lutz (1932)
Phasmatidae *Carausius morosus*	General locomotion	Scotophase	Eidmann (1956)
Acrididae *Schistocerca gregaria*	General locomotion	Photophase	Odhiambo (1966)
LEPIDOPTERA Noctuidae *Autographa californica*, male	Sex response	Scotophase	Shorey and Gaston (1965)
Heliothis zea, male	Sex response	Scotophase	Shorey and Gaston (1965)
Spodoptera exigua, male	Sex response	Scotophase	Shorey and Gaston (1965)
Trichoplusia ni, male	Sex response	Scotophase	Shorey and Gaston (1965)
Trichoplusia ni, female	Sex response	Scotophase	Shorey (1966)
Crambidae *Crambus trisectus*	Oviposition	Scotophase	Banerjee and Decker (1966a,b)
Crambus teterrellus	Oviposition	Scotophase	Crawford (1966)
Phycitidae *Anagasta kühniella*, females	Flight	Late photophase and early scotophase	Edwards (1962)
Anagasta kühniella, males	Flight	Trimodal— scotophase	Edwards (1962)
Geometridae *Ectropis crepuscularis*	Flight	Late photophase and scotophase	Edwards (1962)

(Continued)

37

TABLE III *(Continued)*

Insect	Behavior	Time of active phase	References
Nepytia phantasmaria, female	Flight	Early scotophase	Edwards (1962)
Nepytia phantasmaria, male	Flight	Bimodal—early and late scotophase	Edwards (1962)
Nepytia phantasmaria, larva	Feeding and locomotion	Scotophase	Edwards (1964b)
Lambdina somniaria Arctiidae	Flight	Scotophase	Edwards (1962)
Halisidota argentata, female	Flight	Scotophase	Edwards (1962)
Halisidota argentata, male	Flight	Trimodal—early, mid, and late scotophase	Edwards (1962)
Halisidota argentata, larva Gelechiidae	Feeding and locomotion	Temperature dependent	Edwards (1964b)
Pectinophora gossypiella Lasiocampidae	Oviposition	Early scotophase	Minis (1965)
Malacosoma pluviale, male	Flight	Bimodal—early and mid-scotophase	Edwards (1962)
Tortricidae *Choristoneura fumiferana*, female	Flight	Late photophase	Edwards (1962)
Choristoneura fumiferana, male Lymantridae	Flight	Late Photophase, scotophase	Edwards (1962)
Orgyia pseudotsugata, male	Flight	Late photophase	Edwards (1965)
Orgyia pseudotsugata, larva	Feeding and locomotion	Photophase	Edwards (1965)
COLEOPTERA Scarabaeidae *Amphimallon majalis*	Flight	Early scotophase	Evans and Gyrisco (1958)
Tenebrionidae *Boletotherus cornutus*	General locomotion	Scotophase	Park and Keller (1932)
HYMENOPTERA Formicidae			

TABLE III (continued)

Insect	Behavior	Time of active phase	References
Atta cephalodes	Foraging	Photophase	Hodgson (1955)
Paraponera clavata, male	Mating flight	Early scotophase	McCluskey (1965)
Veromessor andrei, male	Mating flight	Late scotophase, early photophase	McCluskey (1958)
Iridomyrmex humilis, male	Mating flight	Late photophase	McCluskey (1958)
Solenopsis saevissima, male	Mating flight	Mid-photophase	McCluskey (1963, 1965)
Camponotus clarithorax, male	Mating flight	Late scotophase, early photophase	McCluskey (1965)
Camponotus clarithorax, worker	Foraging	Early scotophase	McCluskey (1965)
DIPTERA			
Tephritidae			
Anastrepha ludens	Sex response	Late photophase, early scotophase	Flitters (1964)
Culicidae			
Aedes aegypti	Flight and feeding	Bimodal—early and late photophase	Gillett (1961)
Aedes aegypti	Oviposition	Late photophase	Haddow and Gillett (1957)
Taeniorhynchus fuscopennatus	Flight and feeding	Bimodal—early and late scotophase	Haddow and Gillett (1958)
Taeniorhynchus fuscopennatus	Oviposition	Bimodal—early and late scotophase	Haddow and Gillett (1958)
Anopheles gambiae	Flight	Early scotophase	Jones *et al.* (1966)
Aedes apicoargenteus	Oviposition	Photophase	Haddow *et al.* (1960)
Aedes africanus	Oviposition	Early scotophase	Haddow *et al.* (1960)
Drosophilidae			
Drosophila robusta	Flight	Late photophase	Roberts (1956)

39

3 □ Photoperiodism and Adult Emergence and Swarming

The adult forms of many insect species have been observed to emerge in greater numbers at one time of the day than at others. Emergence is the imaginal (adult) ecdysis, in which the adult stage emerges from its pupal or final nymphal form. The diel pattern of adult emergence of a given species tends to be correlated with the locomotor activity rhythm and the reproductive behavioral pattern of that species. In populations of the diurnal dragonfly, *Tetragoneuria cynosura*, studied by Lutz (1961), 75% of the adult forms emerging on a given day did so before 9 A.M. Callahan (1958) observed that 95% of the adults of the corn earworm, *Heliothis zea*, emerged between 7 and 11 P.M.; this species displays a nocturnal flight habit. A number of Chironomidae species were found to emerge principally between sunset and midnight, with the maximum numbers emerging near midnight (Palmen, 1955). Many species of small diurnal Diptera have been found to display morning maxima of adult emergence: *Drosophila* (Bünning, 1935), *Dacus tryoni* (Myers, 1952), *Scataphage stercoraris* (Lewis, and Bletchly, 1943), *Pegomyia betae* (Dunnung, 1956). Many additional examples might be cited, but these few are sufficient to illustrate the point that adult emergence is not randomly distributed through the diel cycle, but frequently displays a high degree of specialization.

Under natural field conditions, many environmental factors might be expected to influence the emergence of adult insects. It is also conceivable that different species might have evolved the ability to utilize different natural variables as signals in adjusting their times of emergence. The diel cycles of temperature, humidity, and light intensity might well be involved. The role of photoperiod cannot be determined with exactitude unless these several variables can be controlled. This calls for experimentation under controlled conditions. There have been a number of such laboratory investigations, and although only a small number of insect species have been used, the results have constituted valuable additions to our understanding of the general principles of photoperiodism.

In this chapter we will examine what is currently known about the periodism of adult emergence, and also the periodism of swarming behavior of male nematocerous Diptera. The latter phenomenon is much more complex than is that of adult emergence, and there is far less known about the role of photoperiod in swarming behavior.

ADULT EMERGENCE RHYTHMS

Locomotor activity, such as running or flying, can be shown to be rhythmic because its occurrence in the life of an insect may be observed every day. Daily repetitive behavioral patterns displayed by individual specimens may be recorded over periods of days, weeks, or even months without interruption. Emergence differs from a daily behavioral pattern in one very important characteristic; an individual insect emerges as an adult only once. Emergence is not a recurring event. On what basis then, can one speak of an "emergence rhythm"? Any daily rhythm apparent in the emergence of adult insects must be a population phenomenon, in which the population under observation is treated as constituting a single multi-unit superorganism. In the corporate life of this population, the daily production of adult stages may take the form of a daily rhythm. Such a population rhythm may show endogenous circadian characteristics, and be susceptible to phase regulation by photoperiod, thermoperiod, or other environmental factors. The functional unit of the population as a superorganism is the individual insect, and its developmental physiology must include rhythmic functions controlling the times at which successive developmental stages are attained. The time of emergence of an individual adult insect would be determined by the temporal relationships among the underlying physiological rhythms. Adult emergence rhythms manifested at the population level could, therefore, be regarded as resulting from a high degree of synchronization of the developmental processes among the individual insects making up that population. If photoperiod has a phase-setting effect on the adult emergence rhythm, it would be because of a photoperiodic entrainment of developmental rhythms in the individual insects. And in a resonably homogeneous population, the adult emergence rhythm might be expected to reflect accurately the characteristics of the endogenous rhythms of the members of the population.

General Methods

Among earlier workers, the most widely used method of determining the time of adult emergence was one of simple observation, in which counts were made of adults emerging during specific time periods. Such visual counts usually entailed disturbance of the experimental population because of the necessity of illuminating the culture during the observation process. The simple observation method has sometimes been combined with a trapping technique, so that the adult forms are collected without disturbing the rest of the population. Most relatively recent research has involved the use of automatic trapping and collecting methods. These vary greatly in detail, depending on the size and behavioral characteristics of the insect being studied. Newly emerged adults of small flies, such as *Drosophila*, may be collected by means of an automated system of subjecting the emergence cage to a sharp jolt that will cause the flies to drop from the interior surfaces into a collecting device containing a preservative. Automatic recording of the actual moment of emergence of medium-sized moths was accomplished by suspending the pupae on delicately counterbalanced needles connected to a tracing pen and moving chart paper (Edwards, 1964a). When the moth emerged, its movements caused deflections of the tracing pen.

Experimentation on Adult Emergence

One of the earliest experimental studies of daily emergence of adult insects was that of Bremer (1926), who worked with the Mediterranean flour moth, *Anagasta* (=*Ephestia*) *kühniella*. Under normal daylight conditions, adult emergence occurred almost exclusively during the late afternoon and early evening (late photophase and early scotophase). When the pupae were maintained under a reversed photoperiod, so that they were kept in the dark during the civil day and artificially illuminated during the night, the civil time of greatest adult emergence was also shifted. The reversal of the emergence pattern was not complete, however, in that only about 60% of the daily moth production occurred during the late photophase and early scotophase of the reversed photoperiod. Bremer did not control temperature fluctuations as rigidly as might be desired, in that the pupae were illuminated by means of incandescent bulbs without precautions for maintaining a constant

43

temperature. There remained, therefore, some doubt as to whether the emergence rhythm was phase regulated by photoperiod, thermoperiod, or by a combination of the two.

Adult emergence in *A. kühniella* was further investigated by Scott (1936), with particular emphasis on the role of temperature fluctuations. Scott's conclusions regarding the role of photoperiod must be disregarded, because his methods did not permit adequate control of light exposure. Temperature effects were clearly demonstrated, however. The endogenous nature of the emergence rhythm was also demonstrated; cultures that were held under constant temperature conditions in the dark continued to display an emergence rhythm. The role of the diel temperature cycle was shown to be that of a phase setter, because the greatest adult emergence occurred each day shortly after the time at which the ambient temperature began to fall. Under natural conditions, adult emergence would therefore tend to reach a maximum during the early evening hours, because of the normally declining temperatures. By the use of controlled temperature cycles (thermoperiods) of different durations, it was possible to induce adult moth emergence rhythms with periodicities as short as 16 hours. Scott was unable to induce a 36-hour emergence rhythm by means of a 36-hour thermoperiod, and he concluded that the period of the biological rhythm could not exceed its natural endogenous 24-hour periodicity. The demonstration that a temperature cycle could act as the entraining agent of an endogenous circadian rhythm was the most important contribution of Scott's research.

The problem of the adult emergence rhythm of the Mediterranean flour moth was reinvestigated by Moriarty (1959). In this study, both temperature and light conditions were adequately controlled. Moriarty confirmed Scott's finding that a temperature drop would phase set the emergence rhythm. He found that a 5°C drop in temperature had the effect of phase setting the rhythm, whereas a 5°C rise in temperature had no effect. Photoperiodic entrainment of the emergence rhythm was also demonstrated. Maintaining the insect cultures under constant temperatures but with different photoperiods resulted in a demonstration that the principal time of adult emergence was determined by the time of the onset of the photophase. The adult emergence data (Fig. 10) clearly showed that the maximum incidence of moth emergence occurred from 5 to 12 hours after the beginning of the photophase. When the experimental photoperiod was made up of a very short photophase (4 hours) and a long scotophase (20 hours), the moths tended to emerge

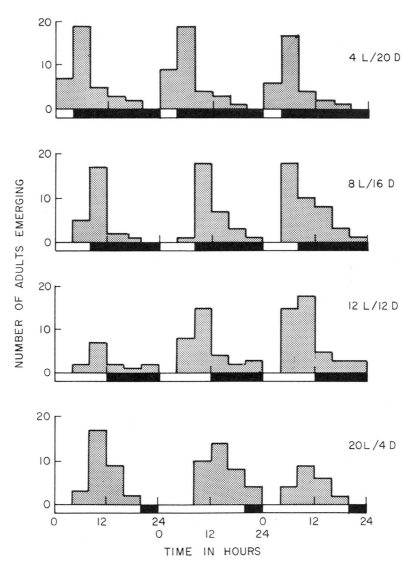

Fig. 10. *Effects of different photoperiods on adult emergence rhythm in the Mediterranean flour moth,* Anagasta kühniella. [*Compiled from data of Moriarty (1959).*]

during the early scotophase. On the other hand, when the photophase was 20 hours in duration, and the scotophase was but 4 hours, emergence tended to occur during the first half of the photophase. These effects strongly suggest that the emergence rhythm was phase set by the change from darkness to light (light-on stimulus) and that the rhythm was so timed that emergence occurred about 8 hours later, quite regardless of the presence or absence of light at the moment of emergence.

These studies of adult emergence in *Anagasta* illustrate the importance of maintaining controlled environmental conditions during experimentation on photoperiodism. But the most significant result of the three investigations is the demonstration that both photoperiod and thermoperiod may be involved in the entrainment of circadian rhythms. The apparent equivalence of a temperature change to a light intensity change in their effects on rhythmic functions poses some problems concerning the nature of possible receptor systems and effector mechanisms. These problems will be discussed in more detail in Chapter 5.

At the beginning of this section on adult emergence rhythms, we made the assumption that such a rhythm is a population phenomenon reflecting the individual developmental rhythms of the members of the population. Now, a question may be asked as to when in the growth of the individual insect are the developmental processes sensitive to the environmental signals that determine the time of the insect's eventual emergence. It is apparent, in most cases, that the developmental rhythms established in the larva will be carried over into the pupal stage, and adult emergence will be determined by such rhythms, unless the rhythms have been reset by temperature or photoperiodic stimuli experienced by the pupa itself. This situation was apparent in the early work on *A. kühniella*; Moriarty (1959), however, exposed only the pupae to experimental photoperiods, and he observed an entraining effect even quite late during pupal development. On the other hand, experimentation with the adult emergence rhythm of the Tephritidae fly *Dacus tryoni* showed adult emergence to be determined by photoperiods experienced during the larval stages; the pupae were insensitive to photoperiod (Bateman, 1955). *Dacus* pupae were found to be responsive to temperature changes, however, and the emergence rhythm could be entrained by experimental thermoperiods. A number of studies have been made of the adult emergence rhythms of *Drosophila* species. These flies are very sensitive to both thermoperiod and photoperiod, and the emergence rhythm may be phase set by temperature or light stimuli experienced during very early larval stages (Bünning, 1935; Pittendrigh, 1954; Brett, 1955; Pittendrigh and Bruce, 1957) or by either photoperiods or brief single light flashes during the pupal stage (Pittendrigh *et al.*, 1958). Since adult emergence may be temporally

46

determined by photoperiodic and thermoperiodic conditions experienced by very early growth stages, as well as during adult differentiation within the pupa, it seems obvious that the emergence of the adult insect is an event controlled by rhythmic functions that are fundamental to the developmental physiology of the insect.

Adult emergence rhythms in *Drosophila* are of particular interest, because of the depth to which they have been studied. Much of the research has been designed to elucidate the relationships between circadian rhythmicity and biological time measurement, and these aspects will be discussed in the following chapter. Only some of the more general features of the adult emergence rhythm will be discussed here. Daily rhythms of *Drosophila* emergence were first reported by Kalmus (1935) and Bünning (1935). It was observed that adult fly emergence tended to occur principally at the beginning of the photophase — that is, the flies displayed a dawn eclosion pattern. Some differences have been reported among the *Drosophila* species studied. For instance, *D. pseudoobscura* populations tend to show daily emergence maxima at from 1 to 2 hours after dawn (or the beginning of the photophase); whereas *D. persimilis* adult emergence was found to reach a peak at about 4 hours after dawn (Pittendrigh, 1958a). *Drosophila melanogaster* cultures showed maximum adult emergence within the first 2 hours of the photophase (Brett, 1955), but some genetic strains may display a bimodal emergence rhythm, with the second emergence maximum occurring in the late hours of the photophase (Harker, 1964). The emergence rhythm of *Drosophila* species has been shown to be entrained by photoperiod and thermoperiod, and to display an endogenous circadian periodicity under conditions of continuous darkness, provided that the experimental population had been exposed to a phase-setting stimulus at some time prior to the beginning of the continuous darkness (Pittendrigh, 1954; Brett, 1955). These concepts are depicted in Fig. 11.

Puparium formation in *Drosophila* cultures does not appear to occur on a rhythmic basis but is more or less randomly distributed within the diel cycle, even in the presence of a photoperiod (Bakker and Nelissen, 1963; Harker, 1965a). One might expect, therefore, that an adult emergence rhythm would be dependent upon the insects having been subjected to phase-setting stimuli at some time during the pupal period. The emergence rhythm is, indeed, sensitive to phase regulation during the pupal period, but also to photoperiods experienced during the larval stages. Brett (1955) demonstrated that experimental cultures of *Drosophila melanogaster* displayed no emergence rhythm if they were

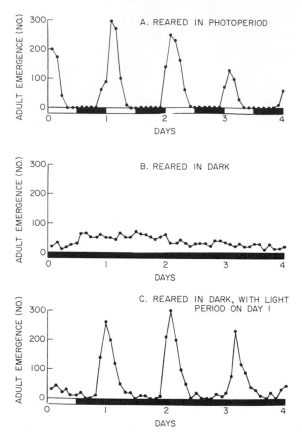

Fig. 11. *Effect of photoperiod, continuous darkness, and an unrepeated light stimulus on the adult emergence rhythm of Drosophila. [Based on experimental data from several sources.]*

maintained in continuous darkness from the egg stage (Fig. 11B). If, however, the cultures were exposed to a brief period of light at any time during larval or pupal development, adult emergence would show rhythmic characteristics in accord with the timing of the imposed light stimulus (Fig. 11C). The phase setting influence of a single light exposure has proved to be astoundingly efficient; Pittendrigh and Bruce (1959) reported that the light impulse from an electronic flash unit (1/2000 second) would phase set the emergence rhythm of dark-reared *Drosophila* cultures. Bunning (1935) found that dark-reared arrhythmic *Drosophila* cultures could be induced to display an adult emergence rhythm simply by transferring the cultures from continuous darkness to continuous light. The subsequent emergence rhythm was phase set in accord with the time of day that the continuous illumination had been initiated.

Light stimulation, but not photoperiod, was involved in both light flashes and continuous illumination treatments of the insect cultures. The effects on adult emergence can be explained only on the basis that the *onset of light* acted as a phase-setting signal that synchronized the rhythmic functions of the individual insects and led to the manifestation of an emergence rhythm in the population as a whole. Such a single light-on stimulus acted as a reference point from which the insects' developmental rhythms were timed. Such phase-setting stimuli have been termed *synchronizers* or *Zeitgeber* (German for "time-givers"). A photoperiod, however, is made up of both a photophase and a scotophase, and therefore contains two possibly phase-setting stimuli—the light-on stimulus and the light-off stimulus—as well as intervening time intervals. That the insect is responsive to the light-off stimulus has been demonstrated in a number of instances. The adult emergence rhythm of *D. pseudoobscura* can be phase set by dark pulses as well as light pulses. Adult emergence is arrhythmic in cultures that have been reared under continuous illumination; transfer of the cultures to continuous darkness causes the appearance of an emergence rhythm (Engelmann, 1966). Dark-reared fly cultures that had been exposed to a light stimulus displayed an emergence rhythm in which maximum numbers of adults were produced at about 24-hour intervals following the onset of light. Light-reared cultures that had been exposed to dark stimulus displayed emergence rhythms in which the first maximum emergence occurred about 12 hours after the onset of darkness and at approximately 24-hour intervals thereafter. It is apparent, therefore, that light and dark stimuli have different timing effects on the emergence rhythm. Both such phase-setting stimuli normally occur everyday when the insects are exposed to the normal diel cycle of daylight and darkness. The time of day at which adult emergence occurs is then a resultant of the temporal relationships between dawn and dusk—that is, daylength.

ADULT EMERGENCE AND SWARMING IN NEMATOCEROUS DIPTERA

Adult emergence rhythms of a number of Chironomidae species were studied by Palmen (1955, 1956, 1958). The ten species studied were brackish water forms found in tideflats of Finland at a latitude of

49

59° 51′ N, and were identified as *Allochironomus crassiforceps*, *Chironomus halophilus*, *Microtendipes pedellus*, *Polypedilum nubeculosum*, *Limnochironomus nervosus*, *Lenzia flavipes*, *Tanytarsus heudensis*, *Monotanytarsus inopertus*, *Cladotanytarsus mancus*, and *Cladotanytarsus atridorsum*. Systematic trapping of the emerging adults in their natural environment showed that in all of the species, adult emergence occurred during the hours following sunset. In the May—June generation, the adult flies tended to emerge in the largest numbers at about midnight, which was about 2 hours after sunset. Very few emerged at any other time of the day. The August generation of adults emerged in the largest numbers an hour or two before midnight, and this seasonal shift was thought to be correlated with the fact that daylengths were shorter and sunsets earlier in August than in June. The diel rhythm of emergence of adult *Allochironomus crassiforceps* displayed a well-defined sex difference, in that the males tended to emerge about 2 hours earlier than the females. No sex differences were detected in the other species studied.

The emergence rhythm of *A. crassiforceps* was shown to be both endogenous and circadian when a pupal population was transferred to controlled conditions of continuous darkness (Palmen, 1958). Among the chironomid species studied by Palmen, adult emergence was confined to the scotophase, and the circadian rhythm appeared to be phase set primarily by the beginning of darkness. Some chironomid species may emerge during the photophase, however; adults of the fresh water midge *Chironomus plumosus* were found to emerge mainly an hour before sunset under Wisconsin summer conditions (Hilsenhoff, 1966). In a study of three terrestrial chironomids, Remmert (1955a,b) reported that *Pseudosmittia arenaria* displayed an adult emergence rhythm in which emergence reached a maximum at about 6 hours after the beginning of the photophase. The other two species—*Limnophyes virgo* and *L. biverticillatus*—did not display detectable emergence rhythms under the conditions of the study.

Clunio marinus is a midge that inhabits the tideland waters of the western coasts of Europe. The larvae live in masses of seaweed, from which adult midges emerge in large numbers every 15 days. This 15-day cycle of adult emergence is suggestive of a lunar or tidal periodism, and field observations have shown that large swarms of adult midges tend to occur a few days after the new moon and on the day after the full moon (Caspers, 1951). Oka and Hashimoto (1959) studied the closely related species *Clunio tsushimensis*, which displays a similar 15-day periodism. On the basis of their finding that oviposition occurred only at the ebb time of the spring tide, and that almost exactly 1.5 synodical months were required for the insect's life cycle. Oka and Hashimoto suggested that the pattern of adult emergence was determined only by these time-related factors. Such an explanation does not seem likely, however, because seasonal temperature cycles in the insect's littoral habitat would greatly modify the time required to complete larval and pupal development. Many *Clunio* populations are found in northern cold waters, where much of the year is spent in a dormant or diapause state; even so, these northern populations also display a 15-day cycle of emergence.

The problem of the developmental periodism of *C. marinus* was investigated by Neumann (1962, 1965, 1966) under controlled laboratory conditions. Cultures from six different geographical populations were maintained, ranging from Helgoland in the North Sea to Santander, Spain. When the larvae were reared under continuous illumination and at a constant temperature, adult emergence was random in daily distribution. Neither diel nor 15-day periodicity was detected. Rearing the larvae under a 12L:12D photoperiod resulted in the appearance of a daily emergence pattern. The geographical population cultures differed in the times of maximum daily adult emergence; the most northern culture (Helgoland) showed an adult emergence maximum during the last few hours of the photophase, and the most southern forms (Santander) emerged during the early scotophase. None of the cultures displayed any tendency toward a 15-day adult emergence cycle.

The adult emergence rhythm was shown to be an endogenous circadian rhythm that could be phase set by photoperiodic stimuli (Fig. 12A). The experiments depicted in Fig. 12 involved the Helgoland culture, and showed that adult emergence was arrhythmic when the insects were reared under continuous light, but an emergence rhythm could be induced by a single 8-hour dark period, following which the rhythm would continue on a circadian basis. From the observation that the first emergence peak occurred 24 hours after the beginning of the exposure to darkness, Neumann concluded that the emergence rhythm was phase set by the light-off stimulus.

Having demonstrated that the adult emergence rhythm of *C. marinus* was regulated by photoperiod, Neumann turned to the problem of the 15-day emergence cycle that was consistently observed under field conditions. Study of the biology of the insect showed that the larvae did not pupate until a few days (2–5) before the predicted time of maximum emergence. It appeared, then, that the 15-day cycle was produced by

51

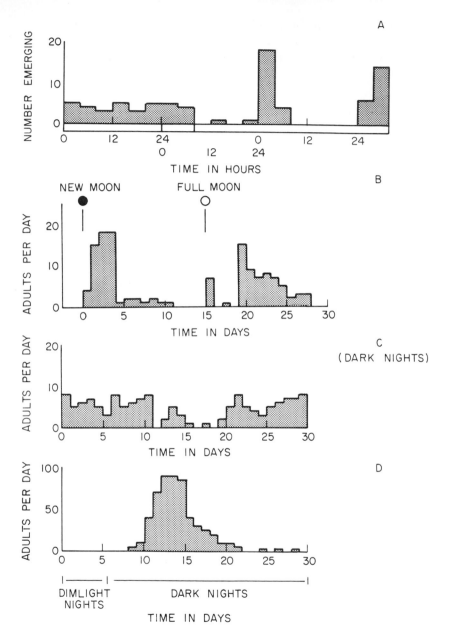

Fig. 12. Adult emergence rhythms in Clunio marinus, as affected by photoperiod and lunar periods. [Adapted from Neumann (1962).]

some periodic factor that regulated larval development during the pre-pupal stages. This hypothesis was tested by exposing a Helgoland culture to natural lighting conditions, but under constant temperature and without any tidal effects. Under these experimental conditions, a 15-day periodism in total adult emergence was observed (Fig. 12B), even though each day's emergence continued to display a diel periodicity. The first emergence maximum occurred on the second to fourth day

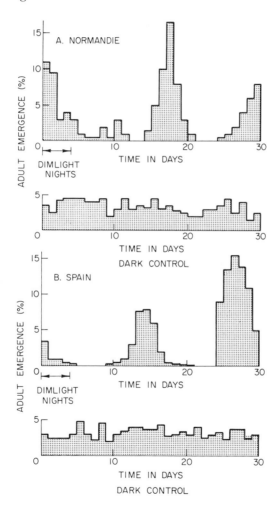

Fig. 13. *Effect of simulated moonlight nights on the adult emergence of two geographical popu-lations of Clunio marinus. [Adapted from Neumann (1966).]*

after the *new moon,* and the second maximum took place on the third day after the *full moon.* Experimental rearings under a 12L:12D photoperiod, in which moonlight nights were simulated by the use of dim light (0.3 lux), showed that emergence reached a maximum in from 12 to 15 days after the beginning of the "moonlight" nights, and that no insects emerged during days of simulated moonlight nights (compare Fig. 12C with 12D). A continuation of this experimental schedule, in which the larvae were exposed to 6 nights of "moonlight" followed by 24 dark nights, produced an emergence rhythm with a 30-day period, but not one with a 15-day period. When these experiments were repeated with different cultures, such as those from Normandie (Fig. 13A) or Spain (Fig. 13B), moonlight nights had the effect of inducing a 15-day cycle of adult emergence. The failure of the Helgoland culture to develop a 15-day adult production schedule has not been explained.

Moonlight, or low intensity light during the scotophase, probably has two effects on the development of the midge larvae. First, it seems probable that moonlight inhibits pupation, and this effect would account for part of the observed emergence rhythm. Such a hypothesis is also consistent with the observation that moonlight suppresses the activity of other aquatic arthropods (Anderson, 1966). The second effect of moonlight on the larvae would be exerted on those that had not yet reached the prepupal instar. Moonlight might influence the temporal programming of larval development such that pupation and emergence would occur about 30 days later.

In addition to daily rhythms of emergence, flight, feeding, and oviposition, many nematocerous species display a flight behavior known as swarming (see Clements, 1963). The swarms are composed of males that aggregate in large numbers, and fly in stereotyped dancelike patterns, sometimes for relatively long periods. Swarms have been divided into two types: (1) the "marker" swarm in which the flying insects fly back and forth in a restricted space in reference to some object that forms a sharp visual contrast against the general background, and (2) the "stand" swarm, in which the aggregation of males fly at higher altitudes than in the previous type and without benefit of obvious visual reference points. Both types of swarms tend to form during morning or evening twilight, and thus occur on a daily basis.

Temperature, time of day, and light intensity appear to be involved in controlling the onset of swarming behavior. Few experimental studies have been carried out on the role of photoperiod in swarming, but the limited existing evidence clearly suggests that swarming is a circadian endogenous phenomenon that may be entrained by the environmental photoperiod. The earliest study touching on this point was that of Bates (1941) with *Anopheles superpictus*. Adult males were maintained at a constant temperature and under a controlled photoperiod of 12L:12D. The transitions from light to dark and again from darkness to light were carefully controlled to simulate the gradual changes in light intensity associated with dusk and dawn under field conditions. Under these experimental conditions, swarming occurred during the artificial dusk period. When the insects were then maintained under continuous dim light, swarming occurred at approximately 24-hour intervals, indicating an endogenous circadian periodism. Swarming of several mosquito species could not be induced at unnatural times of the day by an experimental lowering of the light intensity to an appropriate dusklike level; these species included *Anopheles labranchiae atroparvus* (Cambournac and Hill, 1940), *Anopheles superpictus* (Bates, 1941), *Culex pipiens fatigans* (Nielsen and Nielsen, 1962), and *Aedes triseriatus* (Wright *et al.*, 1966).

It is quite certain that light intensity plays an important role as a releaser of swarming behavior. A number of studies have been made of the influence of light intensity on swarming, and of the modification of its action by such diel factors as temperature changes. Using *C. pipiens fatigans* as their experimental animal, Nielsen and Nielsen (1962) observed that stand swarms began to form at light intensities of about 0.60 log lux, and dispersed when the light intensity reached about 1.60 log lux. Marker swarms began a little later after "sunrise," and the effective light intensities were from 0.92 to 2.11 log lux. Swarms were induced only when the transition from darkness to light was gradual; if the lights were turned on suddenly, the mosquitoes showed excitement, but no swarms were formed. If the dark-to-light transition was quite rapid (requiring only about 15 seconds) some swarming occurred, but only after a delay of several minutes.

The temperatures prevailing during the experimental "dawn" period were also found to influence swarming behavior. The formation of marker swarms was delayed progressively as temperatures rose from 15° to 30°C, indicating that the effective light intensity for the release of swarming was higher at higher temperatures. Light intensities required to terminate swarming were higher at intermediate temperatures (20°–23°C) than at either higher or lower temperatures. Under the decreasing light intensities of simulated sunset, marker swarms appeared only when the ambient temperature was 25°C or higher. Evening twilight stand swarms displayed a broader range of effective temperatures.

The possible role of visual adaptation in the swarming of males of *Culex tarsalis* was investigated by Harwood (1964). Movements of eye pigments in the ommatidia of the mosquitoes during dark and light adaptation were studied. It was found that swarming took place during this adaptation process, and that the insect's eyes had attained a characteristic degree of adaptation at the time that swarming behavior was manifested. The degree of adaptation was measured in terms of an arbitrary "eye index," which was defined as the average cornea diameter: iris diameter ratio. The diameter of the cornea would not change during adaptation, but the diameter of the effective light-admitting orifice (iris) was very small in light-adapted eyes and quite large in dark-adapted eyes. Harwood found that light-adapted eyes of the male mosquitoes showed an eye index of about 21, whereas fully dark-adapted eyes had an eye index of only 4. When the eye index reached a value of approximately 5, swarming occurred. Males of *C. tarsalis* would display swarming behavior under laboratory conditions, even when the transition from darkness to full light was very abrupt. Under such conditions, however, the onset of swarming was delayed for several minutes, but specimens collected and examined at the moment of swarm initiation showed an average eye index of 5.

4 □ Circadian Rhythms and Biological Time Relationships

Insects display individual and population behavioral patterns that recur on a predictable daily basis. These behavioral rhythms usually continue to be manifested when the insects are experimentally isolated from obvious environmental stimuli, such as light and temperature changes, suggesting that the insects possess an innate capacity for measuring the passage of time. Numerous examples of such endogenous circadian rhythms were discussed in the previous chapters, and it was pointed out that the principal role of photoperiod appeared to be that of regulating the timing of the endogenous rhythms, and not that of providing an input of energy to drive the rhythm.

In the present chapter we will examine our current knowledge of the characteristics of circadian rhythms, with emphasis on both their chronometric functions and the mechanisms by which they are influenced (phase set) by photoperiod. Insects are not unique in respect to circadian rhythms; nearly every group of organisms has evolved rhythmic functions. The ubiquity of circadian rhythms points to their fundamental biological importance, and has resulted in extensive experimental study of rhythms in both primitive and highly evolved groups of plants and animals, ranging from single cells, insects, mammals, and man (see recent reviews by Bünning, 1964; Wolfson, 1964; Aschoff, 1965; Sweeney, 1965; and Mills, 1966).

Biological systems that appear to display a capacity for time measurement have been termed "biological clocks." Time relationships are apparently involved not only in the regulation of day-to-day expression of circadian rhythms, but also in well-defined seasonal responses. Seasonal changes in the pelage characteristics of mammals, the flowering of plants, the body form and pigmentation of a number of insects, and the induction of hibernatory states in many different organisms are all examples of the biological effects of the seasonal cycle of daylengths (photoperiods). There might be, therefore, a basis for postulating the existence of a "biological calendar" as well as a "biological clock" in the temporal affairs of organisms.

Great care must be taken in the use of terms such as "biological clock" and "biological time measurement," because there is danger of implying anthropocentric concepts that have no scientific validity. A rhythmic phenomenon in which approximately similar physiological and be-havioral patterns recur endogenously and predictably is susceptible to interpretation as a time-measuring system. However, the detection of a rhythmic biological process does not constitute a demonstration of its time-measuring function. There is a time delay characteristic of any stimulus-response system, whether in terms of milliseconds, hours, days, or months. If such a time relationship is determined by the dy-namics characteristic of the system, it should not be interpreted as con-stituting a clock of some sort. The existence of a biological clock could be deduced only if a degree of temporal freedom could be demon-strated. That is, if a given response to a stimulus were capable of ex-pression at any time following stimulation, but could be held in abeyance until the passage of some arbitrary length of time, the response could then be said to be governed by a biological clock. This is not known to occur in any biological system; all responses are determined. The whole concept of biological time measurement has meaning only insofar as it pertains to the *temporal organization* of the biological system, but is with-out meaning if used to refer to a postulated hour-counting mechanism. Thus, terms such as "periodically consulted biological clocks" and "con-tinuously consulted biological clocks" are both anthropocentric and de-void of biological usefulness. The term *biological clock* will be used in the ensuing discussions, but only in the sense of its symbolizing the set of rhythmic systems determining the temporal organization of the animal. We may legitimately speak of biological time relationships, but not of biological time measurement.

A biological clock might conceivably be of either of two general types: (1) an intermittent, or hourglass system, or (2) a continuously operating rhythmic system. A system of the hourglass type would be one that was set in motion by an environmental signal, such as dawn, and would op-erate until receiving a terminating signal, such as sunset. Its temporal function would be associated with a physiological process such as hormone production or metabolic syntheses occurring only during the photophase or scotophase. The response of the organism would be conditioned by the amounts of end products accumulated during the period of synthesis. An hourglass type of system has been postulated in a number of instances, but appears to be of relatively little general importance in biological time relationships. Such a system would also fail to display any endogenous rhythmicity, since it is, by definition, dependent upon starting and stopping signals of extrinsic origin.

There is, on the other hand, a great deal of evidence that biological time relationships are dependent upon continuously operating rhythmic systems. In order to function as reasonably accurate and biologically useful synchronizing systems, biological clocks might be expected to display three fundamental characteristics: (1) temperature compensation; (2) continuous operation; and (3) susceptibility to phase setting by environmental stimuli such as photoperiod. Each of these characteristics will be discussed in the ensuing sections of this chapter.

TEMPERATURE COMPENSATION OF CIRCADIAN RHYTHMS

The physiological processes of plants and poikilothermic animals are generally sensitive to temperature. Rates of insect growth, metabolism, and general activity tend to be directly proportional to the environmental temperature, within a range of biologically acceptable temperatures (approximately 5°–40°C). The effect of temperature on reaction rates is usually expressed in terms of a *temperature coefficient* (Q_{10}), which for most biological processes will be in the range of 1.5 to 3.0; that is, a 10°C rise in temperature will cause the process rate to increase by a multiple of from 1.5 to 3. On this basis, one might expect that an endogenous rhythm that was not entrained by photoperiod would tend to show a shorter period at higher temperatures than at lower temperatures. The biological clock would tend to run too fast at a high temperature and too slow at a low temperature, and would constitute an exceedingly inaccurate system. A number of studies have shown that such is not the case, and the temperature coefficients of measured circadian rhythms have proved to be very close to unity (from 0.9 to 1.2), (Brown and Webb, 1948; Pittendrigh, 1954; Sweeney and Hastings, 1960). The effect of temperatures on some circadian rhythms in insects is shown in Table IV. Of course, if the environmental temperature is too extreme (below 5°C or above 40°C), the insects will be inactive and no rhythmic behavior will be manifested. But within the normal physiological range of tem-

TABLE IV

Temperature Coefficients for the
Periodicities of Some Circadian Rhythms in Insects

Insect	Rhythm	Temp. (°C)	Observed period (hr)(min)		Temperature coefficient (Q_{10})	Reference
Leucophaea	Locomotion	20	25	6	1.04	Roberts
maderae		30	24	17		(1960)
Drosophila	Adult	16	24	30	1.02	Pittendrigh
pseudoobscura	emergence	26	24	0		(1954)
Periplaneta	Locomotion	19	24	24	1.06	Bünning
americana		29	25	48		(1958)
Apis mellifera	Feeding (trained)	23	24	—	*ca.* 1.00	Wahl
		31	24	—		(1932)
Schistocerca	Cuticle lamella	26	24	—	*ca.* 1.04	Neville
gregaria	deposition	36	23	—		(1965)

perature, the circadian periodicity of endogenous rhythms appears to be only slightly influenced by temperatures.

Temperature does have an effect on rhythmic activities, however. In the first place, the amplitude of a rhythm may be greater at a favorable than at an unfavorable temperature. If the rhythm being observed is one of daily locomotion, a favorably high temperature may result in greater total activity among the insects than would be observed at a lower temperature. But the activity rhythm would continue to display a periodicity of approximately 24 hours; that is, the number of hours between the times of the onset of activity would continue to be about 24 hours. The second principal effect of temperature on circadian rhythms is that of a phase regulator. As will be discussed in a later section, changes in temperature may act as phase-setting stimuli. Thus the rhythm may be phase shifted by a sudden change of temperature, but once a new equilibrium has been established, the rhythm will continue with no change in the length of its period.

The mechanisms by which circadian rhythms are temperature compensated have not been elucidated. It has been suggested, however, that the relative temperature independence of rhythmic functions might indicate the involvement of two or more reaction systems with temperature coefficients that are of opposite sign. If the rhythmic function were rate dependent on a physical process, such an adsorption, which has a negative temperature coefficient, and a subsequent series of enzymatic reactions with positive temperature coefficients, the net process might be relatively temperature independent. Thus, each component of the rhythmic system would display a temperature dependence, but in the overall rhythmic function the individual temperature coefficients would tend to cancel out to produce a resultant coefficient approaching 1.0. There is no experimental evidence to support this hypothesis, however.

Temperature compensation of the biological clock might also be accounted for in terms of temporal cycles of qualitative changes in the programming of metabolic processes. That is, if a controlling system at the molecular level underwent rhythmic changes in the type of end product (messenger RNA, for instance), the physiology of the organism would undergo qualitative changes. Temperature would certainly influence the quantities of metabolic end products, but their chemical identities would have been determined by temperature-independent information-exchange processes at the chromosome level. There is no significant experimental evidence in support of this hypothesis, either.

Continuous Operation of Circadian Rhythms

As amply illustrated by the numerous examples discussed in the previous chapters, daily rhythms of locomotion, feeding, oviposition, and emergence are basically endogenous. They continue to be manifested as circadian rhythms even in the absence of an entraining photoperiod or thermoperiod. If we disregard the possibility of there being entraining signals from the environment that are unknown and uncontrolled by the experimenter, the endogenous characteristic would lead us to believe that the rhythmic functions constituting the biological clock are in continuous operation.

The observable rhythmic behavior may be modified or suppressed by unfavorable environmental conditions without a concomitant suppression of the underlying controlling systems. For this reason, it is thought that the behavioral rhythms themselves do not constitute the biological clock, but are overt indicator processes whose temporal manifestations are determined by a more fundamental biological clock system. This concept may be illustrated by the results of experimentation on the adult emergence rhythm of *Drosophila* species. A *Drosophila* population (laboratory culture) will not show an adult emergence rhythm if it has been maintained in continuous darkness through its entire developmental cycle. If, however, the population is exposed to a short flash of light at any time during the larval stages, an adult emergence rhythm will be manifested (Pittendrigh, 1954; Brett, 1955). It is thought that the light signal has the effect of synchronizing the rhythmic functions of all the members of the population. A single synchronizing signal occurring early in development apparently determines the time of emergence of the adult form of each insect. This means that the physiological rhythms must operate continuously through the larval stages, pupal development, and adult differentiation in order to determine the time of the eclosion event. That the population rhythm of adult emergence may be accurately predicted in relation to a single light signal given during the larval stage, attests to the precision of the insect's biological clock.

In a number of instances, experimenters have entrained circadian rhythmic processes to unnatural photoperiods—such as 12-, 16-, 20-, and 28-hour cycles. Within limits, behavioral rhythms could be forced to adopt such unnatural periods, but upon return to constant conditions of dim light or darkness, the rhythms always reverted to a circadian periodicity. The rhythms have never been observed to maintain artificially impressed unnatural periodicities (Brett, 1955; Harker, 1958, 1961; Pittendrigh, 1960; Roberts, 1962; Moriarty, 1959; Bünning, 1964).

Characteristics of Free-Running Circadian Rhythms

Under constant environmental conditions in which there is no entraining factor, a continuously operating circadian rhythm is said to be *free running*. The characteristics of free-running rhythms have been studied in a number of forms. Particular emphasis has been put on investigation of the time-related properties of free-running rhythms and their relationships to biological clocks.

E. Bünning of the University of Tübingen conducted pioneer studies of daily rhythms in plants, using the rhythmic motions of the leaves of bean seedlings (*Phaseolus multiflorus*). Some of our most basic concepts concerning circadian rhythmicity have come from his research on bean seedlings. Bünning found that the seedling's primary leaves assumed an extended upright position during the daylight hours, but a more drooping position prevailed at night (Fig. 14). When the plants were held under constant conditions, the rhythm of leaf movement continued on an endogenous basis, at least for a few days. Smoked drum tracings of the leaf tip movements showed an undulating rhythm in which the tracing resembled a sine wave (Fig. 14). Bunning distinguished two phases within the daily rhythm: a "tension" phase, normally occurring during the photophase, in which leaf movement was upward; and a "relaxa-

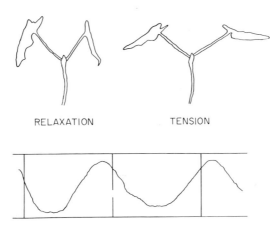

Fig. 14. Circadian rhythm of tension and relaxation in the leaves of a bean seedling. [Adapted from Bünning (1964).]

tion" phase in which leaf movement was downward during the scoto-phase. The tension phase was characterized as being physiologically synthetic and anabolic, requiring an input of energy. The relaxation phase was considered to be more nearly akin to dark metabolism, and was principally catabolic in nature. The leaf movement rhythm could be visualized in terms of a *continuing oscillation* between tension and relaxa-tion phases. The leaf rhythm was interpreted as an *indicator process* pointing to a fundamental time-measuring system in the organism. The fundamental system, or physiological clock, was visualized as a single circadian oscillator to which other rhythmic functions could be coupled. This single oscillator was phase set by dawn—the beginning of the photophase. The tension phase was considered to be from 11 to 13 hours duration, and was followed by the relaxation phase. Since the oscillator was phase set by dawn and not by sunset, the environmental scotophase might or might not coincide with the beginning of the relax-ation phase of the endogenous oscillation, depending on the daylength to which the organism was exposed. In the case of a relatively long day-length (>13 hours), light energy input will continue during the early part of the relaxation phase of the endogenous oscillation, causing a long-day photoperiodic response by the organism. On this basis, Bün-ning has sought to explain the effects of photoperiod on behavioral, biochemical, and developmental phenomena. The Bünning hypothesis offers a single explanation of both phase setting of overt rhythms, such as locomotion in animals and leaf movements in plants, and the photoperiodic induction of such phenomena as plant flowering and insect diapause. For a more complete account of this theory, the reader is referred to Bünning's publications (1960a,b, 1964).

The endogenous oscillator model of the biological clock has proved to be a very useful conceptual basis on which to build. As might be expected, it has been necessary to modify the original concept in a number of ways. In the first place, more than one endogenous oscillator system appears to be necessary to account for most experimental results. On the basis of the appearance of transient phases in the adult emergence rhythm of *Drosophila*, and on differences between temperature and photoperiodic responses of the emergence rhythm, Pittendrigh and his associates found it necessary to postulate the existence of at least two endogenous oscillating systems (Pittendrigh, 1958b; Pittendrigh and Bruce, 1957, 1959; Bruce and Pittendrigh, 1957; Pittendrigh *et al.*, 1958). One of the oscillators was considered to be the pacemaker and to be phase set by photoperiodic stimuli; this oscillator was termed the *Endogenous Self-Sustaining Oscillator A* (ESSO A). The second oscillator was also endogenous and self-sustaining, but was entrained by ESSO A; the second oscillator, called the ESSO B system, was considered to be temperature sensitive, and perhaps also subject to the modifying influences of other physical and chemical factors. The emergence rhythm itself was assumed to be coupled to the B oscillator. It should be recognized that neither Bünning's oscillator nor the ESSO system has been

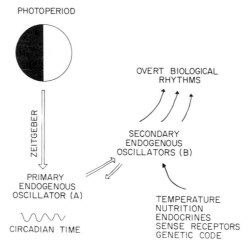

Fig. 15. Hypothetical relationships between endogenous circadian rhythms and photoperiodic entrainment.

demonstrated; they represent theoretical models for the interpretation of photoperiodic responses. And as such, they have been useful but not without limitations. Much experimental data suggest the need for postulating the operation of many ESSO B type rhythms in an organism, each of which may be entrained by the ESSO A oscillator independently. This general concept of circadian rhythms and photoperiodism is depicted diagrammatically in Fig. 15.

Continuous recordings of circadian rhythms, such as leaf movements, have usually been in the form of more-or-less sinusoid curves, as in Fig. 14. Daily rhythms of light production by luminescent microorganisms have also been found to be in sine wave form (Hastings and Sweeney, 1958, 1959), as have oxygen consumption rhythms in a number of different kinds of organisms. For these reasons, most workers have adopted the convention of representing rhythmic functions by curves that oscillate in a sine wave form. This practice is arbitrary, but has the advantage of emphasizing that an oscillation is a continuously changing state. It must be realized, however, that not all indicator processes (locomotor rhythms, for example) can be accurately portrayed by such curves. Neither is it certain that the physiological and molecular processes that lie at the foundation of rhythms can be adequately visualized as following any such form of oscillation.

Some of the terms that will be used in subsequent sections of this chapter are defined in Fig. 16. In the case of an observable rhythmic phenomenon, such as locomotion or adult emergence, the onset of activity occurs at a well-defined point in the rhythm, and constitutes the measurable indicator process; this point we will refer to as the *overt phase*. The rest of the oscillation is hypothetical, but will be referred to as the *overt rhythm*. *Phase angle* is a term used to describe the position of any given point (usually the overt phase) on the curve in relation to the origin. This term reflects the fact that a sine wave is generated by the path followed by a point on the circumference of a moving circle, as diagrammed in Fig. 16. A phase angle of 15° is the equivalent of 1 hour in a 24-hour cycle. However, the period of an endogenous circadian rhythm is seldom exactly 24 hours. For this reason, and because the phase relationship between the circadian rhythm and the environmental phase-setting signals (*Zeitgeber*) may vary, the time scale shown in the figure is in terms of *circadian time*. The circadian time scale has been set at a 24-hour period arbitrarily. The importance of this convention will be more apparent when we consider the problem of photoperiodic entrainment of circadian rhythms. The circadian time scale is based on

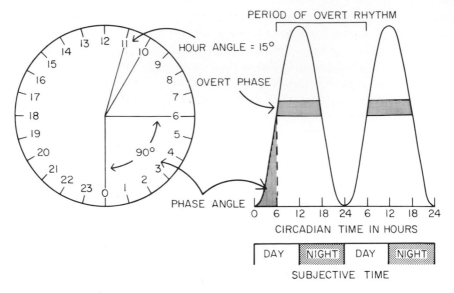

Fig. 16. Some theoretical concepts used in describing circadian functions.

hour 0 as being the time of the beginning of the photophase (dawn), as if the system was entrained to a photoperiod. In the free-running state, there is no photophase or scotophase, but the first 12 circadian hours are considered as corresponding to a daytime state, and this half of the circadian cycle is called the *subjective day*. Circadian hours 12 through 24 are known as the *subjective night*, because the free-running oscillator is assumed to be in a phase that would normally occur during the scotophase of a 12L:12D photoperiod.

A free-running rhythm may have a natural period of greater than or less than 24 hours, thus the term *circadian*. It was once thought that the period of a circadian rhythm was constant within the life of an individual animal, or perhaps within a species. We now know that such is not the case, and that there are factors which influence the period of the free-running rhythm. The free-running rhythm may show changes in period that appear to be spontaneous. Although the rhythm is not hastened by high temperatures nor retarded by low temperatures, it is influenced by light intensity. Also, the insect's previous history of exposure to both light and temperature exerts an influence on the characteristics of its rhythms when in the free-running state.

In a study of the free-running rhythm of locomotor activity in cockroaches, Roberts (1960) compared the periods of the rhythms among individuals of the same species, and also measured the effects of different light intensities. Individual specimens of adult male *Leucophaea maderae* showed free-running activity rhythms that varied in period from 23 hours 16 minutes to 24 hours 0 minutes under conditions of continuous darkness. This variation was between individual insects, not day-to-day variations in individual actographs. When the same group of cockroaches was transferred to continuous dim light, the periods tended to lengthen, and the range was then from 24 hours 2 minutes to 24 hours 45 minutes. The average increase in period length was 36 minutes. The converse effect has been observed among a number of diurnal animals. In these cases, the period of the free-running activity rhythm was shorter under continuous light than under continuous darkness (Harker, 1958, 1964; Bünning, 1964). Continuous light may, of course, be of different intensities, and light intensity has been found to influence the periodicity of free-running rhythms. No systematic studies have been made with insects, but a number of other animal groups have been investigated. In the case of diurnal forms such as birds, reptiles, and protozoa, the periods of the rhythms tended to be inversely proportional to the light intensities to which the animals were exposed. Nocturnal animals, such as mice, reacted in the opposite manner; the higher the intensity of continuous light, the longer the period of the free-running rhythm. The prevalence of these responses among diverse animal forms has led to what is known as *Aschoff's rule* (Aschoff, 1958, 1960). Exactly stated, Aschoff's rule is that: *under conditions of continuous illumination, increasing light intensities tend to lengthen the periods of free-running rhythms in nocturnal animals and to shorten the periods of free-running rhythms in diurnal animals.* This rule cannot be taken as a universally valid generalization, because some exceptions are known. In some nocturnal forms, activity may be entirely suppressed by continuous illumination; such has been observed in the case of dragon fly nymphs, stick insects, and many small aquatic animals (Eidmann, 1956; Serfaty, 1945; Anderson, 1966). Similarly, continuous darkness tends to suppress the activity of some diurnal forms, such as the desert locust, *Schistocerca gregaria* (Odhiambo, 1966).

Previously experienced photoperiods exert an influence on the period length of free-running rhythms. The cockroaches *Blaberus giganteus* and *L. maderae* were maintained in constant darkness, with their individual activity rhythms being recorded (Harker, 1964). They were then transferred to a 12L:12D photoperiod for 5 days, and were then returned to continuous darkness. During the post-photoperiod free run, the length of the period of the activity rhythm differed from its previous value in every insect tested. Harker (1964) demonstrated that the change induced by exposure to the photoperiod was correlated with the *circadian time* that the insects experienced the beginning of the photophase. A cockroach that was in the overt phase of its activity rhythm at the time it was first exposed to light would display an increased period length upon subsequent return to the free-running state. Conversely, if the onset of light occurred several hours after the insect had completed its active phase, the period of the rhythm would subsequently be shorter than its prephotoperiod value. The sign and amount of change were found to be dependent upon the circadian time of the initial photoperiodic entraining stimulus, and the changes so induced were stable under the conditions of continuous darkness.

Some of the behavioral rhythms discussed in Chapter 2 were bimodal in form; there were two periods of activity per diel cycle. Under conditions of continuous darkness or continuous dim illumination, bimodal activity rhythms have been reported in insects that do not display bimodality under natural conditions. Roberts (1960) reported that "secondary" periods of activity occurred with *L. maderae* and *Periplaneta americana* under continuous light, but not when the cockroaches were maintained in darkness.

Photoperiodic Entrainment of Endogenous Rhythms

Under natural conditions, insects are exposed to one sunrise and one sunset each day. Phase regulation of rhythmic functions involves daily adjustments of only a few minutes each day, because of the gradual nature of seasonal changes in daylength. These minor daily adjustments serve to maintain the insect in adaptive synchrony with the environmental photoperiod. The organism's endogenous biological rhythms are thus maintained in entrainment with the exogenous photoperiodic rhythm. There has been much interest in the problem of how entrainment is effected. Research on this problem has involved subjecting insects to extreme and unnatural conditions, and then observing the effects of such conditions on the manifestation of overt rhythms. From the observed effects, attempts have been made to deduce some of the characteristics of the rhythmic systems and the mechanisms of photoperiodic entrainment.

The adult emergence rhythm of *Drosophila* flies has been studied in greater detail than any other insect rhythm, due principally to the intensive research of C. S. Pittendrigh and his associates at Princeton University. Much of the theoretical basis for the ensuing summary of the current understanding of photoperiodic entrainment has been drawn from the published reports of Professor Pittendrigh's research group. It should be pointed out, however, that research biologists are not unanimous in their interpretations of periodic effects, and that not all of the recorded observations can be fully explained by any of the generalized concepts thus far proposed.

Some of the well-defined characteristics of a photoperiodically en-trained rhythm are shown in Fig. 17. This figure depicts the day-to-day pattern of a hypothetical rhythm, which is termed *Overt Rhythm* (OR), the onset (*overt phase*) of which occurs 2 hours after the beginning of the photophase. Under a regularly repeated photoperiod composed of a

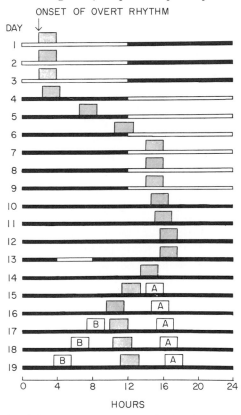

Fig. 17. Characteristics of photoperiodic entrainment of a hypothetical Overt Rhythm.

69

12-hour photophase and a 12-hour scotophase (12L:12D), the overt phase occurred at the same time each day. As shown in the figure, the scotophase of day 3 was experimentally extended into day 4 in order to effect a reversed photoperiod. The Overt Rhythm responded by being delayed on days 4, 5, 6, regaining its normal entrained position (overt phase 2 hours after dawn) on day 7. The transient phases of days 4 to 6 are of interest, because they demonstrate that the Overt Rhythm is susceptible to photoperiodic entrainment. The occurrence of the transient phases also suggests that the entire rhythmic system cannot make a 12-hour phase-setting adjustment in one step. This observation suggests two alternative hypotheses in respect to the mechanism of entrainment: (1) the entire biological clock system can make only limited step-wise adjustments, requiring the manifestation of transient responses; or (2) a fundamental pacemaker rhythm (ESSO A) is phase set immediately upon stimulation and without transient phases, but the Overt Rhythm (ESSO B) follows the pacemaker only gradually, requiring up to several cycles to be fully reentrained. The response data obtained from days 1 through 9 do not provide any basis for choosing between these two hypotheses.

On day 10, the insects were placed under continuous darkness. The Overt Rhythm adopted a 24.5-hour circadian periodicity, as indicated by the time of the overt phase on days 10 through 12. A 4-hour light period was then inserted on the thirteenth day, and its effect on the Overt Rhythm was observed during the subsequent days of continuous darkness. The Overt Rhythm showed transient phases on days 13, 14, and 15; its steady state was attained on day 16, following which it returned to its circadian periodicity of 24.5 hours (days 17, 18, 19).

On the basis of the response to the single light period, we can make a reasonable choice between the two hypotheses posed earlier. The phase-setting effect of the single light period imposed on day 13 suggests that the second of our two alternative interpretations is the more likely to be correct; that is, that the insect's pacemaker rhythm was reset by the light signal, but that transient phases were required for the Overt Rhythm to regain its normal entrainment. Were the first alternative correct, either of two effects should have been observed: (a) If the entire biological clock system were capable of only a limited phase-setting response to the light signal on day 13, the Overt Rhythm should have been manifested at positions "A" on days 15 through 19. This is because the system should have returned to a circadian periodicity when no light stimulus occurred on day 14. (b) If, however, the signal on day 13 had the effect of shortening the period of the Overt Rhythm, so as to move the overt phase toward the time that a similar light stimulation would occur on day 14, the Overt Rhythm should have been observed at positions "B" on days 17 through 19. Under such circumstances, the stabilization of the rhythm and its entrainment to the new light period would be dependent upon several repetitions of the signal. But in the absence of such repeated stimuli, the shortened period of the Overt Rhythm would be maintained, as the rhythm continued to "hunt" for the entrained position. Because a single light pulse cannot be construed as constituting a photoperiod, its effect cannot logically be interpreted in terms of the light signal's having "impressed" a new photoperiodic time relationship on the free-running rhythm.

Although the rhythmic responses diagrammed in Fig. 17 represent a hypothetical experimental series, the concepts illustrated by the "data" presented represent a summary of a great deal of experimental work reported by a number of research programs. Present evidence is strongly in favor of the interpretation that overt rhythms are coupled to an unidentified pacemaker rhythm (ESSO A) that is fundamental to the organism's temporal organization. This fundamental biological clock system is immediately responsive to phase-setting environmental signals. Overt rhythms are coupled to the primary rhythmic system, and the endogenous self-sustaining oscillators of the B type (ESSO B), as discussed in an earlier paragraph.

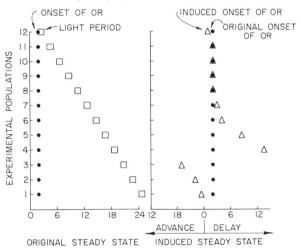

Fig. 18. Effects of single light pulses on the phase setting of a hypothetical Overt Rhythm (OR).

The phase-setting effects of single light pulses (a fraction of a second or an hour or more) have been found to vary greatly, depending on the time of their occurrence. This is illustrated in Fig. 18, which represents another hypothetical series of experiments. As in the previous example, this hypothetical series is designed to summarize the concepts gained through a large body of experimental research. The time scale shown in Fig. 18 is *circadian time*; that is, hour 0 is the beginning of the circadian rhythm and is equivalent to the beginning of the photophase, were the rhythm entrained to a photoperiod. The period of the circadian rhythm has been normalized at 24.0 hours in order to depict the overt phase of the Overt Rhythm at circadian hour 2. Figure 18A shows the time of the Overt Rhythm and the circadian time that each of a series of 12 insect populations were exposed to a single short pulse of light. Other than the single, unrepeated light pulse, the insects were maintained in the dark. Transient phases induced by the light pulse are not shown, but the new steady state of the free-running Overt Rhythm is shown for each of the treated cultures (open triangles in Fig. 18B). It is seen that the circadian time at which the light stimulus was applied determined the direction and extent of the induced phase shifting. Single light pulses applied early in the circadian time schedule had very small effects; those applied between the twelfth and eighteenth circadian hours caused progressively greater phase shifts toward times later than the original onset

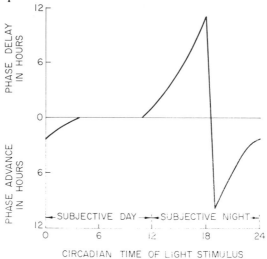

Fig. 19. Effects of single 15-minute light pulses on phase shifts in the adult emergence rhythm of Drosophila pseudoobscura. [Adapted from Pittendrigh (1958b).]

times. A light pulse at the twentieth hour had the opposite effect, and the final steady-state position of the Overt Rhythm was much earlier than the original circadian time.

Using the adult emergence rhythm of *Drosophila pseudoobscura* cultures, Pittendrigh has measured the effects of the circadian time of light stimulation on the direction and extent of phase changes, as shown in Fig. 19 (Pittendrigh, 1958b, 1960, 1961, 1965). Delay phase shifts were observed to be accomplished with only one or two transient phases, and the new steady state was soon attained. Advance phase shifts required up to 6 transient phases before the new steady state was accomplished. Response curves generally similar to Fig. 19 have been obtained for the overt rhythms of a wide variety of plants, mammals, birds, protozoa, and insects (Pittendrigh, 1960, 1961; Roberts, 1962; Harker, 1964; Minis, 1965).

Thus far in this discussion we have not dealt with photoperiods; we have been concerned only with the effects of timed light pulses. To be sure, a photoperiod includes an onset of light (hour 0 on the circadian time scale), but it also includes a duration of light, a cessation of light (onset of the scotophase), and a duration of darkness. In experiments such as those shown in Figs. 18 and 19, in which light pulses were employed to cause phase shifts, the duration of light has been found to influence the responses obtained. For example, the response of the *Drosophila* emergence rhythm to single 12-hour light pulses was similar to that shown in Fig. 19, except that the range of delays and advances was greater, and the curve tended to be shifted to the left so that large phase shifts were observed earlier in the circadian day (Pittendrigh, 1960).

The phase angle between the onset of the photophase and that of the overt rhythm has been found to depend, at least in part, on the nature of the photoperiod. The relationships between daylength and the overt phases of three different insect rhythms are illustrated in Fig. 20. In this figure, hour 0 of the ordinate marks the beginning of the photophases. Points plotted in the stippled areas represent overt phases occurring during the scotophase, and plotted points falling in the white areas represent events occurring during the photophase. Curve A is from the results of Pittendrigh and Minis (1964) on the eclosion rhythm of *D. pseudoobscura*. Very short photophases caused the emergence rhythm to entrain at a predawn phase angle. The phase of the emergence rhythm tended to assume postdawn positions with photophases greater than 6 hours. In the presence of very long daylengths (photo-

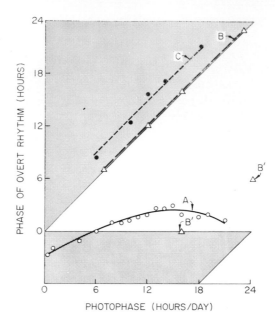

Fig. 20. Effects of daylength on photoperiodic entrainment of three different Overt Rhythms. A = adult emergence rhythm of Drosophila pseudoobscura [based on data of Pittendrigh and Minis (1964)]; B = locomotor activity rhythm of Leucophaea maderae [based on data of Roberts (1962)]; C = ovipositional rhythm of Pectinophora gossypiella [based on data of Minis (1965)]. Stippled areas represent hours of darkness.

phases greater than 16 hours), the phase angle again tended to become smaller.

The ovipositional rhythm of the pink bollworm, *Pectinophora gossypiella,* maintained a constant relationship to the beginning of the scotophase in each of the several daylengths tested (Fig. 20, curve C) (Minis, 1965). The overt phase of the locomotor rhythm in the cockroach *Leucophaea* was also closely entrained to the beginning of the scotophase (curve B) (Roberts, 1962). The cockroach rhythm showed one particularly interesting feature, however; under daylengths of either 16 or 23 hours, the activity rhythm was bimodal (Fig. 20, points B'). The activity manifested at these times occurred during the photophase. Unfortunately no photophases of durations between 16 and 23 hours were tested.

There are good reasons for regarding photoperiodic entrainment as involving the insect's response to two temporally spaced stimuli—the light-on stimulus marking the beginning of the photophase and the light-off stimulus occurring at the onset of the scotophase. The hypothesis that phase regulation is accomplished by an interaction of responses to these two stimuli was tested by Pittendrigh and Minis (1964). In order to minimize the possible physiological effects of long light exposures, a system of *skeletal photoperiods* was used. This involved maintaining the experimental insects in continuous darkness, except for two brief (15-minute) pulses of light each day. One pulse was arbitrarily taken as representing time 0 hours, and the second was given at different times thereafter. The effects of such skeletal photoperiods on the adult emergence rhythm of *Drosophila* and the ovipositional rhythm of *Pectinophora* are shown in Fig. 21. When the two light pulses were 12 or

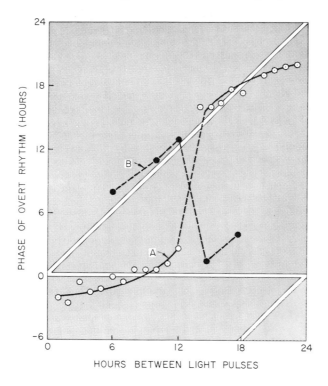

Fig. 21. Effects of skeletal photoperiods (15-minute light pulses) on the entrainment of Overt Rhythms. A = adult emergence rhythm of Drosophila pseudoobscura [based on data of Pittendrigh and Minis (1964)]; B = ovipositional rhythm of Pectinophora gossypiella [based on data of Minis (1965)]. Stippled areas represent hours of darkness.

75

fewer hours apart, entrainment was similar to that observed under short photoperiods (Fig. 20). The skeletal system appeared to be fully equivalent to the corresponding photoperiod, and the rhythmic systems responded to the skeletal "photophase" just as to a normally illuminated photophase. However, as the skeletal photophases exceeded 12 hours duration, the entrainment response underwent a sharp change. There was a phase shift, so that the overt rhythm became entrained as if the shorter of the two skeletal phases were the "photophase" (Fig. 21). It would appear, then, that: (1) photoperiodic entrainment is based on the phase-setting effects of two signals, temporally separated; (2) under normal conditions, the continued presence of light during the photophase prevents the overt rhythm from entraining on the shorter of the two photoperiodic phases. As was discussed earlier (page 73), the duration of light pulses influences their phase-setting effects on free-running circadian rhythms. There is also some evidence that light intensity exerts an influence on the characteristics of phase shifts (Hastings and Sweeney, 1958; Bünning, 1964). The effects of both duration and intensity of light during the photophase is only poorly understood at the present time. There seems little doubt, however, that photoperiodic entrainment involves two temporally spaced stimuli, even though phase-setting effects of single stimuli may be observed with free-running overt rhythms.

Some aspects of photoperiodic entrainment of circadian rhythms can be effectively explained on the basis of the phase-setting responses to different photoperiods, skeletal photoperiods, and single light pulses. Based on these several characteristics of the adult emergence rhythm in *Drosophila*, Pittendrigh and co-workers have formulated a mathematical model of entrainment (Pittendrigh and Minis, 1964; Pittendrigh, 1965). This theory of entrainment was based on empirical observational data on the advances and delays caused by single stimuli delivered at different circadian times (Fig. 19). The entraining photoperiod generates two such phase-setting signals during each 24-hour cycle (light-on and light-off stimuli). The steady-state entrainment represents an equilibrium between the advance and delay phase shifts generated by the two daily photoperiodic stimuli. The endogenous rhythms of the biological clock system run on a circadian basis. The observable phase of an overt rhythm, such as adult emergence, maintains a characteristic phase angle in respect to hour 0 of the circadian time scale. The net phase shift that is involved in the maintenance of a steady-state entrainment to a diel photoperiod must be the difference between the period of the circadian rhythm and the period of the photoperiodic rhythm. That is:

$$T - \tau = \Delta\phi ss$$

where T = the period of the entraining photoperiod (normally 24.0 hours), τ = the circadian period of the endogenous rhythm (>24 hours or <24 hours), and $\Delta\phi ss$ = the net phase shift at equilibrium (steady state). However, $\Delta\phi ss$ is determined by the algebraic sum of the advance and delay phase shifts induced by the light-on and light-off signals generated by the photoperiod. Therefore:

$$T - \tau = (\Delta\phi_1) + (\Delta\phi_2)$$

where $\Delta\phi_1$ and $\Delta\phi_2$ are the phase shifts induced by the two photoperiodic signals.

The circadian rhythm will be entrained by the photoperiod such that the net phase shift per day will be equal to the difference between the circadian and photoperiodic periods. The steady-state phase of the overt rhythm can then be predicted quite accurately, provided that the phase-shift response curve (i.e. Fig. 19) has been determined for the system. Because the response curve is influenced by both signal duration and light intensity, as discussed earlier, the model can produce meaningful predictions of phase relationships only under rigidly controlled conditions. The theoretical model is of value, however, because it constitutes a clear statement of our current understanding of photoperiodic entrainment of endogenous circadian rhythms.

Pittendrigh's theoretical model also yields some information on the temporal limits of entrainment. Again the phase-shift response curve for the rhythm in question supplies the essential data. Theoretically, a circadian rhythm of period can be entrained by any experimental photoperiod having a period T that does not exceed the limits set by the relationship:

$$T_{limit} = \tau + (\Delta\phi_{max})$$

where $\Delta\phi_{max}$ is the maximum phase shift (either advance or delay) effected by a single stimulus. For example, if $\tau = 25$ hours and $\Delta\phi_{max} = 8$ hours, the system could, theoretically, be entrained by any photoperiod in which T was between 17 and 33 hours. T values lying outside of this range would not lead to entrainment, because the system could not attain a steady-state equilibrium.

77

Thermoperiodic Entrainment of Circadian Rhythms

Although temperature has been found to have little effect on the periodicity of endogenous rhythms, a phase-setting influence has been observed in a number of cases. In its natural environment, an insect is exposed to daily fluctuations of temperature, in which the daily maximum usually occurs in the late afternoon and the daily minimum at about dawn. Although much less precise than photoperiod, thermoperiod might also be expected to influence daily behavioral patterns. There is considerable evidence that such is the case, but thermoperiod generally plays a less decisive role than does photoperiod in phase-setting rhythmic functions (Bünning, 1964; Wilkins, 1965).

Locomotor rhythms of the cockroaches *Leucophaea maderae* and *Periplaneta americana* were found to be phase set by thermoperiod in the absence of a photoperiod (Roberts, 1962). In these experiments, the insects were maintained in continuous darkness, and their activity rhythms were free running. They were then exposed to a shallow thermoperiod in which the temperature followed a sinusoid cycle from 22° to 27°C. The cockroaches' activity rhythms were entrained by the thermoperiod so that the overt phase of the rhythm occurred at the time of the maximum daily temperature. When returned to a constant temperature and continued darkness, the activity rhythms resumed a circadian free-running periodicity.

Pittendrigh (1958b) reported experimental results on the effects of a thermoperiod on the adult emergence rhythm of *Drosophila pseudo-obscura*. The fly cultures were entrained to a 12-hour daylength, and a thermoperiod was superimposed on the photoperiod. In different cultures, the minimum daily temperature was made to occur at different times within the photoperiod (Fig. 22). Under natural conditions, *Drosophila* emergence tends to occur at dawn or slightly thereafter, which is also the time of the daily temperature minimum. The same effect was observed in the thermoperiod experiments, but the influence of photoperiod tended to override that of thermoperiod. Fly emergence tended to occur at dawn when the temperature minimum occurred at any time during the scotophase. If the temperature minimum came during the photophase, however, the photoperiodic entrainment of the emergence rhythm was modified, and the overt phase occurred at the time of the minimum temperature.

The adult emergence rhythm of the Mediterranean flour moth, *Anagasta Kühniella,* has been found to be entrained by thermoperiod.

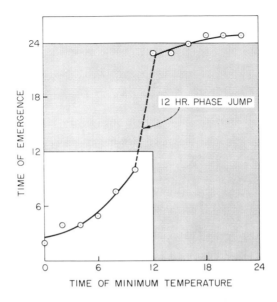

Fig. 22. *Effect of thermoperiod on adult emergence rhythm of Drosophila pseudoobscura populations maintained under a 12L:12D photoperiod. Stippled areas represent hours of darkness.* [*Adapted from Pittendrigh (1958).*]

When thermoperiodically entrained, the moths tended to emerge mainly during the first few hours following the daily temperature maximum (Scott, 1936; Moriarty, 1959). Scott (1936) reported that the insects could be induced to display a 16-hour emergence rhythm if the cultures were held in constant darkness and subjected to a 16-hour temperature rhythm. Upon return to constant temperature, however, the emergence rhythm reverted to a circadian periodicity.

An adult emergence rhythm in the Queensland fruit fly, *Dacus tryoni*, was described by Bateman (1955). Pupae of this species were found to be insensitive to photoperiod; the emergence rhythm was determined by the photoperiods experienced during the egg and larval stages. Interestingly enough, however, Bateman found that the pupae were sensitive to temperature signals, and in the presence of a shallow thermoperiod, adult emergence tended to be concentrated at the beginning of the rising temperature phase of the thermoperiod. Unfortunately, no experiments were run to determine the extent of which thermoperiodic entrainment of the emergence rhythm might be effected.

5 □ Photoperiodism and Physiological Functions

The rhythmic phenomena with which we dealt in the previous chapters were overt expressions of the underlying physiological processes that energized and controlled them. Hypothetical endogenous oscillators (such as ESSO A and ESSO B) must ultimately be identified in terms of biophysical and physiological mechanisms. Photoperiodic control of an overt rhythm would appear to involve: (1) a receptor system, via which photoperiodic information (stimuli) is fed into the biological system, resulting in immediate phase setting of (2) the primary time-related rhythmic mechanism (endogenous oscillator A), which may be a central nervous system function, to which (3) numerous physiological rhythms (endogenous oscillators of type B) are entrained, providing the biochemical and feedback mechanisms that control the manifestation of (4) the overt phase of the photoperiodic response. Some photoperiodic responses, however, are nonrhythmic. Diapause, pigmentation, and polymorphism are examples of nonrhythmic responses to photoperiod; these subject will be explored in Chapters 6, 7, and 8. Because of their nonrhythmic expression, there has long been some controversy as to their relationships to the more obviously circadian responses. In the present chapter, we will discuss what is known about physiological rhythms, so that their probable roles in nonrhythmic developmental phenomena may be more efficiently assessed in the later chapters.

A number of well-defined physiological rhythms have been studied in the higher animals. Daily rhythms of heart beat, body temperature, eosinophil counts, hormone production, liver enzyme activity, and several other processes are known (see Halberg, 1960; Aschoff, 1965; Mills, 1966 for recent reviews). In contrast, there is only fragmentary

81

knowledge concerning the physiological rhythms that may occur in insects. Because of the biological importance of Insecta, and the great usefulness as insects as experimental forms in many areas of biological research, there is great need for exacting research studies of the physiological rhythms in this group of animals. Both the need and the opportunity are emphasized by the observation that dramatic polymorphism is among the photoperiodic responses of many insect species, and polymorphism is a phenomenon that reaches the very heart of the major biological problem of growth and differentiation.

METABOLIC PERIODISM,

Oxygen Consumption Rates

Daily rhythms in the rates of oxygen uptake have been reported in several insect species. An early study by Michal (1931) showed that larvae of the yellow mealworm, *Tenebrio molitor,* displayed a shallow rhythm of oxygen consumption. Other than the observation that the respiratory rhythm had a period of about 24 hours, nothing was reported as to its properties. Campbell (1964) confirmed and greatly extended Michal's observations. She found that the oxygen consumption rate of *Tenebrio* larvae followed a complex rhythmic pattern. Although the highest oxygen uptake rates were observed during the subjective night, the daily rhythm showed several subsidiary peaks and troughs, suggesting that the rhythm had an approximately 6-hour period.

Using a calorimetric method of measuring metabolism, Prat (1956a,b) described rather complex metabolic rhythms in males of the American cockroach, *Periplaneta americana.* Although the heat-production measurements were made in continuous darkness, Prat observed that the insect's metabolic rate was higher during the subjective night than during the subjective day. Irregular metabolic rhythms were also detected among individual grasshoppers of the genus *Melanoplus* and larvae of the greater wax moth, *Galleria mellonella.*

Through the use of continuously recording respirometers, Beck (1963) detected a complex daily rhythm in the oxygen consumption rates in the German cockroach, *Blattella germanica* (Fig. 23). The rhythm was shown to be entrained by photoperiod, in that the positions of the peaks and troughs of the oxygen consumption curve could be altered by experimental changes in the photoperiod. Maximum oxygen consumption rates occurred at about 1 hour after the beginning of the scotophase, and the daily minimum was observed at the onset of the

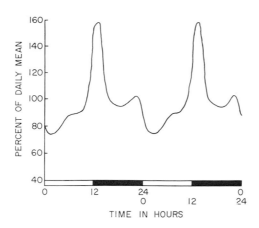

Fig. 23. Photoperiodically entrained oxygen consumption rhythm in adult males of the German cockroach, Blattella germanica. [Adapted from Beck (1963).]

photophase. Further analysis of the oxygen consumption rhythm suggested that the 24-hour rhythm was composed of three subsidiary maxima 8 hours apart (Beck, 1964). It was concluded that the oxygen consumption rhythm possessed an 8-hour period, with the maximum rate being determined by the insect's activity rhythm. Fourier analyses of oxygen consumption rhythms in the American cockroach have also shown the presence of rhythmic components with short, noncircadian periodicity (Richards and Halberg, 1964), but none of the short period rhythms appeared to have either a 6- or an 8-hour periodicity.

Larvae of the European corn borer, *Ostrinia nubilalis*, displayed a daily rhythm of oxygen consumption in which the uptake was at a much higher rate during the scotophase than during the photophase (Beck *et al.*, 1963). That such a rhythm could be attributed to the effects of daily rhythms of feeding and locomotor activity was made highly unlikely by the finding that the oxygen consumption rhythm was clearly detectable during the prolonged larval diapause stage (Fig. 24). Diapausing larvae do not feed and they crawl very little unless disturbed. More detailed study of the respiratory rhythm of the corn borers showed that the rhythm had a period of 8 hours; three complete cycles were recorded each day (Fig. 25). Photoperiodic entrainment was such that the overt phase of the daily maximum coincided with the beginning of the scotophase (Beck, 1964). This rhythm was also shown to be endogenous, as it would continue when the insects were maintained in continuous darkness.

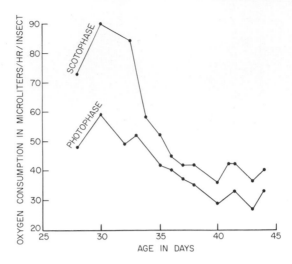

Fig. 24. *Effect of the phase of the photoperiod on oxygen consumption rates in the European corn borer, Ostrinia nubilalis, during diapause. Photoperiod = 12L:12D. [From Beck et al. (1963).]*

Daily rhythms in oxygen consumption rates have been found in a number of insects and other arthropods (Fingerman *et al.*, 1958; Brown, 1959; Rensing, 1964), but whether or not such rhythms are to be expected to occur in all species is still an open question. The ubiquity of

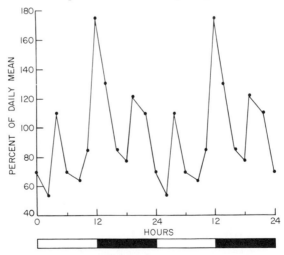

Fig. 25. *Photoperiodically entrained 8-hour rhythm of oxygen consumption rates in larvae of the European corn borer, Ostrinia nubilalis. [From Beck (1964).]*

respiratory rhythms might be anticipated, if for no other reason than the widespread occurrence of general activity rhythms. It should be pointed out, however, that in a few instances rhythmic oxygen consumption rates have been sought but not found (e.g. Moriarty, 1959).

Enzymatic Reactions

The demonstration of activity rhythms and oxygen consumption rhythms would lead one to expect many rhythmic manifestations among enzymatically catalyzed metabolic reaction systems. Rhythmic enzymatic functions have been detected in microorganisms and among the birds and mammals. Few investigations have been devoted to this specific aspect of insect periodism. However, the scattered existing evidence tends to support the concept that enzymatic reactions in insects may display rhythmic components, and the need for detailed investigations is clearly indicated.

Flashing by the firefly *Photinus pyralis* has been shown to occur in the form of an endogenous circadian rhythm (Allard, 1931; Buck, 1937). The fireflies were found to be strongly influenced by both light intensity and intensity changes. Among other effects, Buck reported that a light intensity change from darkness to dim light would induce flashing by the insects, provided that they had been maintained in the dark for 24, 48, 72, or 96 hours. If they had been held in darkness for 12, 36, 60, or 84 hours, the change from darkness to dim illumination did not evoke the flashing response. These observations suggest that the circadian time of stimulation (light-on) played an important role in determining the response. When exposed to continuous dim light, the fireflies began to flash spontaneously for a short time once every 24 hours. The results of this study clearly indicate that the flashing activity of fireflies is coupled to an endogenous rhythmic mechanism.

The biochemistry of light production by *P. pyralis* has been worked out in some detail (McElroy, 1964; Gilmour, 1965). In the presence of adenosine triphosphate (ATP), magnesium ions, oxygen, and the enzyme *luciferase*, the reduced form of the heterocyclic acid *luciferin* is oxidized to an excited state which emits a quantum of light energy. In the insect this process is under nervous system control, the stimulus for flashing coming from branches of the peripheral nerves of the ventral ganglia. A circadian rhythm of flashing activity might be controlled by rhythmic functions within the nervous system, or by metabolic rhythms regulating the availability of ATP, luciferin, or luciferase. Which, if either, of these possibilities is involved in the firefly system is not known.

Bioluminescence in the dinoflagellate *Gonyaulax polyedra* has been shown to be rhythmic, and also to involve a luciferin-luciferase enzymatic reaction (Sweeney and Hastings, 1957; Hastings and Sweeney, 1959). This rhythm was found to be endogenous and entrainable by photoperiod; the light-production phase of the rhythm occurred during the scotophase. Measurements of hourly changes in luciferase activity and luciferin concentration showed both to be rhythmic phenomena (Hastings and Bode, 1962; Bode *et al.*, 1963). Luciferase activity reached its daily maximum in mid-scotophase, with the daily maximum titer of luciferin occurring about 2 hours later. The cells displayed maximum flashing activity at the time when luciferin concentration had reached its maximum level. No comparable studies of the substrate-enzyme relations have been reported for the firefly, but the possibility of such relationships should not be overlooked.

Only a very few instances of rhythmic biochemical changes have been reported as occurring in insects. The hemolymph titer of the sugar trehalose was found to vary according to the time of day in the house cricket, *Acheta domesticus* (Nowosielski and Patton, 1964). Trehalose content of the hemolymph reached its daily maximum during the late scotophase, about 3 hours before the beginning of the photophase. Glycogen analyses of adult mosquitoes, *Culex tarsalis*, were found to show daily fluctuations, with the highest glycogen levels occurring toward the end of the photophase (Takahashi and Harwood, 1964). This glycogen rhythm may have been the result of increased glycogen storage during times of relatively little physical activity, followed by glycogen depletion during the times of active flight and feeding. However, the glycogen synthesis rhythm of the adult mosquito was at least partially determined by the photoperiods under which the larval stages had been reared. This finding suggests that there is more than a simple relationship between the metabolic and activity rhythms in the adult stage. The cycle of glycogen synthesis, storage, and depletion has been found to be controlled by the neurosecretory system of the insect's brain (Handel and Lea, 1965), suggesting neuroendocrine control of the glycogen rhythm. Neuroendocrine control of enzyme synthesis has been demonstrated in a number of cases (Scharrer and Scharrer, 1963; Thomsen and Møller, 1963). And as will be discussed in a subsequent section of this chapter (p. 93), the neurosecretory system appears to be intimately involved in the control of a number of endogenous circadian rhythms and their entrainment by photoperiod.

The best known example of an enzyme that is involved in photo-periodism is the plant pigment *phytochrome* (Borthwick and Hendricks, 1960). Phytochrome occurs in an enzymatically active form when exposed to light, but it changes to an inactive form in the dark. Some, but by no means all, aspects of plant photoperiodism have been explained on the basis of the photodynamics and biochemical action of phyto-chrome (Hamner, 1965). Although the existence of comparable pigment enzymes in insects has been postulated, there is currently no experimental evidence that lends support to the hypothesis. Pigment involvement in photoperiodic stimulus reception seems almost inescapable, but no such system has been demonstrated.

Metabolic processes are universally characterized as enzymatic systems. Biological rhythms, whether behavioral, developmental, or biochemical, must be associated with the functioning of appropriately specific systems of enzymes. The most efficient method for regulating and integrating physiological processes would appear to be through control of enzyme synthesis and the kinetics of enzymatic reactions. In the living cell, deoxyribonucleic acid (DNA) provides the genetic code for the synthesis of short-lived messenger ribonucleic acid (RNA), which in turn forms the templates involved in enzyme and protein synthesis. One of the most appealing hypotheses concerning the fundamental nature of the so-called biological clock is that of Hastings and Sweeney (1959), according to which the primary endogenous oscillating system (ESSO A) is to be found at the molecular level in nucleic acid metabolism. Specifically, the DNA-dependent synthesis of messenger RNA is postulated as the basic rhythmic system. The evidence in support of the hypothesis has come from studies of the luminescence rhythm of the single-celled dinoflagellate *Gonyaulax polyedra,* and there are no pertinent data concerning insect periodism. If valid in single cells, however, the hypothesis is likely to prove to be of general biological significance; it is therefore worthy of brief consideration here.

Two types of light-production rhythms are to be observed in *G. polyedra;* a flashing rhythm and a dimmer background glow rhythm. The glow rhythm shows its maximum light production during the latter part of the scotophase and has been shown to be a photoperiodically entrainable endogenous circadian rhythm. Metabolic inhibitors, such as sodium azide and heavy metal salts were found to exert no effects on the phase setting of the glow rhythm (Hastings and Bode, 1962). Substances known to inhibit DNA, RNA, and protein syntheses were shown

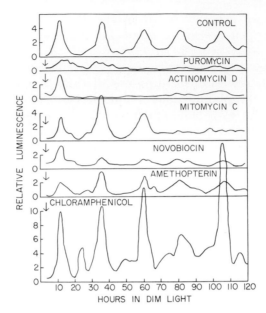

Fig. 26. *Effects of inhibitors on the glow rhythm of Gonyaulax polyedra under free-running conditions of continuous dim illumination. The time of inhibitor administration is indicated by an arrow.* [*Redrawn from Karakashian and Hastings (1963).*]

to exert well-defined effects on the free-running glow rhythm (Fig. 26) (Karakashian and Hastings, 1962, 1963; Hastings and Keynan, 1965). Puromycin, which is known to inhibit protein synthesis, had an immediate suppressing effect on the glow luminescence rhythm; its effect was reversible, and the cells would regain the rhythm with but a slight phase shift. Chloramphenicol also blocks protein synthesis, but is known to stimulate the synthesis of messenger RNA. Its effect on the glow rhythm was to greatly increase the amplitude without affecting the phase. Mitomycin causes a loss of nuclear DNA, and its presence in the cell suspensions caused the glow rhythm to fade out after about three cycles, but without any detectable phase changes. Amethopterin and novobiocin are known to inhibit cellular processes through their blocking DNA synthesis; these substances tended to reduce the amplitude of the glow rhythm, but they had no great effect on the phase setting. Actinomycin D is reputed to be an inhibitor of DNA-dependent RNA synthesis, with its primary biochemical action being that of binding the guanine component of DNA. Actinomycin D was found to inhibit the glow rhythm of the dinoflagellates. Interestingly, the inhibition was manifested only after one cycle of the rhythm, suggesting that the driving biochemical mechanism of a glow peak is determined many hours earlier than its overt expression. Inhibition by actinomycin D could not be reversed; so the possible effects of the inhibitor on phase regulation could not be determined. Hastings and Keynan (1965) concluded that the rhythmicity was, in some unidentified way, dependent on the synthesis of a specific RNA, with this RNA being involved in some process other than (or in addition to) protein synthesis.

Although the RNA-synthesis hypothesis of the biological clock is supported by some experimental evidence, its validity cannot be considered to have been adequately demonstrated to date. It represents a very promising lead, however, and much more investigation is needed. *Gonyaulax* is a single-celled organism, and the pertinence of biochemical investigation of cellular clocks to the problem of metazoan clocks is unclear. Lack of clarity, notwithstanding, most investigators are confident that an understanding of the metazoan system will eventually grow out of an understanding of the cellular system.

Pharmacological Sensitivity

In view of the metabolic and physiological rhythms that have been described in insects and other organisms, the probability would appear to be good that insects should display time-related changes in their sensitivity to insecticides and other pharmacological agents. Circadian rhythms of sensitivity to toxicants were first reported in the German cockroach, *Blattella germanica* (Beck, 1963). Male cockroaches were maintained under a 12L:12D photoperiod and constant temperature (24°C) for 7 days, following which they were transferred to continuous dim illumination. Groups were then treated with a standard dosage of toxicant at different times and returned to continuous dim light for observation. The incidence of mortality was recorded during the first 24 hours after treatment. All treatments were by injection into the hemocoel. Potassium cyanide at the rate of 2 μg per insect caused higher mortality when administered during the subjective night than when given during the subjective day. The insect's sensitivity rhythm showed that potassium cyanide was least toxic at the beginning of the subjective day, but increased in toxicity to reach a maximum in the middle of the subjective night (Fig. 27). Dimetilan (1-dimethylcarbamoyl-5-methyl-3-pyrazolyl dimethylcarbamate) at a dosage of 2.5 μg per insect was also most toxic during the middle of the subjective night, but the minimum sensitivity of the insect occurred during the latter half of the subjective

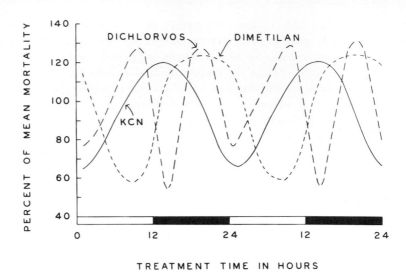

Fig. 27. Rhythmicity in the sensitivity of adult male German cockroaches (Blattella germanica) to three different toxicants.

day. Dichlorvos (2,2-dichlorovinyl dimethylphosphate) at 0.15 μg per insect was most effective during the late subjective day and in the latter half of the subjective night, the sensitivity rhythm displaying a bimodality. Little or no rhythmicity was detected in the cockroach's sensitivity to sodium fluoride, sodium azide, and 2,4-dinitrophenol. A very shallow sensitivity rhythm was detected in the case of DDT [1,1,1-trichloro-2,2-*bis*(p-chlorophenyl) ethane].

Adult females of the two-spotted spider mite, *Tetranychus urticae,* were found to display a daily rhythm of sensitivity to dichlorvos (Polick *et al.,* 1964). The maximum susceptibility to the toxicant occurred at about 2 hours after the onset of light (10L:14D photoperiod). The mites were least sensitive about 2 hours after the beginning of the scotophase. A very complex rhythm of sensitivity was observed in the boll weevil, *Anthonomus grandis* (Cole and Adkisson, 1964, 1965). Adult weevils that had been maintained under different photoperiods (14L:10D, 12L:12D, 10L:14D) were treated with low contact dosages of methyl parathion (*O,O*-dimethyl-*O-p*-nitrophenylphosphorothioate) at different times. After treatment, the beetles were held under continuous illumination during the 24-hour posttreatment observation time. The response rhythm appeared to be phase set by the onset of light, as minimum sensitivity was observed at this time among insects from any of

90

the three photoperiods. Low-sensitivity times occurred at approximately 6-hour intervals, alternating with times of high sensitivity. The 6-hour periodicity of the rhythm was observed in each of the photoperiodic schedules used, but the amplitudes were affected by the photoperiodic regime to which the beetles had been exposed. Decapitation prior to treatment abolished the sensitivity rhythm.

The sensitivity of adult house flies, *Musca domestica*, to insecticides appears to depend upon the photoperiodic cycles experienced by the insects during their development (Fernandez and Randolph, 1966). Flies were reared under different photoperiods, and the adult forms were then exposed to insecticide-coated surfaces and transferred to continuous light conditions for observation. Exposure to the insecticides was initiated 6 hours after the onset of light in each case, and was maintained throughout the 48-hour observation period. This study differed from those discussed above, in that measurements were made of the overall susceptibility to the insecticide, rather than of daily rhythmic changes in susceptibility. The insecticides used were DDT, dieldrin (1,2,3,4, 10,10-hexachloro-6,7-epoxy-1,4,4a,5,6,7,8,8a-octohydro-1,4-*endo*-*exo*-5,8-dimethanonaphthalene), and endrin (1,2,3,4,10,10-hexachloro-6,7-epoxy-1,4,4a,5,6,7,8,8a-octahydro-1,4-*endo*-*endo*-5,8-dimethanonaph-thalene). Flies that had been reared under a 14L:10D photoperiod were more susceptible to any of the three insecticides than were the flies that had been reared under either continuous light or a 10L:14D photoperiod. Although the response differences were small, the data were indicative of significant metabolic differences.

Daily rhythms in the insect's sensitivity to toxicants might be expected to be reflections of rhythmic biochemical processes involved in the metabolism of the toxic chemicals. This has been shown to be the case in the metabolism of disulfoton (*O,O*-diethyl-*S*-[2-(ethylthio)-ethyl] phosphorodithioate) by larvae of the bollworm (corn earworm), *Heliothis zea* (Bull and Lindquist, 1965). In this study, the larvae were reared on a meridic diet at a constant temperature and under either a 14L:10D photoperiod or under continuous dim light. The last instar larvae were injected with a known dosage of radiophosphorus-labeled disulfoton. Groups of larvae were so treated at 2-hour intervals throughout the 24-hour cycle. Four hours after treatment, the larvae and their excreta were extracted. Extracts were fractionated into aqueous and organic solvent phases. The toxic metabolites of disulfoton are thought to be organic solvent-soluble oxidative metabolites; whereas the water-soluble fraction is thought to contain nontoxic hydrolytic products.

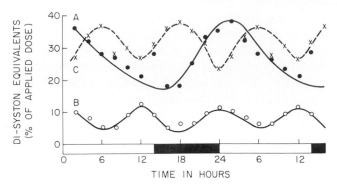

Fig. 28. Effects of photoperiod on the rates of metabolism of disulfoton in larvae of Heliothis zea. A = oxidative metabolites in larval extracts; B = hydrolytic metabolites in larval extracts; C = hydrolytic metabolites in extracts of larval excreta. [Modified from Bull and Lınquist (1965).]

Radiophosphorus counts of the fractions were used as a measure of the metabolism of the administered disulfoton. Extracts of larvae treated at different times within the photoperiod were found to contain different amounts of both hydrolytic and oxidative metabolites (Fig. 28). The formation of hydrolytic products displayed a 24-hour rhythmicity, with the maximum metabolite formation occurring during the middle hours of the scotophase. Production of oxidative metabolites showed two daily maxima—one in the late photophase and a second in the late scotophase. A 12-hour periodicity was also detected in the hydrolytic metabolite content of the excreta. Rhythmic metabolite production was not detectable in groups of larvae that were reared in continuous light. Such apparent nonrhythmicity would be expected, because the circadian times of the individual larvae had not been synchronized through photoperiodic entrainment.

In addition to diel rhythms of sensitivity to toxicants, rhythmic responses to anesthetics and general narcotics have been reported in a very few instances. Nowosielski *et al.* (1964) reported the existence of sensitivity rhythms in house crickets and two-spotted spider mites in respect to the effects of ether, chloroform, and carbon tetrachloride. The cricket displayed maximum sensitivity to these substances during the early scotophase, which is also the time of the insect's greatest locomotor activity. The mite, however, showed minimum sensitivity at that time of the photoperiod. In both arthropods, a phase difference of several hours was observed between the chloroform and carbon tetrachloride sensitivity rhythms.

The ability of insects to withstand other stress factors may also have circadian aspects, as suggested by the findings of Pittendrigh (1961). Pittendrigh measured the ability of *Drosophila* adults to recover from heat stress, and found a correlation with photoperiod. Flies that had been maintained under a long-day photoperiod recovered more rapidly than did those held under a short-day regime.

PERIODISM IN NERVOUS AND ENDOCRINE SYSTEMS

Central Nervous System

Although the central nervous system plays a central role in behavioral patterns that display circadian periodicity, there is little evidence of circadian rhythmicity in the nervous system itself. This statement is made in respect to impulse transmission phenomena only, and not to neurosecretory functions, which will be discussed in a subsequent section. Many neural transmission patterns display rhythmic aspects, but the time factors involved are in the order of milliseconds and do not approach the long periods normally involved in circadian functions. Nevertheless, at least one exception to this generalization has been reported. Rhythmic changes in impulse transmission have been found in the retinula cells of *Dytiscus fasciventris* and a few other coleopterans (Jahn and Crescitelli, 1940; Jahn and Wulff, 1943). Even when the beetles were held in continuous darkness, a circadian cycle of responsiveness to single light stimuli was found. The dark-adapted eye in the subjective night phase was over 1000 times more sensitive than was a dark-adapted eye in the subjective day phase. Conversely, when the insects were light adapted, the eyes were much more sensitive during the subjective day than during the subjective night. Whether in the subjective day or subjective night, dark adaptation led to similar pigment distributions, suggesting that unknown factors were determining the diel periodicity of eye sensitivity.

One of the earliest observations of physiological rhythms in arthropods was that of Kiesel (1894), who observed an endogenous daily rhythm of eye pigment changes. Kiesel's observations were confirmed in 1930, when Welsh (1930) reported that the distal pigment cells in the compound eyes of shrimps (*Macrobrachium olfersii* and *M. acanthurus*) displayed a circadian rhythm of pigment movement. Even under continuous illumination, the pigment migrated distally in the early evening and remained in that position during the subjective night. The eye pigment rhythm paralleled the animal's activity rhythm, and appeared to be controlled by both humoral and central nervous system factors.

93

Neurosecretory System

Decapitation has been shown to destroy the overt manifestation of circadian rhythms in a number of insects. The loss of rhythmicity has most frequently been traced to the loss of the neurosecretory and retrocerebral system functions, rather than the loss of the sensory and association pathways of the brain. The insect neurosecretory system (Fig. 29) includes two or three groups of secretory cells in the brain proper—the medial, lateral, and sometimes, the posterior groups.

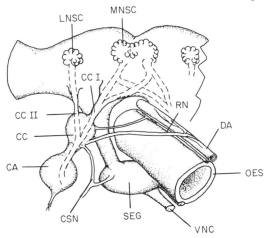

Fig. 29. Typical neuroendocrine complex of an insect (nondipteran). MNSC = medial neurosecretory cells; LNSC = lateral neurosecretory cells; CC = corpus cardiacum; CA = corpus allatum; CC I = corpus cardiacum nerve I; CC II = corpus cardiacum nerve II; CSN = corpus-subesophageal nerve. SEG = subesophageal ganglion; VNC = ventral nerve cord; OES = esophagus; DA = dorsal vessel; RN = recurrent nerve.

In addition to these centers, there are neurosecretory cells of from 2 to 4 types in the subesophageal ganglion, and groups of such cells in each of the other ganglia of the ventral nerve cord (Raabe, 1963; McLeod and Beck, 1963a; Van der Kloot, 1960). The physiological functions to be ascribed to such a plethora of neurosecretory cells are largely unknown. The medial and lateral groups in the brain are known to be involved in the elaboration of the prothoracotropic hormone (the "brain hormone"), with some of the secretory products being translocated in the corpora cardiaca and corpora allata. Axonal translocation of neurosecretory granules has been traced from the medial cells to several peripheral parts of the body, including muscles, aorta, and hindgut, as well as to the corpora cardiaca in such diverse

94

species as *Periplaneta americana* and *Aphis fabae* (Johnson, 1963; Johnson and Bowers, 1963). Such translocation was observed to occur via the stomatogastric nervous system as well as via the ventral nerve cord. It seems quite likely that the complex neurosecretory system of the insect will prove to be of major importance in the control of behavior, growth, and reproduction. This major role is at least adumbrated by the present fragmentary evidence of the role played by the neuroendocrine system in the photoperiodic responses of insects.

Studies have been made of the role of the neuroendocrine system in circadian rhythms of locomotor activity. Using the American cockroach, *P. americana,* Harker (1954, 1955, 1956) observed that either decapitation or exposure to continuous illumination led to a loss of the circadian locomotor rhythm. When an arrhythmic cockroach (from continuous light) was grafted to one showing a normal activity rhythm, it became rhythmic. Such *parabiosis* experiments demonstrated that (1) an activity rhythm could be established in a previously arrhythmic insect; (2) the induced rhythm adopted the phase setting of the originally rhythmic member of the pair; and (3) some blood-borne factor was involved in the induction of the activity rhythm, because the two insects were connected to each other via only the circulatory system. Harker found that rhythmicity could be restored to decapitated cockroaches by the implantation of a subesophageal ganglion that had been taken from a normal rhythmic cockroach. With an implanted subesophageal ganglion, the headless insect would display a circadian locomotor rhythm that was in phase with the rhythm previously shown by the donor of the ganglion. Such induced rhythms would not persist indefinitely, however, indicating a dependence of the ganglion on other internal functions. Harker (1960a,b,c) traced the rhythm-inducing factor of the subesophageal ganglion to two pairs of neurosecretory cells. These cells were located on the lateral aspects of the subesophageal ganglion, one pair on each side.

On the basis of experiments involving ganglion implantation, low temperature effects, and photoperiods (Brown and Harker, 1960), Harker concluded that the subesophageal ganglionic neurosecretory cells maintained an autonomous secretory rhythm. This rhythm, however, was subject to phase regulation by a master control system located in the brain. Surgical removal of the corpora allata and cardiaca resulted in a loss of ability to adjust the activity rhythm to an altered photoperiod, and the activity rhythm itself faded away in about a week, even when under unchanged photoperiodic conditions. These effects were traced to the function of a small nerve that connects the corpora allata-cardiaca with the subesophageal ganglion (Fig. 29, CSN). When this tiny nerve was cut or tied off, the operation had the same effect on the activity rhythm as did extirpation of the corpora. Neurosecretory products were demonstrated to be translocated from the corpora complex to the subesophageal ganglion via the nerve (Harker, 1960c). The conclusion was therefore drawn that photoperiodic entrainment of the locomotor rhythm was normally effected by the neuroendocrine system of the brain, which controlled the circadian secretory rhythm of the subesophageal ganglion via the corpora-subesophageal ganglion nerve.

Although there is general agreement that decapitation destroys a number of rhythmic functions, there is some disagreement concerning the validity of some of Harker's specific conclusions. Surgical removal of the brain only, leaving the subesophageal ganglion intact, did not suppress the circadian locomotor rhythm of the lubber grasshopper, *Romalea microptera* (Fingerman *et al.*, 1958). On the other hand, extirpation of the grasshopper's subesophageal ganglion abolished the activity rhythm, but the reimplantation of subesophageal ganglia did not restore the rhythmic behavior. In experiments on the walking stick, *Carausius morosus*, Eidmann (1956) found that decapitation, brain extirpation, destruction of the anterior brain (protocerebrum), extirpation of the subesophageal ganglion, or section of the circumesophageal connectives would abolish the insect's locomotor activity rhythm. The rhythm could not be reestablished by the implantation of either brains or subesophageal ganglia, however. Using the American cockroach as his experimental animal, Roberts (1965a) was unable to induce an activity rhythm through the implantation of "rhythmic" subesophageal ganglia.

The observation that surgical destruction of the anterior portion of the insect's brain caused a loss of rhythmicity (Eidmann, 1956) is of particular interest, because that part of the brain contains the *pars intercerebralis.* The pars intercerebralis is that area of the brain in which the medial neurosecretory cells are located. Destruction of the optic lobes of the anterior brain did not cause a loss of endogenous rhythmicity, but surgical destruction of the pars intercerebralis resulted in the disappearance of daily activity rhythms in the American cockroach (Roberts, 1965a). If surgical damage, by either incision or microcautery, was confined to tissue lying lateral to the pars intercerebralis, leaving the neurosecretory system uninjured, the insect's activity rhythm was not impaired. The medial and lateral neurosecretory cells have axonal connections to the corpora cardiaca and corpora allata. The functioning of the corpora is, at least in part, dependent on the integrity of these axons. Extirpation of the corpora has been reported to cause a loss of behavioral rhythms in the American cockroach (Harker, 1960b,c) and the desert locust, *Schistocerca gregaria* (Odhiambo, 1966). However, Roberts (1965a,b, 1966) was unable to obtain such an effect, and the circadian activity rhythms of corpora-deprived American cockroaches continued to be manifested.

Studies of some other aspects of insect photoperiodism have also contributed evidence that the neurosecretory system of the brain is of major importance. Working with the effects of photoperiod on body form determination in aphids (*Megoura viciae*), Lees (1960a, 1964) found that the receptor-response system for photoperiodic stimuli was located in the anterior part of the brain. Employing fine optic fibers to transmit light stimuli, Lees observed photoperiod-correlated growth effects only when the mid-dorsal aspect of the anterior brain was stimulated. Stimulation of the eyes or other parts of the insect was ineffective. Lees postulated that direct stimulation of the medial neurosecretory cells was responsible for the photoperiodic determination of body form. Similar conclusions were reached by Shakhbazov (1961) from his study of the effect of photoperiod on diapause development in pupae of the Chinese oak silkworm, *Antheraea pernyi*. The pupal cuticle of this species is quite dark and opaque, except for a small transparent "window" situated directly over the brain. It was found that painting the transparent cuticle with opaque paint prevented photoperiodic responses. The pars intercerebralis was shown to be located immediately under the little window. Shakhbazov's findings were confirmed by other workers (Williams and Adkisson, 1964). The brain was also identified as the receptor system in the photoperiodic induction of diapause in the cabbage worm, *Pieris brassicae* (Claret, 1966a,b). Such experimental results do not demonstrate that the neurosecretory cells are, in themselves, the primary receptors of photoperiodic stimuli; that these cells are intimately involved in the receptor system is very strongly suggested, however.

Although it seems probable that the eyes and optic tracts are normally involved in the reception of photoperiodic stimuli, they do not appear to be the obligate route of stimulation. Some of the evidence discussed above suggests that the optic pathways are not at all involved. A number of workers have masked or removed the compound eyes and ocelli, and have found that photoperiodic responses were not abolished by such treatment (de Wilde *et al.*, 1959; Tanaka, 1950; de Wilde, 1962a). Photoperiodic reception has been attributed to the ocelli in the case of the American cockroach (Harker, 1956), but this observation could not be confirmed by other workers (Roberts, 1965b). Both rhythmic and nonrhythmic overt responses to light may occur in the absence of functional eyes, and nonoptic light reception may play a part in determination of photoperiodic responses (Ball, 1961; de Wilde, 1958; Beck and Alexander, 1964a; Callahan, 1965b). Light sensitivity has been demonstrated to occur in the terminal ganglion of the ventral nerve cord in several arthropods, including Crustaceae (Prosser, 1934; Kennedy, 1958, 1963) and the American cockroach (Ball, 1965).

Rhythmic cycles of secretory activity have been detected within the components of the neuroendocrine system. Circadian rhythmicity, as well as long-term growth-stage changes have been reported. Based on the premise that a relative increase in nuclear size, cell diameter, or organ volume is an indication of a proportional increase in metabolic and secretory activity, rhythmic secretion has been ascribed to medial neurosecretory cells, lateral neurosecretory cells, corpus allatum, and corpus cardiacum. The medial neurosecretory cells of the beetle *Carabus nemoralis* were shown to reach a maximum nuclear size during the late afternoon, at which time the corpus allatum also reached its maximum apparent secretory activity (Klug, 1958). The overt phase of the locomotor activity rhythm of this carabid beetle was observed to occur at the beginning of the scotophase, which was also the time of maximum cell diameter in the insect's corpora allata. Daily variations in corpus allatum volumes were observed in larvae of the cabbage butterfly, *P. brassicae* (Bünning and Joerrens, 1962), and in both neurosecretory cell groups and corpora allata in adult females of the vinegar fly, *Drosophila melanogaster* (Rensing, 1965a,b, 1966; Rensing *et al.*, 1965). In the latter insect, the rhythms were found to be bimodal; maximum activity in terms of nuclear size and numbers of cytoplasmic inclusions occurred about 3 hours after the beginning of the scotophase and again shortly after the beginning of the photophase. The photoperiod employed was 12L : 12D, and the secretory rhythm displayed a 12-hour periodicity. Because no other photoperiods were employed, the exact relationship between photoperiod and overt phases of the secretory rhythm was not determined. A trimodal secretory rhythm was reported to occur in the lateral neurosecretory cells of larval European corn borers, *Ostrinia nubilalis* (Beck, 1964). In this species, maximum cell size occurred immediately

98

following the onset of the photophase, and the other maxima were observed at 8-hour intervals thereafter. In this case, too, the experimental insects were maintained under a 12L:12D photoperiod, and no other photoperiods were tested.

Rhythmic production of 5-hydroxytryptamine by the neurosecretory cells of the brain of a spider, *Leiobunum longipes*, was reported by Fowler and Goodnight (1966). Maximum production occurred during the scotophase at about 6 hours after the onset of darkness. Under tissue culture conditions, the spider brain tissue showed a bimodal secretory rhythm, with the second peak activity occurring in the early photophase. These workers postulated that under normal conditions, the second secretory phase is suppressed by feedback controlling mechanisms. Although the exact physiological role of 5-hydroxytryptamine is unknown, the substance has been shown to be a central nervous system stimulant in higher animals. It has also been implicated in the action of a cardiac stimulant produced by the corpora cardiaca of the cockroach (Davey, 1961a,b, 1962a,b). The substance has also been found to vary rhythmically in the nervous system of mammals, with the daily maximum titer being found at about 8 hours after the onset of the photophase (Fiske, 1964).

Nonneural Endocrine Organs

Prothoracic gland cells of *Drosophila melanogaster* larvae were found to display a daily rhythm of nuclear and nucleolar diameter (Rensing et al., 1965). As was the case with the neuroendocrine system of the adult, the larval prothoracic gland cell rhythm was bimodal, with the nuclear structures reaching maximum dimensions at 12-hour intervals. Fat body cells were also found to show a bimodal daily rhythm of size changes.

The epithelial cells of part of the hindgut (ileum) of mature larvae of the European corn borer were implicated in the production of a hormone (proctodone) involved in the physiology of diapause (Beck and Alexander, 1964b,c). Part of the evidence offered in support of the postulated endocrine function of the ileal cells was the appearance of secretory granules within the cytoplasm. These cytoplasmic inclusions were paraldehyde-fuchsin positive, autofluorescent in the fresh state, and their numbers appeared to vary rhythmically during the diel cycle. The secretory rhythm was shown to have an 8-hour periodicity, with phase setting being effected by photoperiod. The cells appeared to have released their secretory products shortly after the beginning of the scotophase, after which cytoplasmic granules would again accumu-

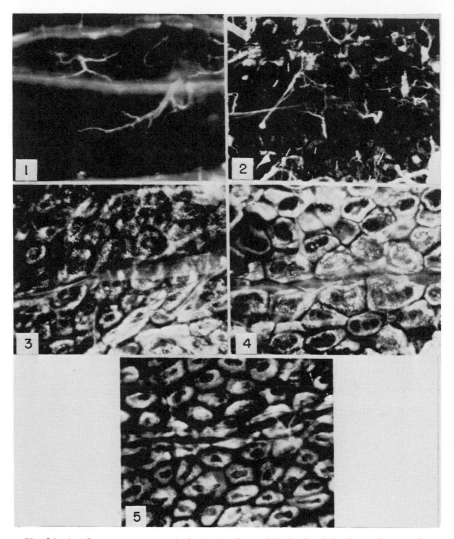

Fig. 30. Autofluorescent secretory inclusions in the epithelial cells of the ileum of mature larvae of the European corn borer, Ostrinia nubilalis, during different phases of the endogenous secretory rhythm. [From Beck et al. (1965a).]

late and again disappear at 8-hour intervals (Fig. 30). Several days were required for the secretory rhythm to become entrained to a new photoperiodic schedule, such as 4-hour change in the clock time of the scotophase (Beck, 1964; Beck and Alexander, 1964b,c; Beck *et al.*, 1965a,b).

100

Multimodality in Circadian Rhythms

Photoperiodically entrainable overt rhythms (such as locomotion, emergence, etc.) may show more than one overt phase per 24-hour cycle, as was discussed in previous chapters. A number of physiological processes have been found to be rhythmic, and among them several have proved to have periods of 6, 8, or 12 hours rather than the expected 24-hour periodicity. Multimodal rhythms have been described in respect to oxygen consumption, neuroendocrine activity, and a number of metabolic processes. These physiological rhythms may be considered legitimate circadian rhythms, nevertheless, because of their demonstrated roles in photoperiodically entrained functions. It seems quite likely that multimodal rhythmic processes may have been overlooked in many investigations because of the methods employed. A schedule of observations based on the presumed existence of a 24-hour rhythm might easily fail to disclose the existence of rhythms of relatively short periodicities.

A multimodality of circadian functions is not a peculiarity of insects, but has been reported in other biological systems as well. A prominent 8-hour component was observed in the complex activity rhythm of the land crab, *Gecarcinus lateralis* (Bliss, 1962), and Aschoff (1966) postulated a bimodal activity rhythm as being a fundamental feature in the higher animals. Hypophysectomy was found to suppress the circadian rhythm of mitosis in the corneal epithelium of the salamander; the rhythm was trimodal in unoperated animals (Scheving and Chiakulas, 1962). And the probable involvement of multimodal circadian functions in plant photoperiodism is at least suggested by some of the experimental data published by a number of investigators.

Most circadian rhythms that have been described appear to be unimodal. Nevertheless, the detection of a wide variety of rhythms showing 6-, 8-, or 12-hour components is of considerable importance to an understanding of the mechanisms underlying photoperiodic and circadian phenomena. It seems probable that, in many cases, a measurable circadian rhythm may result from the phase relationships of two or more interacting physiological processes, each of which may be operating in the form of a short-period rhythm. A unimodal circadian overt rhythm may be driven and controlled by a series of underlying multimodal physiological rhythms.

6 □ Photoperiodism and Growth

Photoperiod is known to have profound effects on the developmental processes of insects. These effects are expressed in the form of observable responses that are as diverse as diapause and seasonal dimorphism. Fundamentally, it would appear that photoperiod might have either or both of two effects on insect development: (1) a growth rate effect, either inhibitory or stimulatory; or (2) an effect on the direction of differentiation, resulting in an influence on the form of the organism.

Little is currently known about the specific physiological mechanisms by which photoperiodic stimuli influence the determination of either growth rates or pathways of differentiation. There may be a rate-controlling effect on growth hormone production, as has been postulated in cases where photoperiod appears to influence the secretory activity of the medial or lateral neurosecretory cells. Photoperiodic effects might also be mediated through the influence of photoperiodic signals on the temporal relationships among a number of integrative mechanisms. These would involve interrelationships among hormone-controlled processes, equilibria among feedback mechanisms, and the like. There is general agreement that the insect responds to the light-on and light-off signals and to the time elapsing between these signals, rather than to the presence, absence, or duration of light energy, per se. There is disagreement, however, as to whether or not the photoperiodic effects are always produced because of phase-regulating influences on endogenous rhythmic functions, rather than on hourglass (or interval timer) types or reaction systems. This problem will be discussed in detail in a later section.

GENERAL PHYSIOLOGY OF INSECT GROWTH

Insect growth is usually characterized as being discontinuous, because it is manifested as a series of molts. At the shedding (*ecdysis*) of the old cuticle, the insect advances to the next growth stage—larval, nymphal, pupal, or adult. Ecdysis is the culmination of a series of events known as the *molting cycle*. The molting cycle and the growth stage attained at ecdysis is considered to be under the control of a three-hormone system.

Prothoracotropic hormone (PTH) is elaborated by the neurosecretory system of the brain and is released into the general circulation via the corpora cardiaca. This hormone stimulates the prothoracic glands (also known as ventral glands, peritracheal glands, and large ring gland cells, in the older literature on different insect orders). The prothoraic glands are stimulated by PTH to secrete the molting hormone, *ecdysone*. Ecdysone, in turn, stimulates the body cells to initiate mitosis, and it also stimulates the epidermal cells to begin elaboration of new cuticular material. The third hormone involved in the growth of immature forms is *juvenile hormone* (JH), also known as neotenin, which is the product of the corpora allata. In the presence of a high titer of JH, the molting cycle produces an additional larval or nymphal stage. If the blood titer of JH is relatively low, a pupal stage is formed, at least in holometabolous species. When JH is absent, or at least in extremely low titer, adult characteristics are manifested in the newly molted insect. For further details on these three hormones and their physiological roles in growth, the reader is referred to the excellent review of Wigglesworth (1964).

Insect growth and differentiation are extremely complex phenomena, and must involve controlling mechanisms of which we currently have little or no knowledge. We have only a fragmentary understanding, for example, of the factors that might determine the amount of JH to be produced by the corpora allata during a given molting cycle. Nor do we understand how the neurosecretory system is controlled, although some photoperiodic effects have been traced to that portion of the brain. In order to account for the effects of photoperiod on insect growth and form, it is necessary to postulate the existence of controlling relationships that are probably in the form of feedback systems.

Insect growth and differentiation are a genetically programmed system, in which the differentiating cells "read" the genetic code, and that coded information determines the cellular processes. The reading of the genetic code appears to be influenced by hormones, such that the genes

104

for "larval synthesis" are read if the JH titer is high, but the genes for pupal or adult development are read when the JH level is low or the hormone is absent (Wigglesworth, 1961). It is well established that ecdysone causes cellular activity at the chromosome level, in the form of visible chromosome puffs (Clever and Karlson, 1960), and some stimulation of mitosis has been shown to occur in response to JH (Wigglesworth, 1964). Although the genetic material determines the growth and form of an insect, the information contained in the genetic array may become available to the cell only under conditions that are determined by the nature and concentrations of hormones produced by cells located elsewhere in the organism.

Environmental information, such as photoperiodic signals, sex attractants, feeding stimulants, is fed into the insect via receptor systems that are part of the insect's nervous system. This input of information may then influence the activities of the neurosecretory system. We do not know whether the neurosecretory cells are the primary receptors of the photoperiodic stimuli, as well as the effectors of the response, or whether the stimuli act via integrative pathways within the central nervous system. In any case, it seems likely that the end result is a modification of the secretory activity of the neurosecretory complex. The products of the neurosecretory cells have a controlling influence over the endocrine output of both the corpora cardiaca and the corpora allata, the subesophageal ganglion, and perhaps other organs as well. These humoral factors may control the ultimate reading of the genetic code by the growing cells. Environmental informational input cannot be considered to be functionally independent of the insect's internal state. Internal feedback systems, such as that described between the ovarioles and corpus allatum (Nayar, 1958; Engelmann, 1957), may also have profound effects on the insect's physiological state and, therefore, on the systems into which photoperiodic stimuli are received.

General activity and feeding rhythms are controlled by the brain and subesophageal ganglion, as was discussed in the previous chapter. But a feedback effect is apparent in which the ingestive activity of the insect may affect the functioning of the neuroendocrine system. The observation that the ingestion of sugars resulted in an acceleration of the heart beat rate was investigated by Davey (1962a). Using the American cockroach, *Periplaneta americana*, Davey traced a sensory input pathway from sugar receptors on the labrum to the frontal ganglion, frontal connectives, and into the brain. In the brain, the sensory impulses were fed into the neural circuits controlling the endocrine activity of the corpora cardiaca. These pathways were from the brain, through the frontal connectives, the recurrent nerve, and the hypocerebral ganglion. As a result of feeding the insect glucose, the corpora cardiaca were stimulated to release a hormonal substance that caused an acceleration of contractions in the dorsal vessel. There was some indication that the subesophageal ganglion might also be involved in the effect of sugar ingestion on heart rate, but its possible role has not been determined.

A more direct involvement of the stomatogastric nervous system in the endocrine regulation of growth was demonstrated by Clarke and Langley (1963a,b), who worked with *Locusta migratoria*. They observed that extirpation of the frontal ganglion or surgical section of the frontal connectives prevented the insects from molting. These investigators concluded that stimuli from the stomatogastric system were involved in the translocation of neurosecretory products from the medial neurosecretory cells to the corpora cardiaca. Feeding activity would thus play a part in the transfer and release of prothoracotropic hormone from the corpora cardiaca, and thereby in the initiation of the molting cycle.

Females of many mosquito species are known to require a blood meal before they are capable of producing eggs. Experimental study of this requirement showed that blood per se was not essential. Midgut distension resulted in the activation of the corpora allata and subsequent maturation of eggs (Larsen, 1958; Larsen and Bodenstein, 1959). This finding was similar to that of Wigglesworth (1934), who observed that abdominal distension following engorgement activated the neuroendocrine system of *Rhodnius prolixus*. The neural pathway was thought to be from abdominal stretch receptors to brain, via the ventral nerve cord. Abdominal proprioceptors might also play a role in the initiation of the molting cycle in larvae of the greater wax moth, *Galleria mellonella* (Edwards, 1966).

In addition to stimuli associated with the feeding process and distension of the abdomen, endocrine functions may be influenced by other types of sensory input. For example, the wheat stem sawfly, *Cephus cinctus*, diapauses as a mature larva in a cocoon, but completion of diapause is delayed if the larva is removed from the cocoon. Larval contact with the walls of the cocoon appeared to be an important factor in the activation of the insect's neuroendocrine system and, therefore, the termination of diapause (Church, 1955a). The titer of JH prevailing during the embryonic development of an aphid (*Megoura viciae*) was found to determine whether the aphid would be an apterous or alate form (Lees, 1961). Relatively high concentrations of JH resulted in the formation of apterous aphids; whereas relatively low JH levels programmed the embryos for alate formation. The production of JH by the parental corpora allata was influenced by the degree of crowding within the aphid colony, with corpora allata activity tending to be suppressed by crowded conditions. Presumably, sensory input resulting from repeated aphid-to-aphid contact caused a partial suppression of JH production and resulted in the formation of winged progeny. Similarly, Highnam and Haskell (1964) found crowding effects on the corpus allatum activity among locusts of the genera *Schistocerca* and *Locusta*. Population density effects in both aphids and locusts were, in all likelihood, mediated by pheromones which acted on the insects' sensory systems. Sensory input into the brain then influenced the endocrine activity of the neurosecretory and retrocerebral system.

The few examples discussed above constitute only a small sampling of the literature on the subject of interactions and feedback systems. They are pointed out here in order to underscore the point that such systems are not only known to occur in insects, but also that they may play an important part in many aspects of insect photoperiodism. Through photoperiodic stimuli, environmental information may be fed into the organismal system, where it may influence the equilibria among complex feedback loops and controlling mechanisms. As the result of such influences, endocrine balances may be shifted and the end effects may be manifested in terms of the programming of development. At the cellular level, the reading and implementation of the genetic code may be affected. We should not expect that photoperiodic stimuli should exert a direct effect on growth processes, but rather that they should act via their effects on the temporal organization of the entire physiological system underlying growth.

Effects of Photoperiod on Growth Rates

On the basis of the demonstration of endogenous circadian rhythms in metabolism, respiration, and hormone production, it might be expected that the growing insect larva would display a daily rhythm in tissue synthesis and growth. In most forms, such a rhythmic growth would be extremely difficult to demonstrate experimentally. In at least one case, however, evidence of rhythmic growth has been reported; deposition of cuticular protein was found to be in the form of daily growth layers in the desert locust, *Schistocerca gregaria* (Neville, 1963, 1965). Deposition of cuticular substance was found to be in the form of an endogenous circadian rhythm which was both temperature compensated and photoperiodically entrainable. Neville (1965) obtained evidence suggesting that rhythmic cuticular deposition occurs in a number of species, including the American cockroach, *Periplaneta americana*, a cave cricket, *Dolichopoda linderi*, and some hemipterans of the family Belastomatidae.

Photoperiod has been shown to influence growth rates in a number of insects, in that developmental rates were found to differ under different daylength conditions. Geyspitz (1953) found that larval growth and molting in a number of lepidopterous species was slower when the caterpillars were reared in daylengths shorter than 17 hours of light per day than when reared in longer daylengths. Danilevskii (1961) published data indicating that larvae of the cutworm *Agrotis occulata* grew more slowly in photoperiods having a 12-hour photophase than in photoperiods with 20 or more hours of light per day. Growth was most rapid when the caterpillars were reared under continuous illumination. Opposite responses to daylength have also been reported, however. Working with a tussock moth species, *Dasychira pudibunda*, Geyspitz and Zarankina (1963) observed that larval growth was accelerated by short daylengths and was slowed by long daylengths. Short-day acceleration of larval growth was also observed in the noctuid *Agrotis triangulum* (Danilevskii, 1961).

From the above examples, it is apparent that caterpillar species differ markedly in the effects of daylength on growth, with some being stimulated by long days and others being inhibited by similar photoperiods. The limited amount of experimental data available tends to suggest that the sign of the response (stimulation or inhibition) is correlated with the effect of photoperiod on the induction of diapause. That is, species in which diapause is induced by short-day photoperiods also display slower growth in response to short days. Conversely, species in which diapause occurs in response to long-day photoperiods tend to show the fastest larval growth under short-day conditions. Thus, Fukaya and Mitsuhashi (1961) observed that growth of the rice stem borer, *Chilo suppressalis*, was slower from the third instar on among larvae destined to diapause than among larvae not so committed. The tendency for prediapause growth to be slower than nondiapause growth cannot be taken as an infallible general rule, however. In some species larval growth rates are unaffected by photoperiod, even though diapause is induced in response to a particular range of daylengths. Larvae of the European corn borer, *Ostrinia nubilalis*, were observed to grow at similar

108

rates in short-day (12L:12D) as in long-day (16L:8D) photoperiods, even though all of the larvae that were reared under the short-day regime were destined to enter the diapause state (Beck and Hanec, 1960; Beck, 1962a).

Diapause is usually defined as being a state of arrested development, and insofar as it is induced by photoperiod it represents a photoperiodic effect on insect growth. However, diapause is a highly specific reaction occurring at well-defined stages of growth, and therefore differs from the general growth rate effects discussed above. Diapause will be considered in Chapters 7 and 8.

Under some conditions, photoperiods may accelerate insect growth without associated daylength effects. This is thought to be caused by the effect of the environmental rhythm on the synchronization of physiological processes within the insect. For example, Messenger (1964) observed that rhythmically fluctuating environmental conditions promoted better growth of the alfalfa aphid, *Therioaphis maculata*, than did rigidly controlled constant conditions. Twenty-four hour cycles of temperature, humidity, and illumination produced the highest rates of survival, growth, and reproduction.

An unexplained effect of light on the growth of insects was reported by Ball (1958). He found that the immature forms of the large milkweed bug, *Oncopeltus fasciatus*, the alfalfa aphid, *T. maculata*, and the German cockroach, *Blattella germanica*, were adversely affected by short daily exposures to light of relatively long wavelengths (red). Reproduction was inhibited in both *Oncopeltus* and *Therioaphis*, and growth was inhibited in *Oncopeltus* and *Blattella*. Although an adverse phase-setting effect of such light pulses does not seem likely, such a possibility has not been ruled out by the work done thus far.

DEVELOPMENTAL RATES AND ADULT EMERGENCE RHYTHMS

A circadian adult emergence rhythm is a population response to exogenous factors, such as photoperiod, and is thought to result from a synchronization of the developmental processes among the members of the population. If this is so, the development of the individual insects must be susceptible to some degree of rate regulation by photoperiodic stimuli. Harker (1965a,b) traced the course of adult differentiation in pupae of *Drosophila melanogaster* in an effort to elucidate the photoperiodic responses involved in the adult emergence rhythm. Harker found four observable anatomical changes that could be used to divide the pupal period into successive stages of adult development. These marker stages were: (1) eversion of the head; (2) the appearance of yellow eye pigment; (3) the appearance of wing pigmentation; and (4) eclosion of the adult fly. In her experiments, the larvae were reared under a controlled photoperiod, and the pupae were maintained in either the same photoperiod or in continuous darkness. Records were then taken of the circadian times at which each pupa reached each of the four successive growth stages and of the number of hours spent in each stage prior to emergence.

The duration of each developmental stage was found to be determined by the circadian time at which the insect attained that stage. For example, the circadian time at which the yellow eye pigment stage was reached determined how many hours would elapse before the next stage—wing pigmentation—would be observable. The term *circadian time* is used here, because pupae that were maintained in continuous darkness followed a developmental schedule that was determined by the photoperiod under which they had been reared as larvae. Essentially similar results were obtained whether the pupae were maintained under their rearing photoperiods or transferred to darkness. This effect suggests that the physiological rhythms underlying adult differentiation were endogenous and were free running under constant conditions.

The relationships between circadian time of stage initiation, photoperiod, and stage duration are illustrated in Fig. 31. The curves shown were replotted from Harker's published data, and show these relationships for the developmental period from "head eversion" to "yellow eye pigment" stages. The response curves for the other two developmental periods—"yellow eye pigment" to "wing pigmentation," and "wing pigmentation" to "eclosion"—were strikingly similar to the responses shown in Fig. 31. In each of the photoperiods tested (4L:20D, 12L:12D, 18L:6D), entry into a growth stage during the first 4 hours after subjective dawn (hour 0) resulted in relatively rapid development. At the fifth circadian hour, a delay was manifested, and a very pronounced delay was associated with the first few hours of the subjective scotophase. Because the different groups of insects had been reared under different photoperiods, the circadian time at which "subjective night" began also differed. Quite obviously, growth stage duration was determined by two types of rhythmic functions—one of which was phase set by the onset of light and the other by the beginning of darkness. Apparently the biological clock system controlling adult development consists

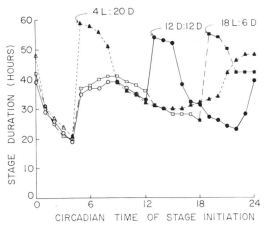

Fig. 31. Effects of photoperiods experienced during larval development and the circadian time of head eversion on the number of hours required to reach the "yellow eye pigment" stage in pupae of Drosophila melanogaster. [Adapted from Harker (1965b).]

of two primary oscillators, rather than just one. On the basis of the effects of light and dark pulses on the emergence rhythm of *Drosophila*, a similar conclusion was reached by Engelmann (1966).

As a result of the successive advances and delays associated with the circadian times that each growth stage is reached, the final event of adult emergence tends to occur at about subjective dawn (Fig. 32). As shown by the data plotted in this figure, pupae reaching the head eversion stage at different circadian times within a 24-hour period will display adult emergence that will be spread over a 3-day period. These data were taken from a 12L : 12D series; the other photoperiods resulted in quite similar patterns, except that there was a tendency toward a bimodal emergence rhythm in the case of the 18L:6D photoperiodic schedule.

Harker observed that the circadian clock system of pupae that were held under continuous darkness could be phase set by a light signal. This would influence the emergence rhythm, because it would change the circadian times at which the insects would be entering the next growth stage. Any pupae that had not yet reached the "head eversion" stage at the time of the imposed light pulse would emerge at times that were determined by the new phase setting. Those insects that had advanced to a later stage at the time of the light stimulus would show intermediate emergence times. In this way, transient phases of emergence, as discussed in an earlier chapter, could be explained.

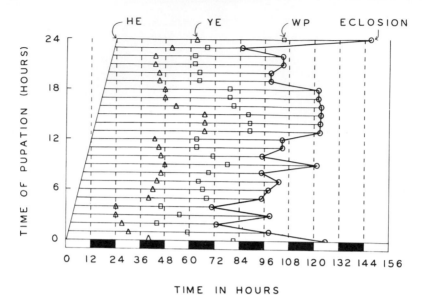

Fig. 32. Time required for adult development and emergence in Drosophila melanogaster, when the initial stage of head eversion occurred at different circadian times. HE = head eversion; YE = yellow eye pigment; WP = wing pigmentation. [Adapted from Harker (1965a).]

EFFECTS OF PHOTOPERIOD ON PIGMENTATION AND BODY FORM

In a number of instances, insect forms that were originally described as different species have subsequently proved to be seasonal forms of but a single species. The classical example of this taxonomic phenomenon is the European nymphalid butterfly *Araschnia levana*. It was originally described as two distinct species—*A. levana* and *A. prorsa*—but it is now known to be one species with two seasonal forms. The levana form is the adult of the overwintering generation, and is a russet-red butterfly with black wing spots. The prorsa form is the adult stage of the summer generation, and is black with white spots. Although long recognized as seasonal forms of a single species, the role of photoperiod in the dimorphism was not demonstrated until the work of Müller (1955). Müller found that both diapause and the levana form coloration were induced by rearing the caterpillars under short-day photoperiods. When exposed to long-day conditions (16 or more hours of light per day) during the larval growth stages, diapause did not occur and the resulting adult butterflies were of the black prorsa form (Müller, 1955, 1960a).

112

Prior to Müller's demonstration, the seasonal dimorphism was generally attributed to seasonal changes in the insect's host plants, or to the physiological effects of prolonged exposure to winter temperatures during the overwintering pupal diapause stage.

There are other known instances of seasonal dimorphism among lepidopterous insects. Caterpillars of *Hylophila prasinana* that were reared under a short-day photoperiod (10L:14D) underwent a pupal diapause before emerging as butterflies. However, caterpillars of the same species that were reared under long-day photoperiods or continuous illumination did not enter a diapause, but the butterflies that emerged were of a form that had been previously described as *Hylophila hongarica*. Similarly, the leaf rollers *Peronea fimbriana* and *Peronea lubricana* have been demonstrated to be seasonal forms of but a single species. Larvae that were reared under long-day conditions gave rise to the orange lubricana form, but those that were reared under short-day photoperiods produced gray adults of the fimbriana form (Danilevskii, 1961).

Although never confused as separate species, a number of other lepidopterans are known to display seasonally associated variations in wing coloration. Daylength has been shown to play a part in determining the wing pigmentation of *Ascia monuste,* with the long-day form being melanic and the short-day form being white (Pease, 1962). Larvae of *Lycaena phlaeas daimio* that were reared under long-day photoperiods (>14-hour photophase) became dark-colored butterflies, but short-day conditions (<13-hour photophase) produced light-colored adults (Sakai and Masaki, 1965). Differences in wing pigmentation were observed in *Heliothis zea,* the bollworm, reared under different conditions of photoperiod and temperature. The pigmentation differences appeared to be somewhat more closely associated with temperature than daylength, however (Phillips and Newsom, 1966).

In the several examples of seasonal dimorphism among the Lepidoptera, one form is most typically associated with the overwintering, diapausing generation, and the other morphic form is usually typical of the summertime, nondiapause generation. This leads to the question of whether or not diapause induction and form determination are expressions of the same physiological mechanism. The alternative interpretation is that although both effects are responses to photoperiod, they are mediated by different genetic loci and different physiological mechanisms. There are no conclusive experimental data on which to determine the validity of either hypothesis. The results reported by Sakai and

113

Masaki (1965), with *L. phlaeas daimio,* tend to support the latter hypothesis, however. They found that larval diapause could be averted by the use of relatively high rearing temperatures, despite the presence of a short-day photoperiod. The wing pigmentation of the adults, however, was of the short-day type, even though the insects had not experienced a period of diapause.

Seasonal dimorphism among the Lepidoptera is confined mainly to differences in wing pigmentation. Among some other insect groups, seasonal dimorphism may involve the form of the wings rather than its color pattern. The gryllid *Nemobius yezoensis* was observed to be micropterous (short winged) under field conditions, but when the nymphs were reared in the laboratory under long-day photoperiods (16 or more hours of light per day), some of the resulting adults were macropterous (long winged) (Masaki and Oyama, 1963). Long days also tended to result in larger and heavier adult forms than did short days (12L:12D). In rearing experiments with the cricket *Gryllodes sigillatus,* McFarlane (1964) concluded that wing form was determined by a combination of temperature, diet, and photoperiod, as well as by genetic factors. The possibility that photoperiod may be involved in determining the morphological phases of the locusts *Schistocerca gregaria* and *Locusta migratoria migratorioides* has been suggested (Papillon, 1965; Albrecht and Cassier, 1965). The incidence of the gregarious phase was found to increase significantly when the nymphs were reared under conditions of relatively long daylengths (photophases of >16 hours). At most, photoperiod might have a modifying effect on locust phase determination, as the phases appear to be influenced mainly by temperature, humidity, and population density.

Photoperiod has been shown to be a factor in the determination of seasonal dimorphism in a number of homopterous species. The rice leafhopper, *Nephotettix cincticeps,* displays two adult forms — a small, short-winged form that is seen mainly in the spring; and a larger, long-winged form that occurs mainly in the summer. The short-winged form has been shown to be produced from diapausing nymphs under the influence of short daylengths. Under long-day conditions, the nymphs did not enter diapause, and the adults were of the long-winged form (Danilevskii, 1961). A similar dependence of wing length and diapause induction on photoperiod was observed in the planthopper *Delphacodes striatella.* Another delphacid planthopper, *Stenocranus minutus,* was found to have a photoperiodically induced reproductive diapause, in which the individuals that were destined to enter the diapause state

114

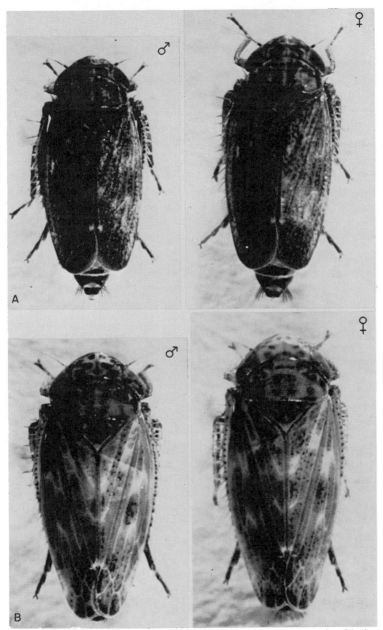

Fig. 33. Seasonal forms of the leafhopper *Euscelis plebejus*. *A = Short-day induced incisus form; B = long-day induced plebejus-form.* [*Photographs by courtesy of H. J. Müller.*]

were larger than those that did not go into diapause (Müller, 1958). The aleyrodid *Aleurochiton complanatus* shows a seasonal dimorphism in the "pupal" stage. Seasonal forms of this white fly were investigated by Müller (1962a,b,c), who found that the pale, nondiapause summer form of pupa was formed under long-day conditions (photophases of >17 hours), and the darker diapause pupae prevailed when the insects were reared under photoperiods in which the photophase was less than 16 hours duration.

The role of photoperiod in the seasonal dimorphism of species of Cicadellidae, genus *Euscelis*, was investigated by Müller in a long series of publications (Müller, 1954, 1957, 1960a,b, 1961, 1965). Müller has demonstrated that the leafhoppers that were originally described as the species *E. plebejus* and *E. incisus* are seasonal dimorphs of but a single

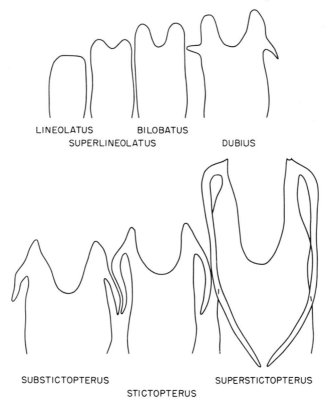

LINEOLATUS   BILOBATUS

SUPERLINEOLATUS   DUBIUS

SUBSTICTOPTERUS   SUPERSTICTOPTERUS

STICTOPTERUS

Fig. 34. Outline drawings of aedeagus forms in seasonal specimens of Euscelis linoleatus. [Adapted from Müller (1957).]

species, which is properly designated as *E. plebejus*. The leafhopper *E. linoleatus* was found to be represented by a complex of seven different seasonal forms: *linoleatus, superlinoleatus, bilobatus, dubius, substictopterus, stictopterus,* and *superstictopterus*. Several of these seasonal forms were once described as separate species.

The seasonal forms of *Euscelis* differ from each other in body size and relative wing length (Fig. 33), but the most important differences are found in the size and shape of the aedeagus of the male genitalia. The dimensions of the aedeagus have been used by Müller as an index of the effects of photoperiod on the growth and form of the leafhoppers (Fig. 34). The relationship between daylength and aedeagus width among leafhoppers that were reared at a constant temperature (30°C) is depicted in Fig. 35.

The increase in size of male genitalia with increasing daylengths suggests that the growth rate of the insect is higher under long-day than under short-day conditions. The effect is not on all aspects of growth, however, as the nymphal stadia were not observed to have been shortened by the influence of relatively long daylengths. Müller concluded that photoperiod influenced the allometric growth relationships among different body parts. If the durations of nymphal stadia were independent of photoperiod, different body sizes and genital forms could result from photoperiodic regulation of the rates of differentia-

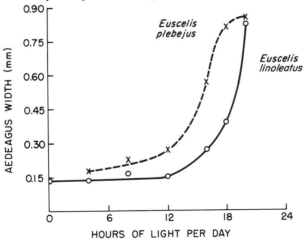

Fig. 35. *Effect of daylength on the width of the aedeagus of two species of leafhoppers, Euscelis plebejus and E. linoleatus. [Adapted from Müller (1957).]*

tion. This interpretation would account for the observed differences in size and form of the aedeagus without necessitating the postulation of separate "long-day" and "short-day" differentiation processes. According to this view, the photoperiodic effects are brought about by the effect of daylength on the *extent* rather than the *direction* of form determination.

Temperature was found to have modifying effects on the photoperiodic control of aedeagus growth. A relatively low constant rearing temperature (such as 15° or 20°C) shifted the photoperiodic response curve slightly toward the short-day response, as compared to the responses obtained at 30°C. The form of the aedeagus was also influenced to a small degree by partial starvation and by excessively high humidity. These effects were relatively minor, however, and exerted no more than a modifying effect on the basic response to photoperiod.

Leafhoppers are plant-feeding forms, and in Müller's experiments they were reared on living plants. Because the effects of photoperiod on plant life are frequently very pronounced, a question might arise concerning the apparent responses of the insects. Is the effect of daylength on the insect itself, or is it primarily on the host plant and thereby indirectly on the insect? An experimental arrangement, in which leafhopper nymphs were allowed access to foodplants at only specified times of the day, made it possible to rear the insects under photoperiods that differed from the photoperiods to which the host plants were exposed. The results clearly demonstrated that the effect of photoperiod were on the leafhoppers themselves, and not via the photophysiology of the plants.

Euscelis form determination was found to be determined mainly by the photoperiods experienced by the middle nymphal instars; the first and last instars were insensitive to photoperiod. Under natural conditions, the short-day forms of leafhoppers are observed during the spring and the autumn; the long-day forms are present in mid- and late-summer. The question of whether the actual daylength or the rate of daylength change is responsible for form determination was also investigated by Müller. He found that the actual daylengths experienced during the responsive nymphal stages was the determining factor. The aedeagus form of the adult male was determined by the mean daylength experienced by the middle nymphal instars. The same responses were obtained under constant, decreasing, or increasing daylength schedules, provided, of course, that the different photoperiodic regimes had similar mean values.

118

Experiments with *E. plebejus* have demonstrated that the insect will respond to skeletal photoperiods (Table V). Daylengths of 20 or 22 hours of light per day induced plebejus form adult males. Daylengths of only 12 hours induced the incisus form. If 1 or 2 hours of darkness was alternated with 11 or 10 hours of light, the incisus form was produced. Short 30-minute dark signals were ineffective. The effectiveness of 1-hour dark signals spaced 12 hours apart was the same as that of a 12L:12D photoperiod. As was discussed in Chapter 4, such results demonstrated that the photoperiodic response was induced through the timing of light-on and light-off signals, rather than in response to the duration of light or darkness, per se. In this respect, the photoperiodism of form determination appears to be similar to that of behavioral and adult emergence rhythms.

TABLE V

Effect of Skeletal Photoperiods
on Aedeagus Form in *Euscelis plebejus*[a]

Photoperiodic schedule	Aedeagus width (mm)	Aedeagus form
12L:12D	0.27	incisus
11L:1D:11L:1D	0.24	incisus
10L:2D:10L:2D	0.12	incisus
11.5L:0.5D:11.5L:0.5D	0.67	plebejus
20L:4D	0.62	plebejus

[a]Data of Müller (1957).

PHOTOPERIOD AND APHID POLYMORPHISM

The seasonal biology of aphids is not only complex, but also is widely variable among the numerous species. Polymorphism is the rule in this group of insects and is intimately associated with their complex seasonal biology. Aphids tend to change both their host plant specificity and their mode of reproduction as the seasons advance. As a result, all possible combinations of host plant alternation and alternation of generations are to be found within the family Aphididae. Before considering the current state of knowledge concerning the role of photoperiod in aphid biology, a general consideration of the typical seasonal biology may be of value (Fig. 36).

Egg. Most typically, the fertilized egg is the overwintering form of an aphid species. The eggs are deposited on the species' primary host plant in the autumn, and they pass the winter in a state of diapause.

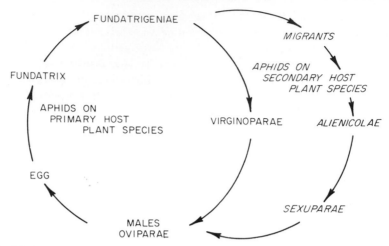

Fig. 36. A generalized seasonal biology of aphids.

Upon hatching in the spring, the eggs give rise to nymphs that become adult females; no males are produced. These springtime females are called *fundatrices*.

Fundatrix. The fundatrix is also known as the "stem mother," and is, with rare exceptions, wingless. These apterous females reproduce by viviparous parthenogenesis. The fundatrices are found only on the primary host plant in those cases where the aphid species shows a seasonal alternation of hosts. All of the offspring of the fundatrices are apterous females known as *fundatrigeniae*.

Fundatrigeniae. These females, too, reproduce by parthenogenetic viviparity. Being apterous, they are confined to the primary host plant on which they were born. The offspring of the fundatrigeniae mature to become females of the same body form and mode of reproduction as their parent. Thus there are from two to several generations of fundatrigeniae during the early part of the growing season. After a few generations of fundatrigeniae have been produced, winged offspring will appear. In some species a few of the alates are males, but the more usual case is that the alate aphids will be female migratory forms.

Migrants. These winged females leave the primary host plant, and settle on the summer, or secondary, host plant species. The migrant forms of aphid species that do not display host alternation will settle on host plants similar to that from which they came, or on any other acceptable plant species. The migrants are also parthenogenetic, viviparous reproducers, and the first generation of offspring will usually be entirely apterous. The progeny of the migrants are all females, and are sometimes called *alienicolae*.

Alienicolae. Starting with the progeny of the migrant generation, there are usually several generations of alienicolae. These forms are all parthenogenetic females, and they may be either winged or wingless. Toward the end of the growing season—late summer or early autumn—a generation is produced that may, in some species, be of a distinctive body form, and is called the *sexuparae*.

Sexuparae. These are female autumn migrants that leave the secondary host plant and return to the primary host plant species. The sexupara is, of course, an alate form. Reproduction is viviparous and parthenogenetic, as in the previous forms. The progeny of the sexuparae are the sexual males and females of the species. In some aphid species, there are two types of sexuparae: *gynoparae*, whose progeny are exclusively females; and *androparae* that give birth to only males. In most aphids, the sexuparae produce offspring of both sexes.

Oviparae and Males. The sexual females are called oviparae, and are apterous in nearly all species. They mate with the alate males, and reproduction is oviparous. The eggs are deposited on the primary host plant, and pass the winter in a state of diapause.

Modifications. Not all of the seasonal forms described above are to be observed in the life cycle of every species of aphid. Many display a greatly simplified seasonal cycle. Aphids that are not obliged to change host plant species at some time during the summer will tend to have a less complex polymorphism than do those in which host alternation is obligatory. Migrants, alienicolae, and sexuparae may not appear as distinct morphological types in aphid species that do not change hosts. Even in such cases, however, alternation of generations is still manifested, and the springtime fundatrices are followed by a succession of fundatrigeniae generations (usually known as *virginoparae*), and the males and oviparous females are produced in the late summer and autumn. Winged forms that disseminate the species to other host plants may be produced sporadically during the summer. The production of such alates is apparently attributable to crowded conditions on the host plant, rather than to photoperiod. In host-alternating species, the appearance of alate migrants and sexuparae is more frequently a seasonal response that involves the insects' reactions to daylength.

Under laboratory and greenhouse conditions of constant temperature, favorable photoperiod, and optimum host plant growth, many aphid species may be cultured parthenogenetically through hundreds of generations without the production of the sexual forms. The sexual forms of some aphid species have never been observed, even in the field. In such cases, the perpetuation of the species appears to be entirely parthenogenetic, and overwintering is accomplished in the form of cold-hardy viviparous virginoparae. Even in some species where males and oviparae have been observed, certain geographical populations reproduce only parthenogenetically.

Factors Influencing Form Determination

A great many studies have been made of polymorphism in aphids, in efforts to elucidate the ecological and physiological factors influencing the differentiation of the several seasonal forms. Biochemical changes in the host plant have often been implicated in seasonal changes in aphid generations. Protein and sugar contents of the plant sap, the water relations of the plant, and senescence effects in the foliage have all been suggested as playing a part in the determination of aphid polymorphism. Environmental temperatures and humidity levels at the leaf surface have also been implicated. The reader is referred to the review articles of Kennedy and Stroyan (1959) and Lees (1966) for a detailed discussion of these several factors. The role of photoperiod in form determination has been demonstrated in a number of instances, and will be discussed below. It should be noted, however, that not all aspects of aphid polymorphism are likely to be explicable on the basis of photoperiod or any other single environmental variable. Undoubtedly there are a number of interacting factors that contribute to the determination of aphid body form.

Form determination occurs during embryonic development. At the time that an aphid nymph is born, its eventual adult form has already been determined, even though the insect must pass through a series of nymphal instars before the adult stage is realized. The newborn aphid nymph already contains the early embryos of some of its own progeny, and some aspects of their adult forms have also been determined. This means that a photoperiodic effect may be manifested a full generation later.

The adult body form of the aphid is determined during embryonic development, and the earliest determination is that of sex. The determination of sex occurs during the late embryonic stages of the *parent*. Parthenogenetically produced aphids are diploid in chromosome number, and sex determination is by the XX–XO system. Meiosis of the aphid oocyte involves the formation of but one polar body. In the formation of the male egg, the X chromosomes pair to form a bivalent, but they fail to replicate. As a result, one whole X chromosome passes into the polar body, and the developing egg is left with but one X chromosome. This process is of interest in the subject of polymorphism, because the production of male (XO) and female (XX) progeny is not a random process. Whether or not the X chromosomes replicate appears to be controlled, so that males are produced only at certain times (Lees, 1961).

Somewhat later during embryonic development, the female embryo will be determined as to whether its adult form will be that of a virginopara (fundatrigenia) or ovipara. This determination may occur many days before birth, and the most advanced embryos contained in a third instar nymph will have been already determined as to both sex and reproductive type (Lees, 1961). The "decision" as to whether a virginoparous female offspring will be alate or apterous is made relatively late in embryogenesis. Apterous or alate determination may be delayed until the last 24 to 48 hours prior to the birth of the nymph (Shull, 1928; Lees, 1959a, 1960b).

Photoperiod and Form Determination

Three aspects of aphid polymorphism have been studied from the standpoint of photoperiodism. They are (1) alate versus apterous determination; (2) the production of males; and (3) virginoparous versus oviparous determination.

The study of insect photoperiodism may be said to have begun in 1923 with the work of Marcovitch (1923, 1924), who demonstrated that the alate autumn migrants (sexuparae) of the rosy apple aphid, *Dysaphis plantaginea*, were produced in response to short-day photoperiods. This aphid species was known as *Aphis sorbi* at the time of Marcovitch's publications. The aphid's photoperiodic response was demonstrated experimentally by maintaining the aphids on their summer hosts (plantain) under artificial short days for a period of about 7 weeks. The short days employed were of but 7.5 hours of light per day, and by this procedure sexuparae were produced in June. Alate sexuparae would not appear until late September under natural field conditions. Similarly, Marcovitch was able to induce sexuparae production in colonies of *Aphis rumicis* and *Capitophorus hippophaes*. Marcovitch was uncertain as to whether the action of photoperiod was on the aphids themselves, rather than on the insects' host plant and thereby an indirect effect on the aphids. He considered the latter hypothesis the more likely, probably because his investigations had been prompted by Garner and Allard's pioneering work on plant photoperiodism (Garner and Allard, 1920). Shull (1928, 1929), working with the potato aphid, *Macrosiphum euphorbiae*, showed that the formation of winged sexuparae was a short-day photoperiodic response of the aphids, independent of the photoperiodic responses of the host plant.

Although Marcovitch suggested that spring migrants of the rosy apple aphid might also be induced by photoperiods, in this case the long daylengths of late spring, he was unable to demonstrate such an effect. Under the influence of long-day photoperiods, some alate aphids were produced after the third generation of fundatrigeniae, but they were not numerous. He observed that the alate spring migrants appeared mainly in crowded colonies, and suggested that alate determination might be influenced by the aphid population density on the plant. This observation has been confirmed in the case of several aphid species (Wilson, 1938; Bonnemaison, 1951, 1958, 1964, 1965a; Lees, 1959a,b, 1961). Bonnemaison (1964, 1965a, 1966a,b,c) showed that alate sexupara production by the rosy apple aphid is induced by a combination of short-day photoperiods and crowded colony conditions.

A detailed study of the effects of temperature and photoperiod on wing determination in the potato aphid was conducted by Shull (1926, 1928, 1929, 1930, 1932, 1938, 1942). The primary host of this species is rose, and Shull's experimentation was with the parthenogenetic (alienicolae) on the secondary host, the common potato. Shull apparently dealt with factors inducing the production of the winged sexuparae, although he did not specifically identify the alates as being sexuparae. When parthenogenetically reproducing potato aphids were transferred from long-day conditions to short-day conditions (daylengths <12 hours), they continued to give birth to apterous progeny for about 48 hours. After that time, the progeny were predominantly alates. Light intensities from 37 to 10,000 lux were equally effective, and photoperiodic effects were detectable at light intensities as low as 5 lux. The correlation between daylength and percentage of alate offspring is illustrated in Fig. 37. These data show that daylengths that were shorter than 12 hours induced a very high incidence of winged progeny. Daylengths greater than 12 hours tended to suppress alate production. The transition from a preponderance of alate to apterous offspring was very sharp, indicating a critical daylength of between 12 and 13 hours. The term *critical daylength* is used to designate the

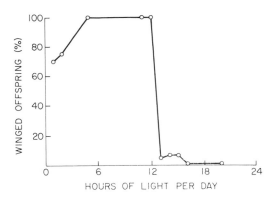

Fig. 37. Effect of daylength on the incidence of winged offspring among apterous virginoparae of the potato aphid, Macrosiphum euphorbiae. [Adapted from Shull (1929).]

daylength that represents a transition point at which the photoperiodic response switches from one mode of expression to another.

The natural diel photoperiod is of 24-hour duration, and any experimental alteration of the duration of either photophase or scotophase necessarily involves an alteration of the other phase, in order to maintain the 24-hour period of the light-dark rhythm. By the use of experimental photoperiods of unnatural length, it is possible to determine the relative importance of the duration of one phase while holding the other phase at a constant value. Shull (1929) used such a technique to measure the effects of different light:dark ratios on the photoperiodism of the potato aphid. The most effective phase durations for alate production was found to be 6 hours in the case of the photophase and 12 hours in the case of the scotophase (Table VI). A 12-hour scotophase combined with photophases of from 2 to 6 hours induced high incidences of winged progeny. On the other hand, a 6-hour photophase combined with scotophases of from 11 to 20 or more hours was also quite effective.

Production of alate sexuparae of *Dysaphis plantaginea* was found to be closely associated with a 12-hour scotophase, even when combined with photophases of from 12 to 48 hours (Bonnemaison, 1966a,b,c). Ovipara determination in the vetch aphid, *Megoura viciae*, has also been reported to be most effectively produced by photoperiods with 12-hour scotophases combined with any of a wide range of photophases (Lees, 1965).

There is good evidence that every aphid embryo is a presumptive alate form. Wing anlagen were found to be present in the early nymphal instars of *Macrosiphum euphorbiae*, whether the nymphs were destined

125

TABLE VI

Effects of Different Unnatural Photoperiods on Production
of Alate offspring by the Potato Aphid, *Macrosiphum euphorbiae*[a]

6-Hour photophase		12-Hour scotophase	
Scotophase (hr)	Alate progeny (%)	Photophase (hr)	Alate progeny (%)
1	0.0	1	31.8
2	0.0	2	74.3
4	0.0	3	74.3
6	4.3	4	73.6
8	1.6	6	74.4
10	8.4	8	58.9
11	49.1	10	54.6
12	83.3	12	31.7
13	86.0	16	13.4
14	83.0	20	2.5
16	69.3	24	2.1
18	65.3	28	2.4
20	53.4		

[a]Compiled from data of Shull (1929).

to become alate or apterous imagoes (Shull, 1938). This finding has
been confirmed with the cowpea aphid, *Aphis craccivora* (Johnson and
Birks, 1960), and the vetch aphid, *Megoura viciae* (Lees, 1961). The
apterous condition may be regarded, therefore, as a secondary condition in which normal wing differentiation has been suppressed. In body
form, development of sense organs, sclerotization, and pigmentation,
as well as in the absence of wings, an adult apterous aphid bears a strong
resemblance to a nymph. Alatae, on the other hand, are usually quite
different from nymphs in all of these several characteristics. For this
reason, it has been suggested that an apterous aphid represents a neo-
tenic (juvenilized) adult. There is experimental evidence that the
apterous state is related to a hyperactivity of the corpora allata in the
production of juvenile hormone. Lees (1961) reported that wing development and other anatomical characteristics typical of the alate
form could be partially suppressed by topical applications of JH con-
centrates to the early instars of alate-determined vetch aphid nymphs.
White (1965) demonstrated that the organ size and apparent secretory
activity of the corpora allata differed between apterous- and alate-determined nymphs of the cabbage aphid, *Brevicoryne brassicae*. During the
last two nymphal stages, the apterous-determined nymphs possessed

much larger corpora allata than did nymphs destined to become alatae. Upon reaching the adult stage, the corpora allata of the alates increased markedly in size; whereas the allata of the apterous forms decreased in both volume and secretory activity.

The role of photoperiod in the production of male aphids is quite uncertain at the present time. As discussed above, sex is determined at the time of the meiotic division, and although male determination is not a random phenomenon, little is known of the controlling mechanism. In his work on the vetch aphid, Lees (1959a) could detect no effect of photoperiod on male determination, but attributed male production to the effects of temperature and age of the reproducing females. Males tended to occur most frequently among the progeny of a virginopara during the middle of her reproductive life; none were produced by young females and very few appeared among the offspring of virginoparae that were approaching senility. Intermediate temperatures (ca. 15°C) induced a greater production of males than did either lower or higher temperatures.

Some effects of photoperiod, age, and temperature were reported by Kenten (1955) in a study of polymorphism of the pea aphid, *Acyrthosiphon pisum*. In this species, males were not numbered among the offspring of young females, nor were they produced by virginoparae that had been reared under a long-day photoperiod (16L:8D). However, large numbers of males were produced in the latter half of the reproductive lives of virginoparae that had been reared under an 8-hour daylength (8L:16D) at an intermediate temperature (13°–20°C). The virginoparae of the rosy apple aphid, *Dysaphis plantaginea*, apparently produced males in response to short-day photoperiods (12L:12D) experienced during their nymphal stages (Bonnemaison, 1958, 1965b). Male production was found to be strongly suppressed among long-day-reared females of the cabbage aphid, *Brevicoryne brassicae*, and the green peach aphid, *Myzus persicae* (Bonnemaison, 1951).

The sexual oviparous female aphid is produced in response to short-day photoperiods in a number of species (Table VII). In species that have an alternation of hosts, the sexual forms are the progeny of the sexuparae. As discussed above, the alate sexuparae may be produced in response to photoperiods, and the progeny of the sexuparae — alate males and apterous oviparae — are not susceptible to further form determination by photoperiod or other environmental factors. Their body form was determined by that of their parents. The situation is different,

TABLE VII
Aphids in Which the Seasonal Production of Sexual
Oviparae Has Been Shown to Be a Short-Day Photoperiodic Response

Species	Common name	References
Acyrthosiphon pisum	Pea Aphid	Kenten (1955)
Aphis chloris		Wilson (1938)
Aphis fabae	Bean aphid	Marcovitch (1924), deFluiter (1950), Davidson (1929)
Aphis forbesi	Strawberry root aphid	Marcovitch (1923)
Brevicoryne brassicae	Cabbage aphid	Bonnemaison (1951)
Dysaphis plantaginea	Rosy apple aphid	Marcovitch (1923), Bonnemaison (1951, 1964)
Macrosiphum euphorbiae	Potato aphid	MacGillvray and Anderson (1964)
Megoura viciae	Vetch aphid	Lees (1959a)
Myzus persicae	Green peach aphid	Bonnemaison (1951)

however, among aphid species that do not have an obligatory alternation of hosts. In these aphids, a sexupara form generation may not appear, and the oviparae are produced from virginopara parents. A female embryo may be determined as either a virginopara or as an ovipara. Photoperiod has been shown to play an important role in determining the virginopara-ovipara developmental alternatives. Virginopara-ovipara determination has been studied in great detail by A. D. Lees, with *Megoura viciae* as the experimental insect (Lees, 1959a,b, 1960a,b, 1961, 1963, 1964, 1965, 1966). Parthenogenetically reproducing populations of this aphid may be maintained indefinitely under optimum conditions. The population studied by Lees had been greenhouse cultured for many years on broad bean plants (*Vicia faba*) at a temperature of 15°C and a daylength of 16 hours. Under these conditions, only virginoparae and a few males were produced; oviparae never appeared in the cultures. Short-day determination of oviparae was demonstrated by transferring newly born first instar nymphs from the standard culturing photoperiod (16L:8D) to a short-day photoperiod (12L:12D). When the transferred aphids reached the adult stage, they all became virginoparae, suggesting that form determination had occurred during the embryonic stages. The female progeny of these aphids were exclusively oviparae, however.

When virginoparae were reared from the first instar throughout their lives under different photoperiods, their progeny were almost

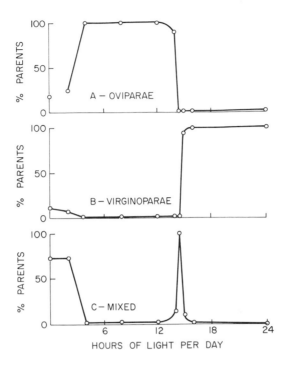

Fig. 38. *Effect of daylength on the determination of virginoparous and oviparous progeny of virginoparae of Megoura viciae.* [*Adapted from Lees (1959a).*]

exclusively oviparae if the experimental daylengths were shorter than 14.5 hours. Virginoparous offspring predominated when the daylengths were greater than 14.5 hours (Fig. 38). The critical daylength for female form determination appeared to lie between 14.5 and 15.0 hours (Lees, 1959a). A subsequent precise determination of the critical day-length showed it to be 14 hours and 55 minutes at a temperature of 15°C (Lees, 1963). In photophases shorter than the critical daylength, most of the parental aphids produced only oviparae; whereas most produced virginoparae when reared in photophases longer than the critical value. The photoperiodic response was found to be temperature sensitive, however. The critical daylength tended to decrease with increasing ambient temperature at a rate of 15 minutes per 5°C. If the aphids were held at temperatures of 23°C or higher, the photoperiodic reaction was not manifested, and all female progeny were virginoparae, even under short-day photoperiods.

Virginoparae that were reared at about the critical daylength tended to produce both virginoparous and oviparous offspring. Within the reproductive life of an individual aphid, the progeny types were not randomly distributed. An aphid would give birth to a succession of one form, and then would switch to the production of the other form. This pattern of reproduction suggested that the morphological determination of the offspring was controlled by the maternal system rather than by the embryonic system. On the basis of these observations, Lees (1960b, 1963, 1966) has postulated the operation of a "maternal switching system," probably endocrine in nature, and he has elucidated many of its functional features.

Each adult virginopara of the vetch aphid was found to contain 18 ovarioles, each with about 6 developing embryos. The earliest of these embryos was found to have begun its development at a time when the parental aphid was itself still an embryo. Such a compression of generations means that a reproducing virginopara contains the early embryonic

TABLE VIII

Sequences of Female Progeny of Individual Apterous
Virginoparae of *Megoura viciae* That Were Transferred Between Long-
Day (16L:8D) and Short-Day (12L:12D) Photoperiods at Different Life Stages[a]

Incidence (%) of virginoparae (V) and oviparae (O)
among progeny of parents transferred at indicated growth stage

Offspring batch	1st instar		3rd instar		Teneral adult		Parturition beginning		With about 20 offspring		With about 45 offspring	
	V	O	V	O	V	O	V	O	V	O	V	O
Transferred from short-day to long-day												
1	100	0	0	100	0	100	0	100	0	100	0	100
2	100	0	73	27	0	100	0	100	0	100	0	100
3	100	0	100	0	9	91	77	23	0	100	0	100
4	100	0	100	0	100	0	100	0	80	20	0	100
5	100	0	100	0	100	0	100	0	100	0	0	100
Transferred from long-day to short-day												
1	0	100	100	0	100	0	100	0	100	0	100	0
2	0	100	100	0	100	0	100	0	100	0	100	0
3	0	100	50	50	100	0	100	0	100	0	100	0
4	0	100	0	100	100	0	100	0	100	0	100	0
5	0	100	0	100	0	100	18	82	100	0	100	0

[a]Based on data of Lees (1959a).

stages of her grandchildren. Because the embryos move down the ovariole as they develop, the oldest embryo in a given ovariole will be at about
the same age and position as the oldest in each of the other ovarioles.
This means that a group of about 18 progeny should be born at about
the same time and with very nearly identical developmental histories.
Such a group was referred to as a "batch" by Lees, and he has used the
form determination of successive batches as a criterion of the state of
the maternal switching mechanism at different times in the ontogeny of
the parent aphid, and as a means of determining the developmental
stage at which the embryo is susceptible to form-determining factors.

Virginopara-determined aphid nymphs were reared under either
short (12L:12D) or long (16L:8D) daylengths, and were transferred
into the opposite photoperiod at different stages of development. The
proportions of virginoparae and oviparae among their female offspring
were then observed through 5 successive batches (Table VIII). The
switching from one progeny type to the other was very abrupt, and its
time of occurrence was dependent upon the parental age at the time of
transfer from one photoperiod to the other. From experiments of this
type, Lees concluded that ovipara-virginopara determination occurred
at about midway during embryonic development, and that form is
determined by a maternal switching mechanism to which the embryos
can respond for only a very short specific time during their growth.
Thus, the very youngest embryos had not yet become sensitive at the
time that the maternal system was switched from ovipara to virginopara
induction, or vice versa; whereas the nearly mature embryos had already
been determined and were no longer influenced by the switching of
inducing mechanisms of the maternal system. It was also observed
that the aphids could be switched from ovipara to virginopara determination more readily than in the opposite direction. This effect was
attributed to an accumulative effect of long-day photoperiods, suggesting
that even brief exposures to long days early in development might exert
a partial activating effect upon the insect's response to subsequent exposures to long days (Lees, 1963). A similar long-day accumulation has
been described in studies of diapause, and this phenomenon will be
discussed in the following chapter.

Highly precise illumination of different parts of the aphid's body led
to the conclusion that the parent aphid's brain was the site of photoperiodic reception. It was postulated that the maternal switching
mechanism was located in the brain—probably the neuroendocrine
system—or that it was at least controlled from the brain (Lees, 1964).

131

There is a time factor in the effects of photoperiod on aphid poly-morphism, and this factor is closely related to the seasonal ontogeny of the species. In his original work on the rosy apple aphid, Marcovitch (1923) found that fundatrices that were hatched and maintained under short-day conditions would give rise to aphid populations that produced oviparae in about 3 months. During that 3 months, several generations of parthenogenetically reproducing forms were formed before any ovip-arous aphids appeared. The fundatrices and at least a few generations of fundatrigeniae were not sensitive to the ovipara-inducing action of the experimental short-day photoperiod. A similar insensitivity of early spring generations was observed by Wilson (1938) in *Aphis chloris*. In this species short-day induction of oviparae did not occur prior to the seventh parthenogenetic generation following the fundatrix. Wilson suggested that a "time factor" was involved, rather than a required number of generations. Bonnemaison (1951) attributed the phenome-non to what he termed the "fundatrix factor." The fundatrix factor was postulated to be a physiological process that became progressively less influential as the aphid colony advanced in age. Some workers have preferred to explain the phenomenon on the basis of a required num-ber of generations that must be produced before the aphid population can become capable of developing sexual forms. The experimental work of Bonnemaison (1951) and Lees (1960b, 1963) has clearly shown, however, that the passage of time is the important factor, rather than numbers of generations. In his studies with the vetch aphid, Lees has termed the time factor as an "interval timer."

Starting with the fundatrigeniae produced by a fundatrix, Lees established a series of parthenogenetic clones under conditions of 15°C and a 12L:12D photoperiod. Each clone was perpetuated by two line-ages: a "first-born" and a "last-born" lineage. The first-born lineage consisted of the earliest progeny of the previous generation; con-versely, the last-born lineage was maintained by preserving progeny produced late in the reproductive life of the parental generation. The two lineages of each clone were identical in age, as measured in numbers of days removed from the original fundatrix ancestor. But the lineages differed in generation numbers, because at the time that the first-born lineage was in the sixth generation, the last-born group might have attained only the fourth generation. Under these conditions, oviparae were produced at about the same day-of-age in both lineages. There was some clone-to-clone variation in the time of ovipara production, but the population response was clearly related to the age of the entire

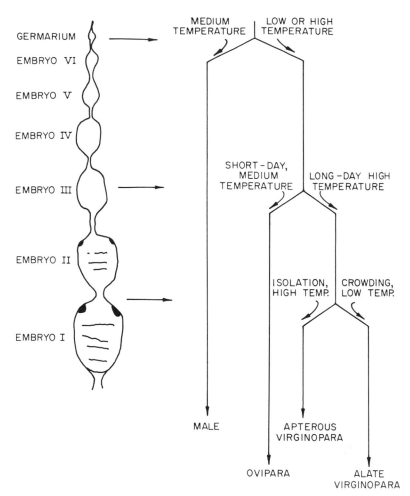

Fig. 39, Developmental alternatives in the polymorphism of the aphid Megoura vivciae. [Adapted from Lees (1961).]

clone rather than to the lineage generation number. Similar clones and lineages that were maintained under long-day photoperiods (16L:8D) produced virginoparae indefinitely, but at about the time that the short-day clones began to produce oviparae, the long-day clones were found to be capable of producing oviparae in the generation following a transfer to short-day conditions. Apparently, the "interval timer" operated similarly under either photoperiod, and each clone became

133

responsive to photoperiod at about the same age. Lees concluded that the interval timer was, in some way, involved in the establishment or control of the maternal switching mechanism.

Aphid polymorphism involves a number of alternative developmental pathways. Which of these alternatives is to be followed by the embryo is determined by time, temperature, and photoperiod, as well as by internal factors such as age, endocrine function, and nutritional state. Lees (1961, 1966) visualized form determination as involving a series of "choices" between alternative developmental pathways, some of which were closed at certain times and during certain developmental stages. Lees' general form determination hypothesis is shown in Fig. 39. As is apparent in the figure, as well as in the foregoing discussion, photoperiod plays an important part in the biology of aphids, but it is not the only determining factor. This hypothetical series of developmental pathways does not include a consideration of the "interval timer" effects discussed in the previous paragraph. The operation of the interval timer would result in the nonavailability of some developmental alternatives at times in the ontogeny of the aphid colony. Some of these modifications of the developmental alternatives are summarized in Table IX.

TABLE IX
Developmental Alternatives That Are Open (O) or Closed (C) to
Embryos of Different Parental Forms of the Aphid *Megoura viciae*[a]

Parental form	Embryonic polymorphic alternatives					
	Male or Female		Ovipara or Virginopara		Aptera or Alata	
Fundatrix	C	O	C	O	O	C
Fundatrigenia	C	O	C	O	O	O
Virginoparae						
Alate	O	O	O	O	O	C
Apterae	O	O	O	O	O	O

[a]Based on Lees (1961).

134

7 □ Photoperiodism and Diapause

Diapause is a genetically determined state of suppressed development, the manifestation of which may be induced by environmental factors. Diapause is an important adaptive mechanism for insect survival during periods of unfavorable environmental conditions, such as low winter temperatures, extreme summer heat, periods of dryness, and seasons in which appropriate food materials are absent. Simple dormancy, such as heat- and cold-torpor, differs from diapause in that the dormant state is most frequently a direct response to deleterious physical forces. Diapause, on the other hand, most typically begins long before the onset of unfavorable physical conditions, and may not be terminated until long after the disappearance of such conditions. In some species, diapause is *obligatory*, and every individual of every generation undergoes a period of diapause as part of its life history. Most insect species display a *facultative* diapause; that is, a diapause that may or may not be manifested in a given individual or population, depending on the environmental conditions prevailing during certain critical stages of the insect's development.

The well-established fact that diapause is genetically determined implies the existence of biophysical and physiological mechanisms by which the diapause state is instituted, maintained, and eventually terminated. Much research has been devoted to insect diapause, with the greatest emphasis on an elucidation of the genetics, physiological mechanisms, and the role of environmental factors. Moisture, diet, temperature, and daylength have all been implicated as being involved in the induction of the diapause state. But of these several factors, daylength has, on the whole, proved to be of the greatest importance, although the effects of photoperiod may be modified or even nullified some of the other influences mentioned above.

Diapause may occur at any growth stage—egg, larva or nymph, pre-pupa, pupa, or adult. Within the developmental biology of any given species, however, diapause will occur only at a quite specific growth stage or instar. Relatively few insect species have been found to be capable of diapausing at more than one point in their life cycle. Although manifested at a genetically predetermined life stage, diapause may have been induced via responses to photoperiods experienced much earlier in development. The classic example of this phenomenon is to be observed in the commercial silkworm, *Bombyx mori*. This species displays an embryonic diapause, but the diapause occurs in response to photoperiods experienced by the female parent during its late embryonic life (Kogure, 1933). In such a case, there is a full generation between determination and manifestation. This type of parental determination of the diapause of progeny has been detected in a number of species, and is apparently much more common than was previously suspected.

Adult diapause is most frequently induced by photoperiods experienced by the insect during its larval stages, and both larval and pupal diapauses may be in response to the environmental conditions—day-lengths, etc.—prevailing during embryonic and early larval stages. The occurrence of diapause at a specific developmental stage in response to photoperiodic stimuli experienced at an earlier (also specific in most cases) developmental stage, or even by the parental generation, poses some interesting biological problems. How can the insect's developmental program be modified by environmental stimuli so that diapause is manifested at a stage subsequent to that at which the stimuli were received? Does "diapause or nondiapause" constitute a developmental alternative, comparable to the form-determination alternatives discussed in the previous chapter?

Seasonal polymorphism is closely associated with diapause phenomena in many cases. In the butterfly *Araschnia levana,* the levana form is the adult stage of those individuals that spent the winter in a pupal diapause that had been induced by short-day photoperiods to which the larvae had been exposed. The prorsa form butterfly is the adult of a nondiapausing individual; that is, one that spent its larval life under the influence of long daylengths. The same relationship between form and diapause has been observed in the polymorphic leafhopper species studied by H. J. Müller. *Euscelis plebejus* specimens were found to vary greatly in the anatomy of the male genitalia, with the genitalial form being determined by the daylengths to which the immature stages had been exposed. The plebejus form prevailed under long-day conditions; whereas the incisus form predominated when the insects were reared under short-day photoperiods. The latter form is the seasonal form that overwinters in a state of diapause, and the diapause has been shown to be a short-day photoperiodic response.

In his work on the polymorphism of the aphid *Megoura viciae*, A. D. Lees has dealt mainly with the developmental alternative of oviparous or virginoparous modes of reproduction. Short daylengths were found to lead to the production of oviparae and long daylengths promoted the production of virginoparae. Oviparous aphids lay eggs, and these eggs enter an embryonic diapause in which they pass the winter. The developmental pathway that leads to the sexually reproducing aphid is also the pathway of diapause determination. A quite similar relationship between photoperiod, reproduction, and diapause has been reported as occurring in the Cladoceran *Daphnia pulex* (Stross and Hill, 1965). This animal was found to reproduce parthenogenetically during the summer, but under the influence of short-day photoperiods a sexual generation appeared and diapausing eggs were produced.

The association of form determination and diapause determination is also well illustrated by the seasonal life history of a mite, *Tetranychus urticae*. This mite overwinters as adult females in diapause, and the diapause state is apparently a response to short-day photoperiods. However, exposure of the early spring generations to short days did not induce diapause; the mite populations became sensitive to short-day photoperiods only after 4 generations of nondiapausing individuals had been produced (Dubynina, 1965). This observation is in striking accord with Lees' finding that young aphid clones could not produce oviparae in response to short daylengths (Lees, 1960a). Oviparae production could occur after the passage of about 50 days and several generations from the first post-fundatrix generation, leading to the postulation of an "interval timer" controlling mechanism. In both instances— aphids and mites—a diapause state was involved in the short-day effect, with the same sort of hypothetical interval timer perhaps being operative.

The parasitic wasp *Nasonia vitripennis* (family Pteromalidae) enters diapause as a mature larva. Experimental work on this insect showed that the larvae were committed to either diapause or nondiapause developmental pathways, depending on the temperatures and photoperiods experienced by their female parent (Saunders, 1962, 1965a,b,

1966a,b). The adult female wasps tended to produce nondiapause progeny early in their reproductive life, and diapause-committed larvae late in life. Under the influence of low temperatures or short-day photoperiods, the wasps switched from nondiapause- to diapause-committed progeny very early in ther reproductive lives. Under high temperatures and long-day photoperiods, the switch to the production of diapause-determined progeny was delayed until the females were nearly senile. Saunders (1965b) has suggested that a maternal switching mechanism comparable to that postulated by Lees might be operating.

As discussed in the previous chapter, the developmental rate displayed by a given arbitrary stage of adult differentiation in *Drosophila* pupae was determined by the circadian time at which the insect entered that developmental stage. Thus for example, the number of hours that would be required for a pupa to advance from the "head eversion" stage to the "yellow eye pigment" stage was determined by the circadian hour at which the "head eversion" stage had been reached (see Fig. 31). It would appear that at critical points of stage initiation, subsequent development was programmed in respect to rate. The programming was probably determined by the physiological state of the insect at those critical points in time. The slowest development programmed in the *Drosophila* stages was a matter of only 50 to 60 hours for the completion of an arbitrary growth stage. If, however, developmental rates could be programmed at much lower rates, so that each stage might require from 500 to 600 hours for completion, a diapause-like state would be apparent. In known instances of pupal diapause, however, adult development is suppressed at much earlier stages than in this example. The principal concept with which we are concerned, however, is that the insect develops to a point in time at which subsequent growth patterns are programmed in accord with the genetic and physiological states of the organism at that moment. Such programming involves determination of form (as in polymorphism) and rate, including such phenomena ad adult emergence rhythms and the state of diapause. By this theoretical view, behavioral and physiological rhythms, form determination, and diapause determination are all related to the interaction of the genetic potential and the temporal organization of the insect.

Diapause was defined above as being a state of suppressed developmental rate. Older definitions have specified that diapause is a state of arrested growth and development (Andrewartha, 1952; Lees, 1955, 1956). The term "arrested" implies a zero rate of developmental processes, and allows no possibility of different degrees or intensities of diapause. This limitation leads to difficulties in dealing with diapause phenomena, because of the necessity of recognizing that some developmental changes must occur during diapause. At the minimum, such changes are those processes that lead to the termination of diapause and the resumption of development at the expected "normal" rate. The growth and developmental processes that occur during the diapause period have been termed *diapause development* (Andrewartha, 1952). Obviously, there is an inconsistency associated with any reference to development that occurs during a time in which development has been arrested. The use of the more relative term "suppression" avoids this difficulty, and also has the advantage of meaningful application to instances where developmental rates remain measurable, even though development is very slow and the insect is obviously in a state of diapause.

Diapause is not a rhythmic event, because it occurs but once in the life of an individual insect. In this respect, diapause resembles adult emergence and form determination. The diapause state is very rarely accompanied by morphological characteristics that permit immediate easy identification of either diapausing or nondiapausing insects. Insects in diapause are usually identified on the basis of the negative criteria of suppressed developmental and metabolic rates. This means that an insect can be identified as being in diapause only by comparing its physiological state with that of an arbitrary norm assumed to represent the nondiapause condition. These factors tend to complicate the study of the physiology of diapause, and also to obscure the exact role of circadian functions in the induction and termination of the diapause state.

PHOTOPERIODIC INDUCTION OF DIAPAUSE

Two publications in 1933 announced the discovery of an effect of photoperiod on insect diapause. Sabrosky *et al.* (1933) reported that adult and nymphal diapause of the pigmy grasshopper, *Acrydium arenosum*, could be prevented by maintaining the insects under continuous illumination. In what has become known as a classical paper, Kogure (1933) published a detailed study of the role of daylength on the incidence of embryonic diapause in the silkworm *Bombyx mori*. Since the time of these two pioneer studies, more papers have been published on diapause than on any other aspect of insect photoperiodism.

In studies of the effects of photoperiod on the induction of diapause, the experimental insects are usually reared for all or part of their life

139

cycle under controlled conditions of light, diet, and temperature. The diapause response is most frequently measured in terms of the *percentage incidence of diapause* within the experimental population. If different day-lengths induce different incidences of diapause among groups of other-wise fully comparable insects, the effect of photoperiod on diapause incidence can be plotted as a *diapause induction response curve*.

Types of Diapause Induction Curves

When percentage incidence of diapause is plotted against daylength, diapause induction curves of the types shown in Fig. 40 may be obtained. *Type I* induction curves are typical of a great many species. This type of response to daylength is also known as a *long-day response*, in that relatively long daylengths tend to favor continuous (nondiapause) growth and development. Low ambient temperatures tend to cause the response curve to be shifted toward the right, so that the occurrence of diapause at the longer daylengths will be favored. Conversely, relatively high temperatures will cause the response curve to be shifted toward

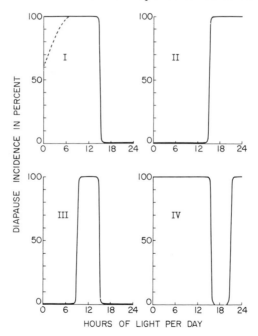

Fig. 40. *Different types of diapause incidence–daylength relationships observed among insects. Type I = long-day response type; II = short-day response type; III = short-day–long-day response type; and IV = long-day–short-day response type.*

the short-day end of the scale. The exact shape and position of the curve will, of course, vary among the species that display this general type of diapause induction response. One frequent variable is the effect of very short photophases, such as 0, 2, or 4 hours. In some species, the diapause incidence at these daylengths will be less than 100% (indicated by the dashed line in Fig. 40, type I). However, this portion of the response curve shows only a gradual increase in diapause incidence as the daylengths are increased from 0 (continuous darkness) to 6 or 8 hours. Such a gradual response is probably not comparable to the critical daylength displayed at between 14 and 16 hours of light per day. The *critical daylength*, or point of transition between very high and very low incidences of diapause, is usually quite sharply defined. The concept of critical daylength in relation to diapause incidence will be discussed in a subsequent section. A few examples of insect species displaying the type I diapause induction response curve are: the Colorado potato beetle, *Leptinotarsa decemlineata* (de Wilde, 1958); *Acronycta rumicis* (Danilevskii, 1961); the pink bollworm, *Pectinophora gossypiella* (Adkisson *et al.*, 1963); and the spider mite, *Metatetranychus ulmi* (Lees, 1953,a, b).

The *type II* diapause induction response curve is the reciprocal of type I. Insects that display the type II response have been called *short-day* forms, because development without diapause is promoted by the shorter daylengths. The critical daylength shown in Fig. 40 for the type II response lies between 14 and 16 hours, although this is both species and temperature dependent. The effect of temperature on type II response is usually opposite to its effect on type I. Relatively high ambient temperatures tend to promote diapause induction; that is the critical daylength is shortened. And relatively low temperatures tend to decrease the incidence of diapause. Although by no means as widespread as type I, a number of insect species have been found to display the type II response. Some of them are: the commercial silkworm, *Bombyx mori* (Kogure, 1933); the geometrid *Abraxas miranda* (Masaki, 1956, 1959); and some strains of the cabbage noctuid *Mamestra brassicae* (Masaki and Sakai, 1965).

Type III response photoperiod shows two well-defined critical daylengths. For this reason, the type III reaction might be termed *a short-day—long-day response*. At the very short daylengths (0 to 8 hours in the example shown in Fig. 40), no diapause incidence is observed. Complete incidence of diapause is observed at daylengths of from 10 to 14 hours. A second critical daylength is found between 14 and 16 hours, but daylengths of 16 or more hours are not diapause inducing. In this type of

141

response curve diapause is induced by only a relatively narrow range (ca. 8 hours) of daylengths. Low environmental temperatures tend to broaden the range of diapause-inducing photophases, and high temperatures tend to reduce the range. In this type of insect response to photoperiod, neither continuous illumination nor continuous darkness is diapause inducing. This characteristic is in sharp contrast to that of type I, where constant darkness tends to promote the induction of diapause and continuous illumination does not. The converse characteristics are shown by type II, where continuous illumination tends to enhance the incidence of diapause; whereas continuous darkness results in a nondiapause growth pattern. Daylengths shorter than about 8 hours represent conditions that are never encountered by insects in their natural habitats during the growing season. The short-day portion of the type III diapause induction curve is of no apparent ecological significance, but it may be of interest from a more theoretical standpoint. The insect's responses to experimental photoperiods with extremely short photophases may provide information as to the nature of the response mechanisms. Examples of insects displaying the type III diapause induction response curve include the European corn borer, *Ostrinia nubilalis* (Beck, 1962a); the oriental fruit moth, *Grapholitha molesta* (Dickson, 1949); the cabbage worm, *Pieris brassicae* (Danilevskii, 1961); and the mirid, *Lygus hesperus* (Beards and Strong, 1966).

The type IV response to daylength has been demonstrated in only a few insect species, all of which are lepidopterans: *Leucoma salicis*, *Euproctis chrysorrhea*, *Euproctis similis* (Geyspitz, 1953), and the peach fruit moth, *Carposina niponensis* (Toshima *et al.*, 1961). Type IV response was also observed in a northern Asia race of the European corn borer (Danilevskii, 1961). As may be observed from the shape of the diapause induction curves, type IV is the converse of type III, and is characterized by an absence of diapause incidence over a very restricted range of relatively long daylengths. All other photoperiodic conditions result in a high incidence of diapause. This type of response might be termed as a *long-day — short-day response*. The effects of temperature on this type of response have not been determined, but the expectation would be that a relatively high temperature would tend to narrow the nondiapause range of daylengths.

The Critical Daylength

The concept of a critical daylength displayed by a species or geographical population is frequently encountered in literature on photoperiod-

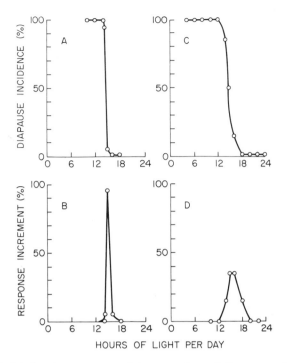

Fig. 41. Critical daylengths as measures of the mean photoperiodic response thresholds of insect populations. For further explanation see text.

ism. The term was defined above as being the point in the photoperiodic response curve at which the sign of the response changed. That is, the incidence of diapause changed from extremely high to very low, or as in the case of the aphids discussed in the previous chapter, progeny production changed from virginopara production to ovipara production. It should be observed that the concept of critical daylength is usually applied to population responses, as in the percentage incidence of diapause. The photophase duration described as the critical daylength is, therefore, an estimate of the mean response threshold of the population being studied. The characteristics of critical daylengths are illustrated in Fig. 41. Figure 41A shows the effect of daylength on the incidence of diapause in an insect population that displays a well-defined critical daylength. Diapause incidence, in this example, was very high at all daylengths shorter than 14.5 hours, but very low when the daylengths were 15 or more hours. The critical daylength might, therefore, be estimated as between 14.5 and 15 hours of light per day.

If the increment of response to increasing daylength is plotted (Fig. 41B), it may be seen that about 90% of the population was responsive to the difference between a daylength of 14.5 hours and one of 15.0 hours. The observed variance was very small, and the result was a dramatically sharp transition between a high diapause incidence and an exceedingly low incidence.

A less well-defined critical daylength is illustrated in Fig. 41C. In this case, the critical daylength was estimated as being between 13 and 16 hours of light per day. When plotted as response increments per unit change in daylength, the data showed a very broad response range (Fig. 41D). Only 35% of the population responded to the difference between daylengths of 13 and 14 hours, and another 35% being responsive to additional hour of light. Because of the relatively great variance in the population responses, the critical daylength was rather poorly defined.

At any given daylength, each insect will or will not be committed to diapause, depending on its individual response threshold, which is undoubtedly a genetic characteristic. The accuracy with which the critical daylength may be measured experimentally can be taken as an approximation of the genetic variability of the particular population under observation.

Temperature and Thermoperiods

Temperature exerts two different effects on the induction of diapause, depending on whether the temperature is constant or fluctuating through a daily cycle (thermoperiod). When the environmental temperature is constant, the critical daylength displayed by populations of experimental insects may vary according to the temperature employed, and some of these effects were briefly mentioned above. The exact effect of different constant temperatures on critical daylengths differs widely among insect species. The critical daylength for ovipara production by the aphid *Megoura viciae* was found to decrease approximately 15 minutes for every 5°C rise in ambient temperature (Lees, 1963). Approximately similar changes in critical daylengths values were observed in diapause induction of *Ostrinia nubilalis* (Beck and Hanec, 1960) and *Pieris brassicae* (Bünning and Joerrens, 1962). Much greater effects have been reported in other species, however. A 5°C change in the constant ambient temperature induced a 1-hour change in the critical daylength for diapause induction in the Asiatic bollworm, *Chloridae obsoleta* (Goryshin, 1958), 1.5 hours change in the value for the noctuid *Acronycta rumicis* (Danilevskii, 1961), and as much as a 2-hour change in the case of *Pectinophora malvella* (Kuznetsova, 1962). Goryshin (1964) suggested that, as a general rule, the critical daylength for diapause induction among lepidopterans is usually shifted from 1 to 1.5 hours per 5°C change in ambient temperature. However, the dipterans *Pegomyia hyosciami* and *Hylemia brassicae* were shown to be highly sensitive, as a 7°C temperature difference (from 18° to 25°C) caused a 4.5-hour shift of critical daylength with *Pegomyia* and a 3-hour shift in the case of *Hylemia* (Zabirov, 1961).

Different levels of constant temperature may have effects on diapause induction other than that of influencing critical daylength. Temperature may considerably modify, or even abolish, the insect's reaction to photoperiod. Such an effect was seen in the case of the vetch aphid, where short-day photoperiods did not induce the production of oviparous females when the ambient temperature was relatively high (>20°C) (Lees, 1959a). Photoperiodic induction of diapause may also be abolished by relatively high environmental temperatures. The cabbage worm, *Pieris brassicae*, offers an example of such an effect, as shown in Fig. 42 (Danilevskii, 1961). Pupal diapause in this species was not induced at any temperature when the insects were reared under constant illumination. In continuous darkness, however, low rearing temperatures resulted in a high incidence of diapause; at 20°C and higher, however, only nondiapause pupae were obtained. Because both continuous illumination and continuous darkness are aperiodic, the diapause-inducing effect of low temperatures and continuous dark might suggest a non-

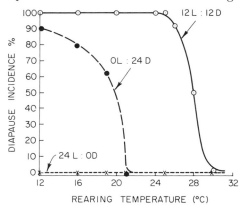

Fig. 42. *Effects of different temperature and light conditions on induction of pupal diapause in Pieris brassicae.* [*Adapted from Danilevskii (1961).*]

145

photoperiodic mechanism of diapause determination. Short-day photo-periods (12L:12D) caused 100% diapause incidence at all temperatures below about 25°C. Temperatures above 28°C completely averted dia-pause induction, even in the presence of the short daylength. High-temperature prevention of photoperiodic induction of diapause has also been reported for a number of other species: the oriental fruit moth, *Grapholitha molesta* (Dickson, 1949); the codling moth, *Carpocapsa pomonella* (Dickson, 1949); the fruit tree spider mite, *Metatetranychus ulmi* (Lees, 1950); the root maggot *Euxesta notata* (McLeod, 1964); and the bollworm *Chloridea obsoleta* (Danilevskii, 1961).

Of the above listed insects, two are of further interest because of unusual temperature effects on the photoperiodic induction of dia-pause. In *Grapholitha molesta* and *Chloridea obsoleta*, diapause was not induced when the ambient temperatures were either relatively high or low. Diapause was induced by short-day photoperiods only at tempera-tures lying in the middle of the range of effective rearing temperatures (21° − 26°C, approximately).

The so-called "short-day" insects − Fig. 40, type II − such as the com-mercial silkworm, *Bombyx mori*, are known to respond to temperature-photoperiod combinations in a manner that is opposite to the examples discussed above. In the short-day species, relatively high temperatures tend to increase the incidence of diapause by shortening the critical daylength. The critical daylength value is shifted toward the long-day end of the scale by relatively low rearing temperatures, which tends to decrease the incidence of diapause among insects exposed to daylengths of intermediate values.

Insects in their natural environments seldom, if ever, experience constant temperature conditions. The environmental temperatures tend to fluctuate through a daily cycle. Although the daily rhythm of temperature changes is never as precise as a photoperiodic rhythm, it nevertheless forms a *thermoperiodic rhythm*. The effect of thermoperiod on rhythmic biological systems has not been investigated to any great extent. The substitution of thermoperiodic signals for photoperiodic signals in phase regulation of circadian rhythms has been reported, however. Some information is also available on the role of thermo-period in diapause induction, and on the combined effects of photo-period and thermoperiod.

The European corn borer, *Ostrinia nubilalis*, overwinters as a mature larva in diapause. This diapause has been shown to be induced by short-day photoperiods experienced during the period of larval feeding and growth (Mutchmor and Beckel, 1958, 1959; Beck and Hanec, 1960). When the larvae were reared at a constant temperature of 26°C, the critical daylength was found to be approximately 15 hours (Beck and Hanec, 1960). The effect of thermoperiod on the induction of diapause was tested at that daylength (Beck, 1962a,b). A relatively shallow temperature cycle was used, in which the high temperature was 31°C and the low temperature was 21°C, giving a daily mean of 26°C. The incidence of diapause was very high when the cool phase of the thermoperiod occurred during the scotophase, but was very low when the warm phase coincided with the scotophase (Table X). The response data clearly showed that diapause incidence was influenced by the temperature of the scotophase. With such a shallow thermoperiod and a relatively high mean temperature, diapause incidence was very low when the insects were reared under continuous darkness. A thermoperiod with greater amplitude and lower mean was found to induce nearly 100% diapause incidence among borer larvae reared in continuous darkness (Beck, 1962b). This thermoperiod consisted of 11 hours at 31°C, 1 hour of declining temperature, 11 hours at 10°C, and 1 hour of rising temperature. Such a thermoperiod appeared to be nearly as effective as a 12L:12D photoperiod and a constant temperature. "Long-day" thermoperiods, in which the warm phase prevailed for 16 hours per day,

TABLE X

Effect of Thermoperiod on the Photoperiodic Induction
of Diapause in the European Corn Borer, *Ostrinia nubilalis*

Temperature during photoperiod (15L:9D)		Diapause
15-hr photophase (°C)	9-hr scotophase (°C)	incidence (%)
31	31	15
26	26	64
21	21	95
21	31	15
31	21	96

Temperature during darkness (0L:24D)	Diapause
24-hr scotophase (°C)	incidence (%)
31	0
26	0
21	15

were not as effective as long-day photoperiods in the avoidance of diapause, however (McLeod, 1963).

Under the conditions of its natural environment, the European corn borer would be exposed to a temperature rhythm in which the night temperatures would be lower than the daytime temperatures. The normal synchrony of thermoperiod and photoperiod prevails when the low-temperature phase of the thermoperiod coincides with the scotophase, and it was this combination that most effectively induced diapause under controlled laboratory conditions. In a study of a physiological rhythm of secretion in gland cells of corn borer larvae, Beck *et al.* (1965a) observed that the phases of the secretory rhythm were more precisely defined when the larvae had been held in a synchronized photoperiod and thermoperiod than when exposed only to a photoperiod at a constant temperature.

Goryshin (1964) studied the effects of combined thermoperiods and photoperiods on the induction of pupal diapause in three lepidopterous species: the sorrel dagger moth, *Acronycta rumicis;* the satin moth, *Leucoma salicis,* and the cabbage butterfly, *Pieris brassicae.* In all three species, thermoperiod had a definite influence on the incidence of diapause. Low scotophase temperatures tended to increase the incidence of diapause, and high scotophase temperatures tended to suppress diapause. Scotophase temperatures had little influence when the daylengths were very long (>18 hours). A thermoperiod with an amplitude of 10°C (21°–31°C) and a half-cycle length of 12 hours (analogous to a 12L:12D photoperiod) was found to exert a diapause-inducing effect on dark-reared larvae of the pink bollworm, *Pectinophora gossypiella* (Menaker and Gross, 1965). The thermoperiodic effect on this species was rather weak, however, in that diapause incidence was only slightly increased over that observed when the larvae were reared at constant temperatures in continuous darkness.

From the foregoing discussion, it is quite apparent that temperature plays a part in the determination of diapause. When insects are reared under constant conditions, the temperature level influences the photoperiodic responses in that it is one of the factors determining the mean threshold of response (critical daylength). At relatively low rearing temperatures, diapause may be induced at all photoperiods; conversely, there may be no photoperiodic induction of diapause under relatively high temperature conditions. These effects may indicate that the temperature extremes lead to a bypassing of the photoperiodic response system, or they may be the result of the critical daylength's having been shifted to a point lying outside of the range of photoperiods to which the insects were exposed. The second major temperature effect on insect periodism is that of the cycling temperature, or thermoperiod. Thermoperiod may, under some circumstances, substitute for photoperiod in the determination of diapause. Thermoperiod may also modify the insects' response to photoperiod; the photoperiodic effects may be reduced when the high-temperature phase of the thermoperiod coincides with the scotophase, or they may be intensified when the low-temperature phase occurs during the scotophase.

Dietary Effects

Because plants are developing, changing biological systems, the diet of a phytophagous insect does not remain biochemically uniform during the growing season. In the case of a multivoltine insect species, the food plant of the spring generation may be quite different from that on which late summer or early autumn generations feed. The possibility that diapause determination is associated with the biochemical composition and water content of the host plant has been considered by many workers. Some evidence in support of such a hypothesis was marshalled through field observations and limited laboratory experimentation before the possible importance of daylength was appreciated. The early work on this problem was also handicapped by a lack of techniques for culturing insects on synthetic media under controlled conditions. These limitations render the conclusions reached by early workers of little value. With the development of stable artificial dietary media and of instrumentation for the control of photoperiod, it is now possible to study the influence of dietary composition on the induction of diapause.

In the few properly controlled studies that have been done, diet has been found to have a relatively minor influence on diapause. Food deprivation has been shown to induce diapause in a few instances (Lees, 1955; Burges, 1962). In most cases, however, the composition of the insect's diet has proved to be either without any effect, or to exert a minor modifying influence on the insect's photoperiodic responses. Lees (1952, 1953a,b) reported that under controlled photoperiodic conditions, the mite *Metatetranychus ulmi* would produce diapause eggs if the leaves of the food plant were either senescent or had been fed on extensively by previous generations of mites. Under less extreme nutritional deprivation, the incidence of diapause was controlled by

149

temperature and photoperiod, and not at all by the biochemical composition of the host plant.

The pink bollworm, *Pectinophora gossypiella*, feeds in the cotton boll, mainly on the developing seeds. As the season progresses, the seeds and fiber tend to become partially desiccated, and the oil content of the seeds rises markedly. An early study of diapause in this species led Squire (1939) to conclude that the incidence of diapause was inversely proportional to the water content of the insect's natural diet. A semisynthetic diet was developed for this insect in 1956 by Vanderzant and Reiser. These workers observed that the incidence of diapause was in an approximate proportionality to the fat (corn oil) content of the diet. This finding suggested that the oil content of the insect's natural food might influence the induction of diapause. Combined photoperiodic and dietary studies yielded experimental results that tended to support such a hypothesis (Bull and Adkisson, 1960, 1962; Adkisson, 1961). The effect of the lipid content of the diet was found to be of secondary importance, however. Diapause was shown to be primarily a response to short-day photoperiods. At photoperiods approximating the critical daylengths, the incidence of diapause was higher on diets containing relatively higher fat concentrations. The effect of the dietary fat level was to determine, at least in part, the critical daylength. Under the influence of a nondiapause-inducing long day (14L:10D), high dietary fat levels did not lead to an increased incidence of diapause. In a study of a closely related lepidopteran—*Pectinophora malvella*—Kuznetsova (1962) observed that the larval food plant influenced the critical daylength for diapause induction, but he did not identify the dietary components responsible. Goryshin (1958) also reported that larval food plants exerted a minor influence on the critical daylengths for the induction of diapause in the bollworm *Chloridea obsoleta*.

The Colorado potato beetle, *Leptinotarsa decemlineata*, undergoes a facultative diapause in the adult stage. Although induced mainly by short-day photoperiods experienced by the newly emerged adult beetles, photoperiods to which the larval stages were exposed also influence the adult response (de Wilde, 1954, 1958). The question of the role of the host plant in the determination of diapause has been investigated by a number of workers. Jermy and Saringer (1955) could detect no nutritional effects; feeding the young beetles young potato foliage did not prevent diapause. These workers concluded that temperature and photoperiod were the only inducing factors. Larczenko (1957), however, reported having detected a correlation between the incidence of diapause and the lipid:protein ratio in the plant material eaten by the beetles. As the lipid:protein ratio increased, the incidence of diapause also increased. Such results suggest a similarity between the Colorado potato beetle and the pink bollworm, in that relatively high dietary lipid concentrations tend to exert a diapause-promoting effect. However, Wegorek (1960) could not confirm Larczenko's results, and concluded that diapause is a response primarily to photoperiods. Feeding newly emerged potato beetles on foliage that had been perfused with any of a multitude of different chemicals had slight, if any, influence on the observed incidence of diapause (Rodionova, 1962).

Although not yet tested under controlled laboratory conditions, there are a number of observations that lend at least limited credence to the hypothesis that diapause incidence may be slightly influenced by nutritional effects. There is need for carefully controlled study of the relationships between the insect's diet and its photoperiodic responses.

Photoperiodic Termination of Diapause

Just as the diapause state may occur in response to photoperiods, so photoperiods may also hasten the termination of diapause. Such a diapause-terminating effect was first observed by Baker (1935) in a study of the larval diapause of mosquito species that inhabit tree holes (*Anopheles barberi* and *Aedes triseriatus*). Short-day photoperiods induced the diapause, and long-day photoperiods were effective in ending it. Diapause-terminating effects of photoperiods have now been reported for a number of insect species. In addition to the mosquitoes mentioned above, dipterous insects in which diapause has been shown to be terminated in response to long daylengths include the pitcher midge, *Metriocnemus knabi* (Paris and Jenner, 1959); the root maggot *Euxesta notata* (McLeod, 1964); and the midge *Chironomus tentans* (Engelmann and Shappirio, 1965). Among the Coleoptera, diapause in the sweet clover weevil, *Sitona cylindricollis*, occurs in the adult stage in response to the short-day photoperiods experienced by the larvae; this diapause may be terminated by exposing the young adults to long-day photoperiods (Hans, 1961). Short-day induced diapause of young adult Colorado potato beetles may also be terminated by exposing the insects to several days of long-day photoperiods (de Wilde *et al.*, 1959). The trichopterans of the genus *Limnephilus* undergo an estival diapause in the adult stage

151

(Novak and Sehnal, 1963). These insects are of the so-called "short-day" type, in that diapause is induced by long-day photoperiods. Diapause was found to be terminable in response to short-day photoperiods. The reproductive diapause of adults of the hemipteran *Lygus hesperus* was observed to be terminated by exposure to long day-lengths (Beards and Strong, 1966). Photoperiodic termination of larval and pupal diapauses among species of Lepidoptera has been observed in a number of cases; these include *Dendrolimus pini* (Danilevskii, 1961), *Christoneura fumiferana* (Harvey, 1958), *Antheraea peryni* (Shakhbazov, 1961), *Ostrinia nubilalis* (McLeod and Beck, 1963b), *Pectinophora gossypiella* (Bell and Adkisson, 1964), and *Hyalophora cecropia* (Mansingh and Smallman, 1966). Among the Odonata, diapause termination in response to long-day photoperiods has been reported in *Tetragoneuria cynosura* (Lutz and Jenner, 1960), *Neotetrum pulchellum* (Montgomery and Macklin, 1962), *Anax imperator* (Corbet, 1956), and *Aeschna cyanea* (Schaller, 1965).

As far as is currently known, the diapause of most species is not terminated by photoperiod. The diapause state may be of very long duration (many months or more than a year) and eventually come to an end "spontaneously," or its completion may be hastened by exposure of the insects to several weeks of low winterlike temperatures. Such chilled insects then develop rapidly upon being returned to optimal incubation temperatures, and diapause may be considered to have been terminated. Even in the many instances where photoperiod has been shown to influence the rate at which the diapause state is completed, or terminated, daylength may not be the only factor involved. The effects of photoperiod may be enhanced or modified by the environmental temperature, sensory stimuli, water availability, chemicals, and by the "intensity" of the diapause state.

Temperature

Because diapause in most insect species requires that the insect be exposed to low temperatures for a prolonged period as a prerequisite for the resumption of active growth and development, the concept of *diapause development* has arisen (Andrewartha, 1952). Diapause development has been defined as the physiological development that goes on during diapause in preparation for the resumption of morphogenesis. The apparent necessity for a diapausing insect to spend weeks or months at low (usually $2°-8°C$) temperatures led to the concept that the biochemical mechanisms of diapause development were

152

characterized by very low temperature optima. In general, it was thought that diapause development involved the degradation of growth-inhibiting metabolites or "diapause hormones," or the repair of some biochemical defect in the physiological system that controlled the rate of growth processes. The biochemical processes that are influenced by low temperature exposure of the diapausing insect have not been demonstrated. There has been no experimental confirmation of the postulated role of either growth-inhibiting metabolites or diapause hormones.

If diapause is regarded as a developmental stage, rather than a biochemical breakdown, diapause development is the process of completing that stage of development. The term *diapause termination* should then be used in the sense of termination through the *completion* of programmed developmental stage, and not in the sense of the *correction* of a defective growth mechanism. The demonstration that diapause completion may be hastened by exposing the insects to growth-promoting photoperiods (usually long-day), has shown that diapause development is not an exclusively low-temperature phenomenon. Nothing is known of the mechanisms by which either low temperatures of photoperiods hasten the completion of the diapause stage. There have been very few studies on the combined effects of low temperature and photoperiod; more research is needed to clarify this subject.

The European corn borer, *Ostrinia nubilalis,* overwinters as a mature larva, and its diapause was long considered to be of the type requiring many weeks of low environmental temperature for termination (Babcock, 1924, 1927). Diapause development in this species was found to be accelerated by long-day photoperiods, however, and diapause could be brought to termination without the intervention of low temperatures (Beck and Apple, 1961; McLeod and Beck, 1963b). Storage of diapausing larvae at 5°C for 6 weeks prior to exposure to long-day conditions only slightly enhanced the rate of diapause termination, as compared to similar larvae that were stored at 30°C before transfer to the long daylengths (McLeod and Beck, 1963b). Storage at the higher temperature resulted in greater mortality than did the low-temperature storage, probably because of the higher rates of fat body reserve expenditure.

Sensory Factors

The possible importance of nonphotoperiodic sensory stimuli in the termination of diapause was suggested by the work of Church (1955a) with the wheat stem sawfly, *Cephus cinctus.* This species passes the winter as a mature larva in diapause, and the larva is normally situated in a cocoonlike hibernaculum in the stem of the host plant. Church observed that if the diapausing larvae were removed from their cocoons, they failed to pupate, even though they had received sufficient low-temperature exposure to have completed diapause development. Physical contact with the walls of the cocoon appeared to pay a part in the insect's normal development. In the absence of such contact stimulation, the pupal molting cycle was apparently not initiated.

Quite apart from any sensory stimulation associated with photoperiods, an input of sensory stimuli has been shown to be of considerable influence on the functioning of the insect endocrine system (Wigglesworth, 1934; Davey, 1962a; Lees, 1961; Thomsen and Møller, 1963; Highnam and Haskell, 1964; Edwards, 1966). How such sensory factors influence photoperiodic responses and diapause development is quite unknown.

Diapause has been terminated by the application of physical stimuli in a number of instances. Electrical shocks, acid treatments, physical wounding, and restricted singeing have all been shown to speed the completion of diapause in specific instances (Lees, 1955). Nothing is known about the basis of such effects, and no general rule has been formulated concerning the actions of such drastic treatments.

Water

Water very frequently plays an important role in diapause. The percentage water content of the insect usually declines from the onset of diapause, and reaches a stable level that, in many cases, represents a surprising degree of desiccation. This decrease in water content is probably an important part of the process of becoming cold-hardy, and thus represents an adaptation for winter survival (Hodson, 1937; Salt, 1961). In the cases of aestival diapause, where high temperatures and aridity prevail, the decrease in water content may be caused by an unavoidable transpiration from spiracles and integument, despite the relative impermeability of these organ systems. Although the diapausing insect typically shows a relatively low water content, water loss is not considered to be a diapause-inducing factor. Such loss occurs after the insect has entered the diapause state, and in fact some forms may lose and absorb water several times during the course of the diapause period (Andrewartha, 1952). In most species, water is actively absorbed or imbibed at the end of diapause, and such water uptake may

154

frequently be a necessary preliminary to the resumption of active growth and development.

The role of water loss and reabsorption in diapause development has been studied by a number of workers, but in some ways the results have been inconclusive and frequently conflicting. Slifer (1946) described the termination of diapause in the eggs of *Melanoplus differentialis* as resulting from the experimental application of xylol and other lipid solvents. The solvents removed the outer waxy layers of the chorion, and the eggs would then absorb large quantities of water. With the influx of water, diapause was terminated and embryonic development was resumed. As pointed out by both Andrewartha (1952) and Lees (1955), the eggs of some grasshopper species typically absorb water during the course of diapause, but water uptake alone does not seem likely to be the diapause-terminating factor. Egg diapause in some other orthopterans, such as the cricket *Acheta commodus*, is preceded by a marked absorption of water (Hogan, 1961).

Koidsumi (1952) described experiments in which the larval diapause of the rice stem borer, *Chilo suppressalis*, was terminated in response to abrasion of the integument. The abraded integument allowed a rapid water exchange with the environment, and when abraded larvae were held in the presence of free water, they absorbed large amounts and diapause was terminated. However, this technique was ineffective with the closely related European corn borer (Beck and Alexander, 1964a). Most investigators have concluded that experimental artifices designed to introduce water into diapausing insects will lead to the termination of diapause only if the insect's diapause development has already been completed, so that the lack of tissue water has becoming the limiting factor preventing immediate resumption of growth (Church, 1955b; van Dinther, 1961; Wellso and Adkisson, 1964).

Access to free water has long been known to be a requirement for pupation of overwintered larvae of the European corn borer (Babcock, 1924; Monchadskii, 1935). Under field conditions, the water content of overwintering borers was found to decline from a prediapause level of about 80% to a stable level of about 50% by midwinter (Beck and Hanec, 1960; Hanec and Beck, 1960). This partial desiccation was normally alleviated by the imbibition of water during the spring, and until the water level of the insect's body was restored to normal, the borer was incapable of pupation. The uptake of water was found to be by active drinking, and not by absorption through the cuticle (Mellanby, 1958; Monchadskii, 1935; Beck, 1967). Beck (1967) reported that partially dehydrated diapausing borers would imbibe about 50μl of water during the first 24 hours in which water was made available to them.

Roubaud (1928) postulated that partial dehydration was required during the course of diapause development in the European corn borer, and both water loss and subsequent rehydration were essential steps in the termination of diapause. This idea has been shown to be incorrect; partial dehydration is not required for the completion of the diapause stage. Borer larvae can be maintained in a fully hydrated state and will complete diapause development when incubated at 30°C under the influence of a long-day photoperiod (McLeod and Beck, 1963b).

In a study of the roles of water and photoperiod on diapause development (Beck, 1967), diapausing European corn borer larvae were incubated under different combinations of moisture and daylength. When diapause-committed borers were transferred to a long-day photoperiod (16L:8D) immediately upon reaching larval maturity, the average time required to complete diapause development and to pupate was about 30 days, if contact moisture was present throughout the incubation period. Under short-day conditions (12L:12D) similar borers required over 120 days to attain the pupal stage. Neither photoperiod led to completion of the diapause stage if the larvae were deprived of access to water. When diapausing larvae were held in a long-day under dry conditions for the first 20 days of diapause, and were given water on the twenty-first day, the average time to pupation was about 30 days from the beginning of the diapause period. These results suggested that the 20 days of water deprivation neither prevented nor accelerated diapause development. Once water was made available to the larvae, they completed their development at the same rate as they would have had water been accessible throughout the incubation period. When diapausing borers were held dry under long-day conditions for 30 days, they lost about 30% of their original body weight. Upon being given water, they regained their original weight by imbibition. The average time to pupation was then 40 days (10 days after receiving water). Apparently the photoperiodically controlled aspects of diapause development were completed by the twentieth long-day, regardless of water availability, but the developmental events leading to pupation were inhibited by a lack of water.

Pupation is a postdiapause event. The European corn borer's requirement for water prior to pupation might also be interpreted as a postdiapause requirement. However, the validity of such an interpretation depends on what criterion is used to mark the end of the diapause state. The borer diapauses as a mature larva that has finished its feeding, and displays some of the early phases of prepupal differentiation; it diapauses as an early prepupa. The initiation of the molting cycle leading to pupation may properly be taken as marking the end of diapause. The activation of the neuroendrocrine system and the secretion of prothoracotropic hormone would constitute the first postdiapause physiological event in such a larval diapause, just as it is the generally accepted criterion for the termination of pupal diapause in a wide variety of species. By this criterion, however, the lack of body water prevents the completion of diapause development, and the insect's need for water imbibition is not a postdiapause requirement. In experiments with the European corn borer, it was found that the neuroendocrine system was not activated until after the water requirement had been met (Beck, 1967). Diapause development was postulated to be a two-phase developmental process. The first phase is thought to be rate controlled by photoperiod, and the second phase probably includes the activation of the neuroendocrine system. Completion of the second phase is dependent upon an appropriate water balance in the insect.

Chemical Effects

The treatment of grasshopper eggs with xylol had a diapause-terminating effect, as discussed above, which was interpreted as being the result of water absorption by the egg. Vapors of fat solvents, such as carbon tetrachloride, xylol, and toluene, have also been reported to terminate the diapause state in larvae of the sugar beet webworm, *Loxostege sticticalis* (Pepper, 1937). In some instances, treatment of diapausing forms with fat solvent vapors has been found to terminate diapause, but without a stimulation of water uptake (Lees, 1955). It is thought that in such cases diapause is terminated by either (1) an unidentified chemical effect on the insect's metabolism, or (2) a shock or injury effect that results in the elevation of both metabolic and developmental rates.

A number of pharmaceutical chemicals were administered to diapausing larvae of the European corn borer in attempts to terminate diapause (Beck and Alexander, 1964a), but with uniformly negative results. The substances used were mainly central nervous system stimulants for man and higher animals, but they had no observable effects on the borer larvae. Hogan (1961, 1962) reported that urea and some ammonium compounds would greatly accelerate the termination of embry-

157

onic diapause in a cricket, *Acheta commodus*. When these substances were tested on the corn borer, it was found that relatively massive doses (400–800 μg/larva) injected into the diapausing larvae resulted in the termination of diapause. Ammonium acetate was found to be the most effective (Beck and Alexander, 1964a). Other nitrogenous compounds and suspected metabolic intermediates did not stimulate diapause development. The ammonium acetate treatment did not eliminate the effect of photoperiod on diapause development, however. Diapause was most rapidly terminated when the larvae were treated with 400 μg of ammonium acetate and held under a long-day photoperiod, in which case the average time from treatment to pupation was 10 days.

Intensity of Diapause

The duration and stability of diapause vary among insect species, and also among the individuals of a given species. In some cases diapause is little more than a transitory delay in the developmental sequence, but in others the diapause state may persist for several years. Diapause in the latter case is said to be more intense than in the former. Diapause always involves a suppression of metabolic rate, as measured by oxygen consumption, and developmental rate. Intensity of diapause is generally thought to be inversely proportional to these rates, or directly proportional to the degree of suppression. Diapausing pupae of *Hyalophora cecropia*, for example, show an oxygen consumption rate that is only about 2% of the prediapause rate (Schneiderman and Williams, 1953). Larval diapause in the European corn borer involves a less drastic reduction of metabolism, and borers in diapause were found to show an oxygen uptake rate that was from 25 to 30% that of nondiapausing larvae (Beck and Hanec, 1960). The pupal diapause of cecropia will persist for 10 months or a year in the absence of low-temperature or photoperiodic treatments, but the larval diapause of the corn borer will end spontaneously in about 13 weeks. From these characteristics, diapause is considered to be of much greater intensity in cecropia pupae than in European corn borer larvae.

Diapause in different insect forms and under different conditions cannot always be compared meaningfully on the basis of rather arbitrary standards of intensity, however. A good example of the limitations of our concepts of relative intensity of diapauses is to be found in the larval diapause of the Khapra beetle, *Trogoderma granarium* (Burges, 1960, 1962). The larvae of this species go into a diapause state if the temperature drops below about 30°C. While in diapause, the larvae move about, feed a little, and may even molt; but they have a lowered metabolic rate and do not complete their growth and development. If the temperature is elevated a few degrees, as from 30° to 35°C, diapause is terminated. Such a diapause would appear to be of very low intensity. Nevertheless, the larvae may remain in diapause for as long as 8 years, which would suggest a very intense diapause.

Photoperiod and temperature have been found to influence the apparent intensity of diapause in a number of different species. These environmental factors are experienced by the prediapause growth stages, but their influence is expressed in the relative intensity of the ensuing diapause. The pupal diapause of the geometrid *Abraxas miranda* has been found to be of two types: a summertime estival diapause and a winter hibernatory diapause. Masaki (1959) observed that the summer diapause was much less intense than the winter diapause. The estival diapause was induced by relatively long daylengths and moderate temperatures, and was of quite short natural duration. The winter diapause, on the other hand, was found to be induced by short-day photoperiods and low temperatures; it was a much more intense, long-lasting diapause. *Mamestra brassicae*, a cabbage-eating noctuid, also has a pupal diapause that may occur in the summer generation as a period of estivation or as an overwintering diapause in the generation that reaches pupation in the autumn (Masaki and Sakai, 1965). In this species, also, the apparent intensity of the diapause depended on the temperatures and photoperiods to which the growing caterpillars had been exposed.

The pink bollworm, *Pectinophora gossypiella*, shows an appreciable incidence of diapause among larvae that were reared in the dark. A thermoperiod was observed to increase the incidence of diapause. The diapause that was induced by either a thermoperiod or a short-day photoperiod was found to be more intense than that induced by continuous darkness alone (Menaker and Gross, 1965). Bell and Adkisson (1964) also observed that the intensity of diapause in pink bollworm larvae was influenced by the photoperiods experienced by the prediapause larval growth stages.

Short-day photoperiods are known to induce the larval diapause of the European corn borer, but the characteristics of the inducing photoperiod was shown to have an influence on the characteristics of the diapause (Beck *et al.*, 1963; McLeod and Beck, 1963b). At daylengths approaching the critical daylength for diapause induction, diapause in-

159

tensity was reduced, as compared to the intensity of diapause occurring in response to daylengths lying in the most effective range. For example, a photoperiod of 13L:11D induced a diapause incidence of about 95%. A 15L:9D photoperiod, on the other hand, induced a diapause incidence of only about 25%. Among the individual borers that went into diapause, the intensity of diapause differed between the two groups according to the inducing daylength. When the diapausing borers were incubated under long-day conditions (16L:8D), those from the 13-hour daylength group required an average of 30 days to reach the pupal stage. The diapausing larvae that had been reared under a 15-hour photophase, however, pupated after an average of only 13.5 days of long-day exposure. Diapause was apparently much less intense in the latter group.

SUMMATION OF PHOTOPERIODIC EFFECTS

Photoperiods experienced by an insect during its early development may modify its responses to photoperiods experienced later. For example, Kogure (1933) found that long-day photoperiods during late embryonic development committed the silkworms, Bombyx mori, to the production of diapause eggs upon reaching the adult moth stage. Short-day photoperiods (diapause averting in this insect) experienced during the larval instars had the effect of modifying the diapause commitment, however, and the moths would produce both diapause and nondiapause batches of eggs.

De Wilde and co-workers (1959) reported that photoperiods experienced by the larvae of the Colorado potato beetle, Leptinotarsa decemlineata, influenced the induction of diapause in the adults. Young adults of this species enter diapause in response to short daylengths experienced during the first several days following emergence. Continuous darkness also has a weak diapause-inducing effect. Diapause incidence among young beetles that were held in darkness was found to be lower if the larval stages had been reared under long-day photoperiods than was the case if they had been reared under the influence of short days. Diapause in the Colorado potato beetle is characterized by a suppression of development of the female reproductive organs. Among beetles that had entered diapause in response to short days, ovarian development was found to be influenced by the photoperiods experienced by the larvae. Ovarian development was more advanced at the onset of diapause among those beetles that had spent their larval

160

stages under long-day conditions than among those that had been under short-day photoperiods. The investigators concluded that there was an accumulative effect of larval and adult photoperiodic treatment, and that the effect was reflected by the state of development of the female reproductive system.

An accumulative effect of long-day photoperiods on the termination of diapause in the European corn borer, *Ostrinia nubilalis*, has also been reported (McLeod and Beck, 1963b; Beck and Alexander, 1964a). Short-day photoperiods did not reverse or cancel the development accomplished under the influence of long days, but had the effect of suppressing developmental rates to the levels typical of the diapause state. Short-day induction of diapause was also found to be less efficient among borers that had been exposed to long days during the first two larval stadia than among borers that had been maintained in short days throughout their development (Beck and Hanec, 1960; Beck *et al.*, 1963).

Long-day photoperiods were also found to have cumulative effects in form determination of the vetch aphid, *Megoura viciae* (Lees, 1960b, 1963). Continuous darkness exerts a weak short-day effect on this species, and under such conditions, form determination of aphid progeny was found to be influenced by photoperiods experienced early in the parental life.

These several examples are sufficient to support the concept that photoperiods experienced during one stage of development may influence the insect's response to photoperiods occurring at a subsequent stage. In general, it has been observed that photoperiods that do not induce diapause determination have a greater cumulative effect than do those tending to induce diapause. Little or no cumulative effects have been observed among insects in which diapause determination can occur only at a sharply defined growth stage. Where the insect's sensitivity to photoperiod extends over a large part of its larval life, the induction of diapause and the intensity of the diapause state have been found to be influenced by the insect's total photoperiodic history. The accumulative effects of photoperiods is an important consideration in the question of the photoperiodic significance of gradually changing daylengths.

DIAPAUSE AND GRADUAL CHANGES IN DAYLENGTHS

Short-day, and in a few cases long-day, induction of diapause has been established beyond reasonable doubt by means of experimentation in which the daily photoperiods were of a fixed, controlled pattern. Such rigid, switch-controlled light-dark alternations do not occur in nature, however, because natural daylengths are subject to daily seasonal incremetal changes. The question has arisen frequently as to what, if any, role these daily incremental changes might play in photoperiodism, particularly in regard to the induction and termination of diapause.

Dickson (1949) investigated this problem with the oriental fruit moth, *Grapholitha molesta,* and concluded that the daily increments of daylength change played no role in diapause induction. The absolute duration of the photoperiodic phases that prevailed during the insect's sensitive stages determined whether or not diapause was to occur. Similarly, diapause egg production by fruit tree spider mites, *Metatetranychus ulmi,* was found to depend on actual phase duration rather than on the rate and direction of daylength changes (Lees, 1953a,b, 1955). Diapause egg production was induced whether the daylengths were decreasing or increasing, provided that the mean daylength employed was shorter than the mite's critical daylength.

The opposite conclusion was drawn by Corbet (1956) in a study of the nymphal diapause of the dragonfly, *Anax imperator.* Corbet observed that, under natural daylight conditions, the nymphs developed without diapause in the spring, at which time the days were becoming progressively longer. In late summer, however, the nymphs were subjected to similar daylengths, but the daily increment of change was in the direction of shorter days; under these conditions the nymphs went into diapause. It was concluded that decreasing daylengths induced diapause, but laboratory experimentation on this point yielded somewhat inconclusive results. Diapause in *Aeschna cyanea* was also terminated in response to increasing daylengths (Schaller, 1965). Working with a different species of dragonfly (*Tetragoneuria cynosura*), Lutz and Jenner (1960, 1964) concluded that actual phase duration was the important factor rather than the direction or amount of daily change of daylength. Lukefahr and co-workers (1964) reported that diapause in the pink bollworm, *Pectinophora gossypiella,* was effectively induced by photoperiods that decreased slowly from 16 to 13 hours of light per day, as well as by constant photoperiods with daylengths of about 14 hours. Their experiments contained dietary as well as photoperiodic variables, however, and the significance of the results is not clear. From his work on the seasonal development of the dermestid beetle *Anthrenus verbasci,* Blake (1960, 1963) concluded that incremental changes in the photoperiod exerted effects on the timing of larval

162

diapause. Larvae that were exposed to increasing daylengths underwent a diapause of shorter duration than did larvae that were exposed to decreasing daylengths. The effect may have been due to the influence of daylength on the rate of diapause completion, however.

Larval diapause in the sorrel dagger moth, *Acronycta rumicis*, was found to be induced by short-day photoperiods, with the critical daylength being 14.5 hours (Danilevskii, 1961). Rearing the larvae under long-day photoperiods in which the daylength was shortened by 10 minutes each day did not result in diapause induction, when the shortest daylength attained was longer than the critical daylength. In this case, diapause induction was not dependent upon decreasing daylengths, but was dependent upon the daylength's being shorter than the critical 14.5 hours. The converse experiments, in which the larvae were reared under short days that were increased 10 minutes per day, produced a very low incidence of diapause. However, the critical daylength had been exceeded as the larvae approached the end of larval development.

At least two factors need to be considered in an interpretation of the effects of decreasing or increasing daylengths. One is the critical daylength, and the other is the cumulative effect of photoperiods experienced during the growth stages in which the insect is sensitive to photoperiod. Thus, under conditions of progressively lengthening days, the tendency for short-day determination of diapause may be overridden by the later long days, unless the growth stage of determination had been completed before the daylengths exceeded the critical value. On the other hand, decreasing daylengths may result in a high incidence of diapause, if the insects were sensitive to photoperiods during the latter part of development, so that the days of lengths below the critical level were the ones to which the insects responded. But if the insect's sensitive period extended over most of its development, long-day photoperiods experienced early in life may have the effect of decreasing the response to later short days, particularly if the shortest days experienced were very little below the critical daylength for diapause induction.

DIAPAUSE AND LIGHT CHARACTERISTICS

Photoperiodic induction of diapause necessarily involves the reception of light by the insect, either as an input of light energy over the span of time known as the photophase or as the reception of light-on and light-off stimuli. In either case it might be expected that the insect would display some response characteristics related to the quantity and quality of the light. Although there have been a number of studies in which data on light characteristics have been reported, no reliable action spectra have been determined. Because a light energy input, a receptor system, and an effector system must be involved in photoperiodism, the amount of energy required to elicit a response should vary according to the characteristics of the receptor pigment complex. Action spectra are therefore needed, in which the amount of energy required to effect a standard response has been determined for different wavelengths of impinging light.

Scattered observations on the light intensities (presumably white light) required for the photoperiodic induction of diapause have indicated that very low energy levels are effective. Kogure (1933) found that silkworm eggs were responsive to light of only 0.1 lux (1 ft-c = 10.76 lux), and the early instar larvae were sensitive to incident light of about 1.0 lux. A similar extreme sensitivity was reported for the midge *Metriocnemus knabi* (Paris and Jenner, 1959). Adults of the Colorado potato beetle, *Leptinotarsa decemlineata*, were observed to be responsive to any white light intensity exceeding about 0.1 lux (de Wilde and Bonga, 1958). Most species appear to be less sensitive than these extreme examples, however. The threshold light intensities required for diapause induction usually are found between 5 and 25 lux (0.5–2+ ft-c).

In contrast to plant photoperiodism, where the effective wavelengths are from 660 to 735 mμ, insect diapause is induced by photophases composed of light of much shorter wavelengths. The most effective wavelengths have been found to lie between about 400 and 550 mμ. The highest production of diapausing silkworm eggs was observed when the photophase was of wavelengths between 350 and 510 mμ. Wavelengths above 610 mμ were not at all effective, and a barely detectable effect was observed at 550 mμ (Kogure, 1933). Maximum incidence of larval diapause was obtained with wavelengths between 400 and 580 mμ, in the case of the Oriental fruit moth, *Grapholitha molesta* (Dickson, 1949). A low incidence of diapause was induced at 660 mμ, but the Oriental fruit moth larvae did not respond to either ultraviolet (360 mμ) or infrared (1400 mμ). Wavelengths as high as 660 mμ are seldom effective in photoperiodic systems, but de Wilde and Bonga (1958) reported that adults of the Colorado potato beetle would respond to wavelengths of about 675 mμ, but not to those above 700 mμ. The upper range of wavelengths that are effective in photoperiodic induction of diapause may be as low as 530 mμ (*Metatetranychus ulmi*, Lees, 1953b). In some

164

species the lower range of effective wavelengths may extend into the ultraviolet, as in the case of silkworm eggs (350 mμ) and pupae of the Chinese oak silkworm, *Antheraea pernyi* (<400 mμ) (Williams *et al.*, 1965).

Pupal diapause in the cabbage butterfly, *Pieris brassicae,* is induced in response to short-day photoperiods. Bünning and Joerrens (1960) reported that the effectiveness of blue and red lights differed, depending on the circadian times at which the insects were exposed. During the first 12 hours after the beginning of the photophase, blue light promoted diapause induction, but red light prevented induction. During the second 12 hours of the circadian time cycle, however, the effect of the two wavelengths was reversed; blue light inhibited and red light promoted the induction of diapause (Fig. 43). On the basis of these results, Bünning and Joerrens postulated that the receptor pigment system underwent circadian changes in sensitivity. Such an interpretation is unnecessarily complicated, however; the response data can be interpreted on a much simpler basis. It seems most likely that the blue wavelengths are stimulating and the red light is equivalent to darkness, regardless of the circadian time of stimulation.

Many insects that live in soil, fleshy fruits, or thick plant stems are, nevertheless, sensitive to photoperiod. One may wonder how such forms detect light intensity changes in the outside environment. In some such cases, the insects display an extremely low response threshold, and suffi-

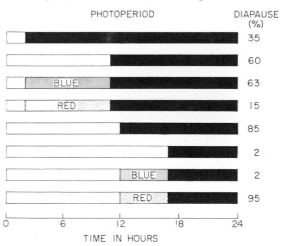

Fig. 43. *Effects of red and blue lights on the induction of diapause in the cabbage butterfly,* Pieris brassicae. *[Based on data of Bünning and Joerrens (1960).]*

cient light to induce photoperiodic responses is presumed to reach them. Callahan (1956a) has suggested that irradiation in the infrared range may play an important role in the photoperiodism of insects that inhabit obscure and shielded environments. Infrared has been tested for possible involvement in photoperiodism in a number of instances, however, with consistently negative results. The number of species examined was relatively small, and the possible importance of infrared light frequencies merits further investigation.

DIAPAUSE AND TIME RELATIONSHIPS

The demonstration of a "critical daylength," above which a given insect species or population displays a very low incidence of diapause, and below which virtually every individual goes into diapause, suggests that the diapause reaction is controlled by a temporal programming system. Species and populations within a species are known to differ in respect to critical daylength, the shape of the diapause-incidence response curve (Fig. 40), and the growth stages at which diapause occurs. As will be discussed in greater detail in the following chapter, the physiological mechanisms involved in diapause induction and termination are probably quite different in the different types of dia-pause—embryonic, larval, pupal, and adult. Diapause has probably evolved independently in different groups of insects, and the several types of diapause may represent different alternatives for solving the problems of phenological synchrony and the survival of adverse seasons. The physiological adaptations involved in the specific expressions of diapause are, in some yet unknown way, controlled via the so-called "biological clock" system. We do not know that this system is funda-mentally similar in different insects that show different photoperiodic responses. The existing evidence points more strongly toward a funda-mental unity in temporal systems than toward a diversity, however. The problem to be considered here has to do with the characteristics of the biological timing systems that are associated with the induction and termination of diapause.

An early hypothesis to explain photoperiodic induction of diapause was that some essential factor (such as a hormone) was synthesized during one phase of the photoperiod and degraded or neutralized during the opposite phase. This would be comparable to an hourglass type of biological clock. Kogure (1933) postulated that the embryonic diapause of the commercial silkworm, *Bombyx mori*, was caused by pro-

166

duction of "hibernation substances" in the larvae and pupae. High temperatures and long daylengths tended to promote the syntheses of these substances, and low temperatures and darkness tended to prevent their production. It should be recalled that the silkworm is one of the so-called "short-day" insects, in which diapause is induced by long-day photoperiods and relatively high temperatures. Larval diapause of the oriental fruit moth, *Grapholitha molesta* was induced by short-day conditions, and Dickson (1949) postulated that a *diapause hormone* was involved. According to Dickson's hypothesis, the diapause hormone was produced during the larval growth stages, and its synthesis was a two-step process. One step of the synthesis was accomplished in the dark, and the other in the light. The dark-promoted synthesis was postulated to be time sensitive, with a scotophase duration of about 11 hours being required for optimum synthesis.

Because diapause induction results from the exposure of the sensitive growth stages of an insect to a succession of daily cycles of an effective photoperiod, de Wilde (1962a) postulated that some unidentified diapause-inducing factor was produced and accumulated until the amount present in the insect was sufficient to evoke the state of diapause. Schneider (1950), Hinton (1957), and Schroder (1957) have also postulated the existence of diapause hormones that are directly responsible for the initiation and maintenance of the diapause state.

Controlled endocrinological experimentation involving the techniques of ligation, organ transplantation, parabiosis, and administration of tissue extracts have consistently failed to yield results that would support the diapause hormone hypothesis. The most notable apparent exception to this general statement is the "diapause hormone" of the silkworm, *Bombyx mori*, but it does not constitute an actual exception. The diapause hormone of the silkworm does not induce diapause in the physiological system within which it acts. The target organ of this hormone is the ovary of the moth, and it has the physiological function of inducing the ovarioles to produce eggs that are programmed for diapause. Injection of highly active silkworm diapause hormone preparations into larvae or pupae will not cause the recipients to go into diapause. The diapause hormone of the silkworm will be discussed in more detail in the next chapter.

Most of the existing experimental evidence supports the hypothesis, first advanced by Wigglesworth (1934), that diapause is the consequence of the absence of a growth hormone. The specific hormone lack may be

167

different among the different types of diapause, as will be discussed in a Chapter 8. The main problem to be examined in the present section has to do with the mechanisms by which photoperiod might regulate hormone production. Way and co-workers (Way *et al.*, 1949; Way and Hopkins, 1950) suggested that the photoperiodically induced pupal diapause of the tomato moth, *Diataraxia oleracea*, was caused by a lack of growth hormones. Because diapause was induced by short-day photoperiods but no diapause occurred when the insects were reared under a long-day regime, these investigators postulated that long daylengths stimulated the production or accumulation of the hormones promoting growth and differentiation.

A biological clock system of the hourglass type, in which some active process builds up during the photophase and is reversed during the scotophase, or vice versa, would be an acceptable working concept if all insects were of either the long-day or the short-day types (Fig. 40, types I and II). If continuous darkness induced diapause but continuous illumination prevented diapause, or if continuous light induced and continuous darkness prevented, one hypothetical reaction could be assigned to the photophase and an opposing reaction could be attributed to the scotophase. But such an hourglass hypothesis does not appear to be meaningful in those cases where photoperiodic induction of diapause occurs in only a limited range of daylengths, and where continuous light and darkness appear to be equal (Fig. 40, types III and IV). In these responses, some additional postulates must be introduced to account for the time factors involved. Some accounting must be made for the fact that diapause-inducing factors are not active in light only or dark only, but that diapause is induced only in response to certain durations and sequences of illumination and darkness. Lees (1953a,b, 1954) pointed out that the postulation of synthesis of active substances during the dark and their subsequent degradation in the presence of light would account for some, but not all, of his experimental data concerning the photoperiodic induction of diapause in the mite *Metatetranychus ulmi*. In general, it would appear that the hourglass model of biological time relationship does not provide an adequate theoretical basis for interpreting the photoperiodic responses of insects.

An alternative to the hourglass hypothesis is that of a continuously operating rhythmic system running on a circadian basis. Some difficulties are encountered with this hypothesis, too. Diapause is not manifested as a rhythmic phenomenon; like adult emergence, discussed in previous chapters, diapause occurs or fails to occur as a single event in

168

the life history of each individual of the insect population. Whereas an emergence rhythm may be detected on a population basis, the onset of diapause cannot be so observed. Circadian rhythms are consistently observed to be insensitive to temperature changes within the biological range of noninhibiting temperatures, but both the incidence of diapause and the critical daylength for diapause induction are temperature dependent. This may mean that the physiological mechanisms controlling the induction and completion of diapause are temperature-sensitive processes that are coupled (entrained) to temperature-independent endogenous rhythms that are responsive to photoperiods. These several difficulties and uncertainties make it necessary to approach the time relationship problem indirectly, through studies of the characteristics of photoperiodic induction and termination of diapause under carefully controlled conditions.

Photophase and Scotophase Duration

The natural diel photoperiod consists of a number of hours of light followed by a number of hours of darkness, and the duration of the photophase plus that of the scotophase must total 24 hours. Experimental alterations in the duration of one of the phases necessarily involve a complementary alteration of the other phase in order to maintain the 24-hour total. In order to investigate the relative importance of the light and dark phases, it is necessary to hold one phase at a constant duration and to vary the other phase systematically. This means, of course, that the overall photoperiod will be shorter or longer than 24 hours.

The relationships between phase duration and diapause incidence in the oriental fruit moth (*Grapholitha molesta*) and the European corn borer (*Ostrinia nubilalis*) are shown in Fig. 44. Both of these lepidopterous species diapause as mature larvae, and both show a type III diapause induction response curve, in which diapause incidence is negligible under either continuous illumination or continuous darkness. The two species show some similarities in the range of effective photoperiods, with *Grapholitha* being somewhat more specific in its requirements for diapause induction; *Ostrinia* responded to a broader range of photophases. Diapause induction was not dependent, in either case, on photoperiods of the normal 24-hour type; nor was induction enhanced by photoperiods that showed any regular ratio of photophase: scotophase durations (1:1, 1:2, or 2:1 ratios). The European corn borer appears to differ from the oriental fruit moth in its reaction to 12-hour

169

scotophases. Scotophases of 12-hour duration, combined with photophases of any duration between 4.5 and 30 hours, effectively induced diapause. The oriental fruit moth, on the other hand, showed no tendency to be more responsive to one phase than to the other, and its response range appeared to be rather symmetrical.

Forms displaying the typical long-day response curve (Fig. 40, type I), in which continuous darkness tends to result in high incidences of diapause, would be expected to show a quite different relationship between phase duration and diapause induction. This is illustrated in Fig. 45,

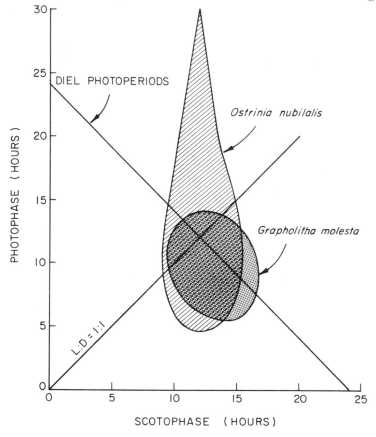

Fig. 44. *Effects of scotophase and photophase durations on larval diapause incidence among oriental fruit moths, Grapholitha molesta, and European corn borers, Ostrinia nubilalis. Shaded areas indicate diapause incidences of 50% or more.* [*Based on data of Dickson (1949) and Beck (1962a).*]

170

which is based on the results of Lees (1953b), who studied the effects of photoperiod on the production of diapausing eggs in the mite *Metatetranychus ulmi*. In this case, too, there was no apparent dependency of diapause induction on exposure to a 24-hour photoperiod; neither was there a simple relationship between diapause induction and the ratio of phase duration. Approximately similar relationships between phase durations and the incidence of diapause might be expected to be found in other species that have been found to display the type I diapause response curve. These would include *Leptinotarsa decemlineata*, *Diataraxia oleracea*, and *Acronycta rumicis*. In the case of the last named species, Goryshin (1963) reported that 1:1 ratios of photophase and scotophase duration induced high incidences of diapause over a very broad range (9L:9D to 36L:36D). However, as shown in Fig. 45, such ratios of light to dark would also induce high incidences of diapause in *M. ulmi*, but without contributing to a clarification of the photoperiodic characteristics required for the induction of diapause.

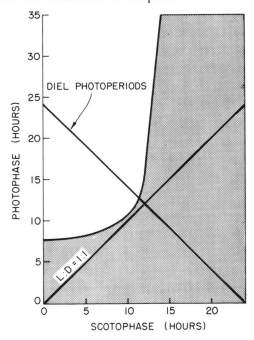

Fig. 45. *Effects of scotophase and photophase durations on the incidence of diapause egg production among females of the fruit tree spider mite, Metatetranychus ulmi. Shaded areas indicate diapause egg production by 50% or more of the female mites. [Adapted from Lees (1953b).]*

Most workers who have studied the problem have agreed that neither light:dark ratios nor adherence to a 24-hour photoperiod is essential to the induction of diapause (Lees, 1955; Danilevskii, 1961; de Wilde, 1962a). Some investigators have come to opposing conclusions, however. Otuka and Santa (1955), working with the cabbage armyworm, *Barathra brassicae*, determined the effects of 1:1 light:dark ratios on the incidence of pupal diapause. Of the ratios they tested, diapause was induced only with the 12L:12D photoperiod. They therefore concluded that only 24-hour photoperiods were effective, and that the maximum incidence of diapause occurred when the photophase and the scotophase were of equal lengths. These conclusions were not justified, however, because Otuka and Santa did not determine the responses to 12-hour photophases or scotophases when combined with opposite phases of different durations, and the 1:1 ratios tested did not include any phase durations that were intermediate between 6 and 12 hours or between 12 and 24 hours. Similarly, Adkisson (1964) concluded that diapause induction in the pink bollworm, *Pectinophora gossypiella*, was closely dependent upon a 24-hour photoperiod and an approximately 1:1 ratio of light to dark. However, Adkisson's published data showed that a 12-hour scotophase combined with a 24-hour photophase resulted in a diapause incidence that was not greatly different from that induced by a 12L:12D regime.

Effects of Light-Breaks on Diapause Induction

The duration of the scotophase has frequently been found to be more critical than photophase duration in the induction of diapause. For this reason, several workers have concluded that if the photoperiodic induction of diapause involves the measurement of time, it must be primarily the duration of the scotophase that determines whether or not diapause will occur. The scotophase has, therefore, been subjected to critical analysis in regard to its importance in diapause and its possible role in time relationships.

Pupal diapause in the cabbage worm, *Pieris brassicae*, was shown to be induced by short daylengths (Bünning and Joerrens, 1960). If the scotophase was interrupted by a short period of light (2 hours), the incidence of diapause was reduced, but the amount of reduction depended upon the time at which the *light-break* occurred (Fig. 46). With a 6-hour photophase and 18-hour scotophase, a 2-hour light-break most effectively prevented diapause when it occurred each day at about 16 hours after the beginning of the photophase. Similarly, in a 12L:12D

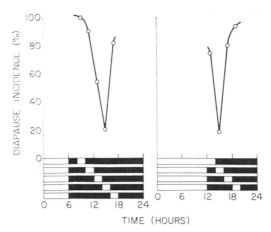

Fig. 46. Effects of 2-hour light-breaks on the incidence of diapause in populations of Pieris brassicae. The incidence of diapause is plotted against the circadian time of the light-break. [Adapted from Bünning (1964).]

photoperiod, diapause induction was prevented by a light-break at 16 hours. Bünning and Joerrens interpreted their results on the basis that diapause induction involves the effects of photoperiods on endogenous circadian rhythms, with circadian time being measured from the onset of the photophase. Light-breaks during the scotophase would tend to avert diapause induction if they occurred at the time of the endogenous cycle at which the insect's light sensitivity was at its maximum. In the case of *P. brassicae*, the maximum light sensitivity must occur at about 16 hours after the beginning of the photophase. The time within the scotophase at which such hypothetical light sensitivity occurs would vary with different photoperiods, because circadian functions are timed only from the beginning of the photophase.

Working with the closely related imported cabbage worm, *Pieris rapae*, Barker and co-workers (Barker, 1963; Barker *et al.*, 1963, 1964) obtained results that were in good agreement with those of Bünning and Joerrens. They found that even very short light pulses (about 0.001 second) would effectively reduce the incidence of diapause, if the light pulse occurred each day at about 14 hours after the onset of the photophase.

Light-breaks of 1 hour were shown to prevent the induction of diapause in the European corn borer, *Ostrinia nubilalis* (Beck, 1962a). In this case the photoperiod used was 11L:13D, which would induce a very high incidence of diapause. When the 13-hour scotophase was

173

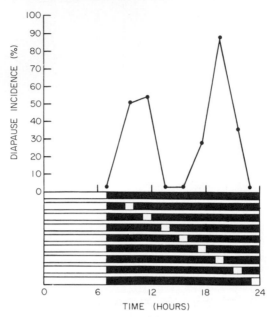

Fig. 47. Effect of 1-hour light-breaks on the induction of diapause in the European corn borer, Ostrinia nubilalis. The incidence of diapause is plotted against the circadian time of the light-break. [Adapted from Beck (1962a).]

interrupted by an hour of light during the middle hour, so that the photoperiodic cycle was 11L:6D:1L:6D, no diapause was induced. Such a light-break occurred 17 hours after the beginning of the photophase. Light-breaks were also applied at different times during a 17-hour scotophase. The uninterrupted 7L:17D photoperiod did not induce a significant incidence of diapause (Fig. 47). When the 1-hour light-breaks were timed to occur at from 13 to 15 hours after the beginning of the photophase, little or no diapause was induced. Light-breaks at either 11 or 19 hours caused high incidences of diapause, however. Since the photophase was 7 hours and the light-break was 1 hour, the borer larvae were exposed to a total of 8 hours of light and 16 hours of dark each day. A 1-hour light-break occurring at hour 19 would be preceded by 12 hours of uninterrupted darkness. And a light-break at hour 11 would be followed by 12 hours of uninterrupted darkness. The incidence of diapause was high among borers exposed to either of these two schedules, and Beck (1962) interpreted the results as being further evidence of the major importance of the 12-hour scotophase in the induction of diapause in this species (see Fig. 44).

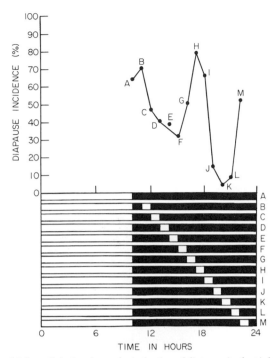

Fig. 48. Effects of 1-hour light-breaks on the induction of diapause in the pink bollworm, Pectino-phora gossypiella. [Adapted from Adkisson (1964).]

This interpretation tended to emphasize the role of the scotophase and to assign little importance to the duration of the photophase in the induction of diapause.

A still more complex response to light-breaks has been observed in the photoperiodic induction of larval diapause in the pink bollworm, *Pectinophora gossypiella* (Adkisson, 1963, 1964, 1965, 1966). A 14-hour scotophase was interrupted at different times by 1-hour light-breaks (Fig. 48). The light-breaks reduced the incidence of diapause most effectively when they occurred at either 15 or about 20 hours after the onset of the photophase (schedules F and K, respectively, in Fig. 48). Photoperiodic schedules B and M contained uninterrupted dark periods of 12 hours, and diapause incidence was relatively high. The longer dark period of schedule F was only 8 hours, and the diapause incidence was very low. However, schedule H included an uninterrupted dark phase of only 7 hours, but a high incidence of diapause was observed. With photoperiodic schedules that involved 1-hour light-breaks occur-

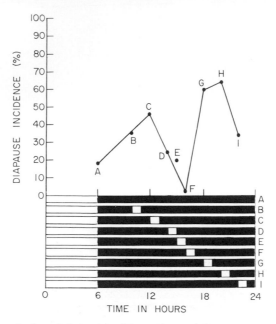

Fig. 49. Effects of 1-hour light-breaks on the incidence of diapause among larvae of the pink bollworm, Pectinophora gossypiella. [Adapted from Adkisson (1964).]

ring at different times during an 18-hour scotophase (Fig. 49), somewhat different relationships were apparent. In these experiments, only schedules C, G, and H induced high incidences of diapause, and these schedules included uninterrupted dark periods of 11, 12, and 14 hours, respectively. And although a light-break at 15 hours after the beginning of the photophase had a diapause-preventing effect, a light-break at 20 hours resulted in a high incidence of diapause. From the observed effects of 1-hour light-breaks inserted at different times during scotophases of different lengths, Adkisson (1964) concluded that diapause was most effectively *prevented* by light-breaks occurring at about 10 hours before the beginning of the photophase or at about 10 hours after the onset of the scotophase. It was concluded that both the light-on signal (onset of photophase) and the light-off signal were involved in the "time-measuring" aspects of diapause induction. This conclusion was consistent with the observation that photoperiods having scotophases under 10 hours duration were ineffective in diapause induction, because the circadian times of maximum light sensitivity would then occur just before and just after the scotophase. With such long-day

176

photoperiods (>14L: <10D), the light-sensitive circadian times would fall within the photophase, and diapause would be averted. Longer scotophases, on the other hand, would cause the times of greatest light sensitivity to occur during the scotophase, and because no light stimuli would be received at these times, diapause would be induced. However, this hypothesis failed to account for the very low incidence of diapause that was induced by a photoperiod of 6L:18D (Fig. 49, schedule A). According to Adkisson's hypothesis, light-sensitive periods should have occurred at the fourteenth circadian hour (10 hours before light-on) and at the sixteenth circadian hour (10 hours after light-off); since both of these light-sensitive times would fall within the 18-hour scotophase, diapause should have been induced in a very high percentage of the pink bollworm larvae.

The occurrence of "light-sensitive times" during the course of a circadian rhythm was first postulated by E. Bünning, and later by several other workers, in efforts to explain the biological effects of light-breaks. It may well be, however, that the concept is not valid; the effect of light-on and light-off stimuli may always be that of phase-setting endogenous rhythms. Light-breaks may represent unnatural phase-setting signals. In this case, photoperiodic schedules with light-breaks during the scotophase should function in a manner comparable to the skeletal photoperiods discussed in an earlier chapter. Minis (1965) attempted to demonstrate that the effects of light-breaks on diapause induction in the pink bollworm were fundamentally comparable to the effects of phase-setting light pulses on ovipositional rhythms of the adult stage of the same species. The results were negative, however, and the hypothesis could not be confirmed. Adkisson (1966) also attempted to interpret the effects of light-breaks on diapause induction in terms of the insects' responses to skeletal photoperiods. He found, however, that different responses were obtained with asymmetrical skeletal photoperiods that were, theoretically, similar. Adkisson concluded that diapause induction in the pink bollworm did not depend solely on the length of the scotophase, but that the duration of both phases was involved.

Oviparae of the vetch aphid, *Megoura viciae*, and most other aphid species deposit eggs that pass the winter in a state of diapause. The aphid ovipara is, therefore, closely associated with the phenomenon of diapause induction. As was discussed in the previous chapter, oviparae of the vetch aphid are produced in response to short-day photoperiods. Professor A. D. Lees has studied the time relationships involved in aphid polymorphism, and the question of whether or not circadian rhythmic functions are involved in determination of the oviparous form. Lees (1965) found that a 12-hour scotophase would result in ovipara production when combined with any photophase of from 12 to about 40 hours duration. The critical scotophase length was about 10.5 hours. When combined with a photophase of 8 hours, any scotophase that exceeded the critical length caused the induction of a very high incidence of ovipara-producing aphids.

The light-break technique was also applied to the aphid problem (Lees, 1965). A 13.5-hour photophase was combined with a 10.5-hour scotophase, within which light-breaks of 1 hour were scheduled at different times. Light-breaks during the first 2 hours or the last 6 hours of the scotophase greatly suppressed ovipara production. Light-breaks that occurred from 3.5 to 4.5 hours after the beginning of the scotophase did not prevent ovipara production. Lees concluded that these effects were independent of the photophase, because the same results were obtained when a 10.5-hour scotophase was combined with a 25.5-hour photophase. Lees interpreted his data as indicating that the biological clock system of the aphid is of the type that measures the duration of only the scotophase. No evidence of circadian rhythmic functions was detected.

Endogenous Rhythms and Diapause

Endogenous rhythms that are susceptible to phase regulation by photoperiodic signals are thought to be involved in the determination of diapause. The rhythmic functions may not display strictly circadian characteristics, however. That is, a biological clock system might function very efficiently within a diel-based environment, without the requirement that the period of the clock itself be approximately 24 hours.

Is there evidence that the insect's photoperiodic clock system depends on endogenous rhythmic functions, whether or not these rhythms show circadian characteristics? Photoperiodically regulated metabolic and endocrine rhythms have been detected in several different insect forms, as was discussed in Chapter 5. And several of these rhythms were found to display noncircadian periodicities of 12, 8, or 6 hours. Diapausing European corn borer larvae, for example, were shown to display an oxygen consumption rate rhythm that continued during the period of diapause (Beck *et al.*, 1963) and showed an 8-hour periodicity, even though it was sensitive to phase setting by a 24-hour photoperiod (Beck,

1964). The demonstration of such rhythms, however, does not constitute proof that they are involved in either the induction or termination of diapause.

Evidence that endogenous rhythmic functions play an important role in diapause has come from three quite dissimilar studies. Diapause in the dermestid beetle *Anthrenus verbasci* was observed to occur at different larval stages, rather than at a specific stage as in most insects. The onset of larval diapause was found to be time dependent; diapause would occur within a beetle culture according to the culture age rather than the insects' developmental stage. The determination of diapause appeared to depend on endogenous rhythmic functions that were not dependent upon external factors such as photoperiod (Blake, 1959).

Evidence of endogenous rhythmicity and diapause determination has also come from a series of studies on diapause development in the European corn borer (Beck, 1964; Beck and Alexander, 1964a; Beck *et al.*, 1965a,b; McLeod and Beck, 1963b). These studies involved experimentation on the photoperiodic requirements for termination of diapause and on the temporal relationships of endocrine functions. The work on photoperiod was based on the well-established concept that endogenous rhythms continue on a free-running basis in continuous darkness. A rhythmic pattern that was established in the insect by several days exposure to a photoperiod should continue on a free-running basis when the insect was transferred to continuous darkness. This was strongly suggested from the results of exposing diapausing corn borer larvae to different photoperiodic schedules (Table XI).

TABLE XI

Effect of Different Photoperiods on Diapause Development in the
European Corn Borer, *Ostrinia nubilalis*. (All Larvae Were Reared in a
Short-Day Photoperiod and Were 22 Days of Age at the Beginning of the Experiment)[a]

Schedule	Photoperiodic treatment		Posttreatment photoperiod	Average time to pupation (days)
	1st 10 days	2nd 10 days		
A	Long-day	Long-day	Long-day	31
B	Long-day	Long-day	Darkness	27
C	Long-day	Darkness	Long-day	29
D	Long-day	Darkness	Darkness	30
E	Long-day	Short-day	Long-day	42
F	Long-day	Short-day	Darkness	>50
G	Long-day	Short-day	Short-day	>50

[a]From Beck and Alexander (1964a).

179

Diapausing corn borers that were 22 days old were exposed to long-day photoperiods (16L:8D) for 10 days. They were then exposed to one of the following treatments for an additional 10 days: (1) short-day (12L:12D), (2) continuous darkness, or (3) long-day (16L:8D). At the end of the second 10-day treatment, the larvae were transferred to one of the three different photoperiodic conditions and were observed for pupation. The average number of days from the beginning of the initial long-day exposure to pupation was recorded. When the diapausing larvae were held in a long-day photoperiod throughout the experiment, the average time to pupation was 31 days (schedule A). Continuous darkness during the posttreatment holding period (schedule B), the second 10-day treatment (schedule C), or both (schedule D) did not alter the rate at which diapause was completed. The rate of development established under the influence of the long-day photoperiod was not changed by subsequent continuous darkness. Under schedule E, however, 10 days of long-day were followed by 10 days of short-day, following which the larvae were again exposed to long-day photoperiods. In this case pupation was delayed by about 10 days, which was equal to the time spent under the influence of the short-day regime. The short-day exposure did not reverse the development accomplished by the first 10 days of long days; the short-day photoperiod apparently reduced the developmental rate to the low level typical of the diapause condition. Diapausing larvae were exposed to long days, followed by short days, and they were then either transferred to darkness (schedule F) or continued under short-day conditions (schedule G). In these cases, the larvae did not pupate within the 50 days of the experiment. Apparently the rate of development established under the influence of the short-day photoperiod was not changed detectably by subsequent continuous darkness. From these experiments, it is apparent that if photoperiodic responses involve the establishment of a pattern of temporal relationships among physiological rhythms, such rhythms must continue endogenously under the aperiodic conditions of continuous darkness.

The incidence of diapause among larvae of the pink bollworm was found to be influenced by the photoperiodic experience of the insects during their late embryonic as well as larval growth stages (Mendker and Gross, 1965). Adkisson (1966) showed that eggs and first instar larvae that were exposed to several days of diapause-inducing short-day photoperiods would not go into diapause if they were subsequently reared under long-day conditions. Eggs and young larvae that were transferred from short-day photoperiods to aperiodic conditions, such as either continuous illumination or continuous darkness, showed a high incidence of diapause. The developmental pattern established under the influence of the short-day photoperiods was not changed by an aperiodic environment.

Evidence of rhythmic functions in metabolic and endocrine systems has been obtained for several insect species. Cell size changes and secretory cycles have been detected in the neuro-secretory systems of the brain and subesophageal ganglion, corpora allata, corpora cardiaca, prothoracic glands, and—in the case of the European corn borer—the proctodone-producing cells of the ileum. In most of these cases, the rhythmic functions appeared to be running at frequencies higher than one cycle per 24 hours, as was discussed in Chapter 5.

The effect of photoperiod on the induction and termination of diapause, and on other developmental processes, might be explicable in terms of phase relationships among a number of interacting physiological rhythms. If there were two (or several) rhythmic processes that stood in a functional relationship to each other, their phase relationships might determine the rate of physiological processes that were dependent on their products. A growth-controlling system might be so envisioned, provided that one important requirement be met. One of the rhythms must be phase set by the light-on signal, and the other by the light-off signal. A photoperiod that would cause the two endogenous rhythms to run in a physiologically unfavorable (*out-of-phase*) relationship to each other might result in a low rate of development, or diapause. Conversely, a photoperiod that resulted in the two rhythms' being *in phase* with each other might exert a growth-stimulating effect.

The only experimental evidence that directly supports such a hypothesis has come from the research on diapause development in the European corn borer. In this insect, the termination of diapause is associated with the initiation of the pupal molting cycle, which is thought to involve the activation of the neuroendocrine system. The activation of the neuroendocrine system of the corn borer's brain appeared to be stimulated by the hormone *proctodone*, which was produced by epithelial cells of the ileum (Beck and Alexander, 1964b,c). An endogenous secretory rhythm was observed in the ileal epithelium, and this rhythm was shown to be phase set by the onset of the scotophase. A secretory rhythm was also detected in the lateral neurosecretory cells of the brain, and this rhythm was apparently phase set by the light-on stimulus of the photoperiod (Beck, 1964). Both rhythms showed an 8-hour periodic-

16 L : 8 D = NO DIAPAUSE

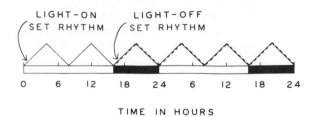

LIGHT−ON   LIGHT−OFF
SET RHYTHM   SET RHYTHM

TIME IN HOURS

15 L : 9 D = CRITICAL DAYLENGTH

TIME IN HOURS

12 L : 12 D = DIAPAUSE

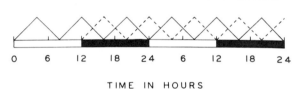

TIME IN HOURS

Fig. 50. Theoretical effects of photoperiod on the phase relationships among rhythms showing an 8-hour periodicity and light and dark sensitivities.

ity. Phase setting would, therefore, be expected to occur once each 24 hours, and the rhythms should run endogenously through two cycles before the next photoperiodic phase-setting signals would be received (Fig. 50).

When diapausing borers are under the influence of a short-day photo-period, such as 12L:12D, the ileal and neurosecretory rhythms would be held in an out-of-phase relationship, because the two phase-setting signals would be separated in time by 1.5 cycles of the 8-hour rhythms (Fig. 50, bottom diagram). However, the two rhythms would be maintained in an in-phase relationship when the insects were held under a 16L:8D photoperiod (Fig. 50, top). A photoperiod approximating the critical daylength would produce an intermediate phase relationship, as shown by the middle diagram of Fig. 50. Beck (1964) postulated that the low rate of diapause development that has been observed under short-day conditions and the high developmental rate that prevails under long-day conditions might be explained on the basis of the phase relationships among endogenous subcircadian rhythms.

The effects of light-breaks on diapause induction in the European corn borer (Fig. 47) showed that the circadian time of the light-break strongly influenced the response. Light-breaks occurring at circadian times of about 11 or 19 hours resulted in high diapause incidences; whereas light-breaks at from the thirteenth to fifteenth circadian hours induced little or no diapause. The time difference between the 11-hour response peak and the 19-hour peak is 8 hours, suggesting that the effect of the light-breaks was on the phase setting of 8-hour physiological rhythms, rather than because of the effect of light on the so-called "light-sensitive" times within a circadian rhythm. The light-break data of Adkisson on diapause induction in the pink bollworm (Figs. 48 and 49) show maxima and minima of diapause incidence that suggest an approximately 6-hour periodicity of underlying physiological rhythms.

Biological clock systems based on light- and dark-sensitive short-period endogenous rhythms could function quite efficiently under either diel or nondiel photoperiods. The limitations of the hourglass hypothesis might be avoided, and the failure of the circadian clock hypothesis to account for the effects of light-breaks and nondiel photo-periods might also be explained. The postulated time relationships among subcircadian rhythms, as discussed above, cannot account for the relatively greater role of the scotophase than that of the photophase that has been observed in the great majority of the photoperiodic responses of both plants and animals. An additional characteristic of the phase relationships must be assumed. This characteristic is that the rhythm that is phase set by the light-on signal (light-set rhythm) is entrained by the dark-set rhythm (Fig. 51). This hypothesis for a biological clock was based on the photoperiodic responses and rhythmic physiological functions of the European corn borer (Beck, 1968). According to this hypothetical model, the dark-set rhythm is always phase set by the onset of the scotophase, and the light-set rhythm is always phase set by the onset of the photophase. But upon phase setting by the onset of light, the light-set rhythm is also entrained to the dark-set rhythm, and the entrainment is maintained when the light-off signal

183

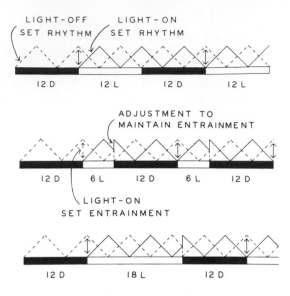

Fig. 51. Hypothetical noncircadian biological clock system involving light-set and dark-set rhythms.

results in a phase setting of the dark-set rhythm. This means that the length of the scotophase largely determines the phase relationships between the two types of rhythms. This hypothesis is illustrated for one diel photoperiod (12L:12D) and two nondiel photoperiods (6L:12D and 18L:12D), all of which induce a diapause incidence of nearly 100% in the European corn borer. Although this hypothetical system is consistent with the experimental results obtained in studies of diapause induction and termination in the corn borer, direct experimental testing has not been possible.

In summary, photoperiodic induction and termination of the diapause state in insects involves complex time relationships. The biological clock system appears to be capable of functioning efficiently in its natural 24-hour based environment, and also under the strain of experimental nondiel conditions. The time-relationship system has been shown to be both rhythmic and endogenous. In at least several cases, noncircadian rhythmic functions have been detected, and these rhythms may play a major role in the insect's temporal organization. Neither the hourglass nor the circadian models of the biological clock is consistent with the bulk of experimental evidence relating photoperiod and diapause. A time-relationship system of noncircadian endogenous rhythms was postulated.

184

8 □ Survey of Photoperiodically Controlled Diapause

Nearly all insect species that are naturally exposed to the vicissitudes of seasonal climatic cycles display a capacity for diapause. Photoperiod has been shown to be a major environmental factor in controlling the induction, maintenance, and termination of diapause in a great many species. As more examples of diapause are subjected to detailed investigation, the number of species in which photoperiod plays a decisive role grows larger. Photoperiod has been shown to be of importance in the induction of diapause even in some tropical forms, although the insects live in an environment in which seasonal changes in daylength are relatively slight.

Some of the general characteristics of the role of photoperiod in the control of diapause were discussed in Chapter 7. In the present chapter, the discussion will be centered on the characteristics of different types of diapause and how they are influenced by photoperiod. Among different insect groups, diapause may occur in the egg, different larval or nymphal instars, pupa, or adult stages. Within each of these types, there may be great differences as to critical daylength, the growth stage at which diapause determination occurs, and the characteristics of the diapause state. At the present time, there is no basis for postulating that the physiological mechanisms underlying the different types of diapause are fundamentally similar. It is tempting to postulate that the biological clock system through which photoperiod exerts its controlling influence might be identical in all organisms, but this hypothesis may also represent an oversimplified view.

Embryonic Diapause

A great multitude of insect species survive adverse seasons by means of eggs in a state of embryonic diapause. The role of photoperiod in the induction of this type of diapause has been demonstrated in only a relatively small number of species, however (Table XII). Undoubtedly a great many more examples will be reported as more species are investigated.

The word "diapause" was originally coined to describe a stage of blastokinesis in which the movements of the embryo around the yolk mass were interrupted between anatrepsis and katatrepsis. The term is now used in a much broader, and generally quite different sense, and is applied to a variety of developmental interruptions occurring in either embryonic or postembryonic development. Embryonic diapause

TABLE XII

Examples of Embryonic Diapause in Which Photoperiodic Control
(Induction or Termination) Has Been Demonstrated or Reasonably Inferred

Order and family	Genus and species	References
LEPIDOPTERA		
Bombycidae	*Bombyx mori* (L.)	Kogure (1933)
Lymantridae	*Orgyia antiqua* (L.)	Kind (1965)
DIPTERA		
Culicidae	*Aedes triseriatus* Say	Kappus (1965)
	Aedes togoi Theobald	Vinogradova (1960, 1965)
HEMIPTERA		
Miridae	*Adelphocoris linoleatus* (Goeze)	Ewen (1966)
HOMOPTERA		
Cicadellidae	*Euscelis plebejus* Fall.	Müller (1957, 1961)
	Euscelis linoleatus Br.	Müller (1957, 1961)
Aphididae	*Dysaphis plantaginea* (Pass.)	Marcovitch (1923, 1924)
	Aphis forbesi weed	Marcovitch (1923, 1924)
	Myzus persicae (Sulzer)	Bonnemaison (1951)
	Brevicoryne brassicae (L.)	Bonnemaison (1951)
	Acyrthosiphon pisum (Harris)	Kenten (1955)
	Macrosiphum euphorbiae (Thomas)	MacGillvray and Anderson (1964)
	Megoura viciae Buck.	Lees (1959a)
ACARINA		
Tetranychidae	*Metatetranychus ulmi* Koch	Lees (1950, 1953a,b)
CLADOCERA		
Daphnidae	*Daphnia pulex* Leydig	Stross and Hill (1965)

186

can occur at any of a large number of developmental states, depending on the species, and is not confined to a stage between anatrepsis and katatrepsis. Some eggs go into diapause at a very early stage—well before the embryo begins to show metamerization (e.g. *Bombyx mori*); or at a later stage in which appendages have begun to differentiate (e.g. *Locusta migratoria* and many other Orthopterans); or at a very late stage in which the embryo has become a larva that is apparently ready to hatch (e.g. *Lymantria dispar* and many other lepidopterans) (Lees. 1955).

Diapausing eggs show very low metabolic rates, as might be expected on the basis that embryonic development has been strongly suppressed, if not virtually arrested. Water loss from eggs in diapause is also typically very slow, and such eggs may remain viable for protracted periods, even though in a state of partial desiccation. The role of water uptake in the termination of embryonic diapause was discussed in the previous chapter.

Photoperiodic determination of embryonic diapause is usually caused by the photoperiods experienced by the parental generation rather than by the eggs themselves. Embryonic diapause is the lymantrid moth *Orygia antiqua* was found to be determined by the photoperiods to which the female parent was exposed during its larval development (Kind, 1965). And as was discussed previously, embryonic diapause in the commercial silkworm was found to be determined during the late embryonic and early larval development of the female parent. Diapause eggs of mites and aphids are also produced in response to photoperiods to which the females had been exposed, and in the case of aphids, the photoperiodic determination occurs very early in development. An apparent exception to this general rule was reported in *Aedes triseriatus* (Kappus, 1965), in which case diapause occurred in response to short-day photoperiods experienced by the embryos from 5 to 8 days after egg deposition. Exposure of the parental generation to short-day or long-day conditions did not influence diapause determination among the progeny.

Diapause induction has been studied intensively in the case of *B. mori*. Because the photoperiods to which the eggs of one generation are exposed determines whether or not diapause will occur in the eggs of the succeeding generation, it is apparent that the action of photoperiod is on the system that determines the developmental program to be followed throughout the life of the insect. Nothing is known of how

187

photoperiodic stimuli effect developmental programming, and investigators have concentrated mainly on an elucidation of the physiological aspects of diapause egg production.

Silkworm eggs are determined in respect to diapause or nondiapause by the ovariole that produced them. Ovarian determination appears to depend upon the presence or absence of a hormone produced by neurosecretory cells of the subesophageal ganglion (Fukuda, 1951, 1952, 1953a,b; Hasegawa, 1952, 1957). Production of the "diapause hormone" by the subesophageal ganglion was shown to be controlled by the brain, for if the brain was extirpated or if the circumesophageal connectives were severed in pupae that were nondiapause determined, the subsequent moths laid diapause eggs. Surgical removal of the subesophageal ganglion from pupae that were diapause-determined resulted in moths that deposited only nondiapause eggs. Hasegawa (1957) partially purified the diapause hormone from pupal extracts, and has subsequently demonstrated that the target organ of the hormone is the ovary (Hasegawa, 1963, 1964; Hasegawa and Yamashita, 1965; Yamashita and Hasegawa, 1965). The current concept of the hormonal pathway leading to the production of diapause-determined eggs is shown in Fig. 52. Morohoshi (1957, 1959) reported that the corpus allatum of the silkworm pupa may be involved in this process. He concluded that the corpus allatum produced a factor that antagonized the action of the diapause hormone and tended to promote the production of eggs of the nondiapause type.

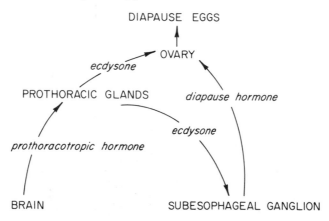

Fig. 52. Hormonal sequence involved in the production of diapause-determined eggs by the silkworm, Bombyx mori. [Adapted from Kobayashi and Ishitoya (1964).]

Embryos of unchilled diapausing silkworm eggs were found to be incapable of development when explanted into hanging drops under tissue culture conditions; nondiapausing embryos developed when so explanted (Takami, 1958). However, when diapausing embryos were cultured in a hanging drop side-by-side with nondiapausing embryos, they were capable of growth (Takami, 1959). From such results, Takami concluded that diapausing eggs contained a growth-inhibiting substance of maternal origin that prevented the embryos from producing the hormones required for their continued development.

Embryonic diapause of the tussock moth *O. antiqua* has been found to be induced by an endocrine mechanism that is similar to that found in the silkworm (Kind, 1965). Neurosecretory production of a diapause hormone by the subesophageal ganglion was demonstrated. The production of diapause-determined eggs by the hemipteran *Adelphocoris linoleatus* may also be the result of such a mechanism (Ewen, 1966).

Larval and Nymphal Diapause

Although it most frequently occurs at a species-specific stage, larval and nymphal diapause may occur during any of the stadia of immature insects. For example, the spruce budworm, *Choristoneura fumiferana*, characteristically diapauses as a second instar larva, but a second period of diapause during a later larval stage has also been observed in some geographical populations (Harvey, 1961). *Dendrolimus pini* and *Dendrolimus sibiricus* larvae have been observed to go into diapause during one or more of several larval stadia, depending on seasonal climatic conditions (Geyspitz, 1965). Nymphs of the dragonfly *Tetragoneuria cynosura* most typically diapause as mature, last instar forms; some, however, require 2 years to complete their development and will diapause at an early instar during the first winter and as mature nymphs during the second winter (Lutz and Jenner, 1964).

A great many holometabolous forms enter diapause as fully grown mature larvae. Because their larval growth period has been completed, and they will pupate upon completion of diapause, without further feeding, they are more properly termed "prepupae." In many species having this type of diapause, the insects show histological and biochemical indications of prepupal differentiation. For this reason, *prepupal diapause* is most properly distinguished from *larval diapause*. Examples of larval and nymphal diapause that are influenced by photoperiod are tabulated in Table XIII, and the instances in which the

189

TABLE XIII

Examples of Larval and Nymphal Diapause in Which Photoperiodic
Control (Induction or Termination) Has Been Demonstrated or Reasonably Inferred

Order and family	Genus and species	References
LEPIDOPTERA		
Olethreutidae	*Grapholitha molesta* (Busck)*	Dickson and Sanders (1945), Dickson (1949)
	Carpocapsa pomonella (L.)*	Dickson (1949)
	*Laspeyresia pomonella**	Shel'deshova (1962)
Zygaenidae	*Harrisinia brillians* (Banes and Dunnough)*	Smith and Langston (1953)
Phaloniidae	*Carposina niponensis* (Walsh.)*	Toshima *et al.* (1961)
Gelechiidae	*Pectinophora gossypiella* (Saunders)*	Bull and Adkisson (1960)
	Gelechia malvella Hübner*	Danilevskii (1961)
	*Pectinophora malvella**	Kuznetsova (1962)
Pyraustidae	*Ostrinia nubilalis* (Hübner)*	Mutchmor and Beckel (1958), Beck and Hanec (1960)
	Loxostege sticticalis (L)*	Danilevskii (1961)
	Loxostege verticalis L.*	Danilevskii (1961)
Phycitidae	*Plodia interpunctella* (Hübner)*	Tzanakakis (1959)
Crambidae	*Chilo suppressalis* (Walker)	Inouye and Kamano (1957)
	Diatraea saccharalis (F.)	Katiyar and Long (1961)
Lasiocampidae	*Dendrolimus pini* L.	Geyspitz (1953, 1965)
	Dendrolimus sibiricus Ischtv.	Geyspitz (1965)
Lycaenidae	*Lycaena phlaeas daimio*	Sakai and Masaki (1965)
Tortricidae	*Choristoneura fumiferana* (Clemens)	Harvey (1957)
	Pandemis corylana F.	Danilevskii (1961)
	Pandemis ribeana Hübner	Danilevskii (1961)
	Capua reticulana Hübner	Danilevskii (1961)
	Cacoecia podana S.C.	Danilevskii (1961)
Lymantridae	*Euproctus similis* Fuessl.	Geyspitz (1953)
	Euproctus chrysorrhoea L.	Geyspitz (1953)
	Leucoma salicis L.	Geyspitz (1953)
Arctiidae	*Arctia caia* L.	Danilevskii (1961)
	Arctia aulica L.	Danilevskii (1961)
	Parasemia plantaginis L.	Danilevskii (1961)
	Lithosia griseola Hübner	Danilevskii (1961)
Noctuidae	*Athetis ambigua* F.	Danilevskii (1961)
	Agrotis C-nigrum L.	Danilevskii (1961)
DIPTERA		
Culicidae	*Anopheles barberi* Coq.	Baker (1935)
	Anopheles plumbeus Steph.	Vinogradova (1962)
	Anopheles bifurcatus L.	Danilevskii (1961)

*Prepupal diapause.

190

TABLE XIII *(Continued)*

Order and Family	Genus and Species	References
	Aedes triseriatus (Say)*	Baker (1935), Love and Whelchel (1955)
	Toxorhynchites rutilus	McCrary and Jenner (1965)
Ceratopogonidae	*Culicoides guttipennis* Coq.	Baker (1935)
Chironomidae	*Chironomus tentans*	Engelmann and Shappirio (1965)
	Clunio marinus Hal.	Neumann (1966)
	*Metriocnemus knabi**	Paris and Jenner (1959)
Otitidae	*Euxesta notata* (Wiedemann)	McLeod (1964)
HYMENOPTERA		
Tenthredinidae	*Athalia colibri* Chr.*	Danilevskii (1961)
	Athalia glabricollis Thompson*	Saringer (1966)
	Lygaeonematus compressicornis F.*	Danilevskii (1961)
Diprionidae	*Neodiprion sertifer* (Geoffrey)*	Sullivan and Wallace (1965)
	Neodiprion rugifrons Middleton*	King and Benjamin (1965)
Braconidae	*Coeloides brunneri*	Ryan (1965)
	Apanteles glomeratus L.*	Danilevskii (1961)
Trichogrammatidae	*Trichogramma evanescens* Wstw	Danilevskii (1961)
Pteromalidae	*Pteromalus puparum* L.*	Masleninkova (1961)
	Nasonia vitripennis (Walk.)*	Saunders (1965b)
NEUROPTERA		
Chrysopidae	*Chrysopa* spp.*	Danilevskii (1961)
COLEOPTERA		
Dermestidae	*Anthrenus verbasci* (L.)	Blake (1960)
OPTHOPTERA		
Gryllidae	*Nemobius yezoensis*	Masaki and Oyama (1963)
	Gryllus campestris	Fuzeau-Braesch (1965, 1966)
Tetrigidae	*Acrydium arenosum*	Sabrosky *et al.* (1933)
ODONATA		
Aeshnidae	*Anax imperator* Leach	Corbet (1956)
Corduliidae	*Tetragoneuria cynosura* (Say)	Lutz and Jenner (1964)
Libellulidae	*Neotetrum pulchellum* (Drury)	Montgomery and Macklin (1962)
HEMIPTERA		
Lygaeidae	*Ischnodemus sabuleti*	Müller (1960a,b)
HOMOPTERA		
Aphididae	*Periphyllus testudinatus*	Bonnemaison (1956)
Cicadellidae	*Nephotettix cincticeps* Uhler	Kisimoto (1959)
Delphacidae	*Delphacodes striatella* Fall	Kisimoto (1956)
ACARINA		
Ixodidae	*Ixodes ricinus*	Belozerov (1964)

diapause is known to be of the prepupal type are identified by an asterisk (*).

Physiological Characteristics

Nymphal, larval, and prepupal diapauses are characterized by a reduced metabolic rate, reduction of body water content (among terrestrial forms), increased accumulation of fat body reserves, and suppression of growth, as compared to nondiapausing individuals of the same species. The diapausing insects are not necessarily quiescent, however, and may move about actively when suitably stimulated. Those that diapause as a prepupa in a cocoon, and those that diapause in a hibernaculum, normally display little or no locomotor activity, but they are capable of coordinated movements and stereotyped behavior patterns under experimental conditions. Diapause is generally considered to be caused and maintained by a temporary failure of the endocrine system to elaborate the hormones that stimulate metabolism and growth. The exact role of photoperiod in the control of this type of diapause is unknown at the biochemical level.

Prepupal diapause occurs only at a very precisely defined point in the developmental sequence of the insect, in regard to the state of tissue and organ differentiation. The female gonads are relatively undifferentiated, and rapid growth of these organs does not take place until after pupation. The male gonads, however, undergo much differentiation during the late larval stages, and at the beginning of diapause spermatogenesis may be well advanced. Spermatogenesis is not only arrested during diapause, but there may also be some regression and resorption of the more advanced cells. Cloutier and Beck (1963) observed that spermatogenesis began in fourth instar larvae of the European corn borer, *Ostrinia nubilalis.* Spermatids were found in the testes of fifth instar larvae, even in larvae that were destined to go into diapause. At the onset of diapause, all spermatocytes that had advanced beyond the pachytene stage underwent degeneration and eventual resorption. Similar observations have been reported for the rice stem borer, *Chilo suppressalis* (Mochida and Yoshimeki, 1962), and the wheat stem sawfly, *Cephus cinctus* (Church, 1955a). The role of endocrine functions in spermatogenesis are not known.

In addition to the testes, a number of other organ systems have been found to have begun differentiation toward the pupal and adult stages at the time of the onset of diapause. These include the midgut (Beck *et al.,* 1950), hindgut (Beck and Alexander, 1964b), central nervous

192

system (Beck *et al.*, 1963), and the hemolymph (Chippendale and Beck, 1966). In respect to the hemolymph, Chippendale and Beck (1966) found that European corn borer larvae showed a distinct shift from a larval blood protein pattern to a prepupal pattern at about 11 or 12 days of larval age. This time of change from larval to prepupal condition also coincided with the time of diapause determination under short-day rearing conditions. No difference in blood picture could be detected between diapause and nondiapause prepupae, however, until the latter had initiated the pupal molting cycle.

Diapause in any postembryonic stage is usually considered to be caused by the absence of the growth-promoting hormones of the neuro-endocrine system. It has been well established that the growth-limiting factor in pupal diapause is the brain's failure to secrete prothoraco-tropic hormone. In larval diapause of the prepupal type, however, the inability of the neuroendocrine system to produce hormones does not seem to be the primary cause of diapause. Although the insect is unable to complete its development until the proper hormones have been produced, the diapause state itself appears to involve rate-limiting factors that suppress development at points preceding the action of prothoracotropic hormone. This effect may be illustrated by the results of Beck (1968), working with the European corn borer and the greater wax moth, *Galleria mellonella*. Whereas the corn borer has a photo-periodically induced prepupal diapause, the wax moth does not have such a diapause and, as far as is known, its development is not influenced by photoperiod. All combinations of reciprocal brain transplantations were made between diapausing prepupae of the corn borer and prepupae of the wax moth. The operated insects were then incu-

TABLE XIV

Pupation of Diapausing European Corn Borers and Prepupal
Greater Wax Moths Following Reciprocal Brain Transplantations[a]

Experimental series	Brain donor	Brain recipient	Posttreatment conditions	Pupation (%)
A	Wax moth	Wax moth	Darkness	100
B	Corn Borer	Wax moth	Darkness	95
C	Corn borer	Corn borer	Long-day	92
D	Corn borer	Corn borer	Short-day	78
E	Wax moth	Corn borer	Long-day	69
F	Wax moth	Corn borer	Short-day	2

[a]Adapted from Beck (1968).

bated under different photoperiodic conditions and observed for pupation (Table XIV).

Wax moth brains implanted into brainless wax moth prepupae resulted in pupation of the recipients (Table XIV, series A), as would be expected on the basis that neither brain nor body was in diapause. Wax moth larvae also pupated normally when they had received brains from diapausing corn borers (series B). This effect should not be expected if the diapausing borer brains were inactive from the standpoint of hormone production. The diapausing borer brains might have been activated by the surgical manipulations involved in explantation and implantation, an interpretation which was supported by the results of series C and D. In these experiments diapausing borer brains were implanted into brainless diapausing borers, and whether held under a long-day or a short-day photoperiod, the recipient larvae pupated. When this effect was first reported (Cloutier *et al.*, 1962), it was suggested that the surgical procedures destroyed a barrier to metabolite exchange between the brain and the hemolymph. As long as such a "brain barrier" was functional, the insect remained in diapause. Once the barrier was broken—via photoperiodic responses under natural conditions, or via surgical damage—diapause was terminated. No direct experimental evidence has been obtained, however, that would lend any support to this hypothesis.

The brains of mature wax moth larvae (prepupae) were also implanted into brainless diapausing corn borers (Table XIV, series E and F). The recipient larvae were held under either short-day or long-day photoperiods; of which only those in the long-day went on to pupate. The recipient borers that were maintained under a short-day photoperiod remained in diapause despite their having received a nondiapause brain.

These experimental results are quite inconsistent with the concept that diapause is caused by a shutdown of the prepupal neuroendocrine system. Apparently such a diapause involves more of the physiological system than just the neuroendocrine organs. Diapause may or may not be terminated by the implantation of a brain system, but the important characteristic of the brain is not whether it came from a diapause or nondiapause donor (Beck, 1968).

Diapause Determination

Photoperiodic determination of diapause must precede the actual manifestation, and there has been some interest in the question of the growth stage at which photoperiod exerts its influence. The photo-period-sensitive stage varies quite widely among different species. Larval diapause may be determined by the photoperiods experienced by the parental generation, as in the case of *Aedes triseriatus* (Love and Whelchel, 1955). Diapause among larvae of the parasitic wasp *Nasonia vitripennis* was found to be determined by the photoperiods experienced by the female parent during her early adult life and also by the age of the female at the time of egg deposition (Saunders, 1962, 1965a,b). Similarly, determination of larval diapause in the braconid *Coeloides brunneri* was found to be in accord with the photoperiodic history of the female parent (Ryan, 1965). In both of these cases, larval diapause was the result of the parental response to short-day photoperiods. The mechanisms by which the photoperiodic responses of the adults control the developmental programming of the larval offspring is quite unknown.

Larval diapause in some forms appears to depend, at least in part, on the photoperiods experienced by the embryonic stages of the insect. Prepupal diapause of the pink bollworm, *Pectinophora gossypiella,* was reported to be induced by short-day photoperiods to which the larvae were exposed, but diapause determination also appeared to be influenced by photoperiods under which the eggs were incubated (Menaker and Gross, 1965; Lukefahr *et al.,* 1964; Adkisson, 1966). Kuznetsova (1962) found that exposure of the eggs of *Pectinophora malvella* to long-day photoperiods tended to prevent short-day induction of diapause at the prepupal stage.

In most cases, larval diapause (including both nymphal and prepupal) is determined by photoperiods to which the larval stages have been exposed. Experimental identification of the larval stages that respond to photoperiod is complicated by a number of factors that markedly influence the results. Temperature is an important factor, and in most cases low temperatures tend to increase the apparent sensitivity to diapause-inducing photoperiods. Because growth rates are lower under relatively low temperatures, the number of inductive photoperiodic cycles to which the insects will be exposed during a given stadium will be greater at a low than at a high temperature. The number of inductive cycles may be quite critical to diapause determination. The most important factor influencing an experimental determination of the photoperiod-sensitive growth stage is the photoperiodic history of the insects themselves. If the critical growth stage is determined in terms of the stage at which the diapause commitment may no longer be reversed, the experimental results will be different from what would be the case if the experiments were directed toward identification of the growth stage at which a commitment to diapause may be effected. Generally, the effects of short-day, diapause-inducing photoperiods are much more readily reversed than are those of long-day regimes.

These several effects may be illustrated by the photoperiodic responses of the European corn borer. When larvae that had been reared under continuous light and 29°C (nondiapause-inducing conditions) were transferred to a 9.5-hour daylength and 18°C, a high incidence of diapause was induced, provided that the transfer had been effected not later than the first day after ecdysis to the fifth (last) instar (Mutchmor and Beckel, 1959). A daylength of 9.5 hours combined with a temperature of 29°C did not induce diapause among borer larvae with a similar developmental history. Working at 26°C, Beck and Hanec (1960) found that diapause could not be induced by exposure of the last instar borer larvae to a short-day photoperiod following a long-day schedule that had prevailed during the earlier stadia. It has been shown that about 10 days are required for the corn borer to adjust to a 4-hour change in the photoperiod (McLeod and Beck, 1963b; Beck et al., 1965a). At 18°C, the fifth larval stadium lasts about 15 days, which would be ample time for the phase adjustment to a diapause-inducing photoperiod. At either 26° or 30°C, however, the stadium is but 3 to 4 days duration, and this short period is insufficient for a short-day induction of diapause. Whereas Mutchmor and Beckel (1958, 1959) concluded that diapause was induced by the temperature and photoperiods experienced by the larvae after the beginning of the final larval stadium, Beck and Hanec (1960) concluded that there was no critically sensitive stage and that diapause incidence was influenced by photoperiods experienced early as well as late in larval development.

The developmental point at which diapause is irreversibly determined among corn borer larvae reared at 30°C and a 12-hour daylength has been measured with some precision, however. Such short-day reared larvae were transferred to long-day conditions (16L:8D) at the ninth, tenth, eleventh, etc., day of larval age, and were then observed for diapause. The results showed that diapause was determined between the eleventh and twelfth day (Table XV) (Beck, 1968). Transfers effected by the eleventh day resulted in no appreciable incidence of diapause, and the borers went on to pupate within 9 or 10 days. Transfer to long-day conditions on the twelfth day or later did not prevent diapause, and the borers required about 30 days of long-day exposure to complete the diapause and advance to the pupal stage.

196

TABLE XV

Effect of Transfer from Short-Day to Long-Day
Rearing Conditions on the Duration of Diapause and the
Age at Pupation of the European Corn Borer *Ostrinia nubilalis*[a]

Larval age at transfer (days)	Average age at pupation (days)	Average time from transfer to pupation (days)
9	18	9
10	19	9
11	21	10
12	40	28
13	41	28
16	48	32
20	52	32

[a]Adapted from Beck (1968).

The number of photoperiodic cycles required to induce diapause depends not only on the environmental temperature, but also on the insect species. As discussed above, the European corn borer was found to require about 10 short-day cycles to effect diapause determination. *Dendrolimus pini* was found to require at least 20 inductive cycles at 20°C, but *Loxostege sticticalis* was committed to diapause after but 7 or 8 days of short daylength (Danilevskii, 1961). Reversal of diapause determination may sometimes be accomplished by even fewer long-day exposures; a single long-day occurring just prior to the last larval molt was found to reduce the incidence of pupal diapause quite sharply in cultures of *Polia oleracea* (Way and Hopkins, 1950).

PUPAL DIAPAUSE

Known instances of photoperiodically controlled pupal diapause are presented as Table XVI. A very great many insect species overwinter as pupae, and the number of forms in which pupal diapause has been shown to be determined by photoperiod will, undoubtedly, increase as the photoperiodic responses of more species are investigated.

Physiological Characteristics

Pupal diapause is characterized by a strongly suppressed metabolic rate, cessation of adult differentiation, and marked resistance to water loss by transpiration. It was once thought that much of the central nervous system was nonfunctional during the pupal diapause, and that diapause was perhaps *caused* by an "electrical silence" of the principal

197

TABLE XVI
Examples of Pupal Diapause in Which Photoperiodic Control
(Induction or Termination) Has Been Demonstrated or Reasonably Inferred

Order and family	Genus and species	References
LEPIDOPTERA		
Noctuidae	*Polia oleracea* (L.)	Way *et al.* (1949); Way and Hopkins (1950)
	Polia contigua Vill.	Danilevskii (1961)
	Polia dissimilis Kn.	Danilevskii (1961)
	Mamestra brassicae (L.)	Otuka and Santa (1955), Masaki (1956)
	Melicleptria scutosa Schiff	Goryshin (1958)
	Trachea atriplicis L.	Danilevskii (1961)
	Heliothis zea (Boddie)	Phillips and Newsom (1966)
	Heliothis virescens (Fabr.)	Phillips and Newsom (1966)
	Acronycta rumicis L.	Danilevskii (1961)
	Acronycta megacephala (Fabr.)	Danilevskii (1961)
	Acronycta leporina L.	Danilevskii (1961)
	Acronycta psi L.	Danilevskii (1961)
	Demas coryli L.	Danilevskii (1961)
	Chloridea obsoleta Fabr.	Goryshin (1958)
	Chloridea dipsacea L.	Goryshin (1958)
Tortricidae	*Argyrotaenia velutinana* (Walker)	Glass (1963)
	Polychrosis botrana Schiff	Danilevskii (1961)
Arctiidae	*Hylophila prasinana* L.	Danilevskii (1961)
	Hyphantria cunea (Drury)	Jermy and Saringer (1955)
	Spilosoma menthastri Esp.	Danilevskii (1961)
	Spilosoma lubricipeda L.	Danilevskii (1961)
Sphingidae	*Manduca sexta* (Johannson)	Rabb (1966)
	Smerinthus ocellatus L.	Danilevskii (1961)
	Smerinthus populi L.	Danilevskii (1961)
Lymantridae	*Dasychira pudibunda* L.	Geyspitz and Zarankina (1963)
	Stilpnotia salicis (L.)	Muller (1960a)
Geometridae	*Abraxas miranda* Butler	Masaki (1959)
Notodontidae	*Lophopteryx camelina* L.	Danilevskii (1961)
	Pygaera pigra Hubn.	Danilevskii (1961)
Papilionidae	*Papilio podalirius* L.	Wohlfahrt (1957)
Pieridae	*Pieris rapae* (L.)	Barker *et al.* (1963)
	Pieris brassicae L.	Way *et al.* (1949)
	Pieris napi L.	Danilevskii (1961)
Nymphalidae	*Araschnia levana* L.	Muller (1955)
Saturniidae	*Antheraea pernyi* Guer	Tanaka (1950)

198

TABLE XVI *(Continued)*

Order and family	Genus and species	References
	Hyalophora cecropia (L.)	Mansingh and Smallman (1966)
	Philosamia cynthia Drury	Pammer (1965)
DIPTERA		
Anthomyiidae	*Pegomya hyosciami* Pz	Zabirov (1961)
	Hylemya brassicae (Bouche)	Hughes (1960), Zabirov (1961)
Muscidae	*Haemotobia irritans* (L.)	Depner (1962)
HOMOPTERA		
Aleyrodidae	*Aleurochiton complanatus*	Müller (1962)

nerve tracts in the brain (Van der Kloot, 1955). This theory of diapause was disproved by Schoonhoven (1963), Tyshchenko (1964), and Tyshchenko and Mandelstam (1965). Tyshchenko demonstrated that a temporary loss of ability to transmit impulses is a normal feature of pupal development in lepidopterans, and not peculiar to those pupae that enter the diapause state.

The endocrinology of pupal diapause has been subjected to intensive investigation by a number of workers. Pupal diapause appears to be controlled entirely by the neuroendocrine system of the brain. During diapause, neither prothoracotropic hormone nor juvenile hormone is secreted (Williams, 1946, 1952; Schneiderman and Gilbert, 1959, 1964). In the absence of these hormones, the prothoracic glands cannot produce ecdysone, and the insect's growth and differentiation is thereby stopped.

Pupal diapause is usually terminated only after a rather prolonged exposure (several weeks or months) to relatively low temperatures (<10°C). In some instances of estival diapause, relatively high temperatures are required. Most diapausing pupae are not sensitive to photoperiod, but a few exceptions to this rule have been discovered. The Cecropia silkworm, *Hyalophora cecropia*, and the Chinese oak silkworm, *Antheraea peryni*, are two such species. The latter species has a pupal diapause that occurs in response to short-day photoperiods experienced during the last two stadia of larval growth (Tanaka, 1950). The pupae, themselves, are also responsive to photoperiod, in that diapause will be indefinitely prolonged by short days, but can be terminated within a few weeks if the pupae are exposed to long-day conditions (Shakhbazov, 1961). Interestingly enough, a patch of transparent cuticle occurs

199

on the head of the pupa, immediately above the brain. Shakhbazov showed that the photoperiodic response could be abolished by painting this "cephalic window" with opaque materials. Williams and Adkisson (1964) showed that a 12-hour daylength had the maximum diapause-promoting effect on this species, and that a 17-hour daylength was the most effective treatment for the termination of diapause. Williams and his co-workers also demonstrated that the effect of photoperiod was exclusively on the brain, presumably the neuroendocrine system, and that the most effective wavelengths of light were between 398 and 510 mμ (Williams *et al.*, 1965).

Diapause Determination

Pupal diapause is determined as a developmental commitment in response to photoperiods experienced during earlier growth stages. Usually, diapause determination occurs during the larval stages. As discussed above, pupal diapause in the Chinese oak silkworm is determined by the photoperiods to which the last two larval instars are exposed. Claret (1966a,b) reported that pupal diapause in the cabbage butterfly, *Pieris brassicae*, is determined in the last two instars (fourth and fifth), but the two stages differed in their sensitivity to photoperiod. When reared under long daylengths (16L:8D), the larvae could not be committed to diapause by transfer to short-day photoperiods (8L:16D) if the transfer was accomplished after the beginning of the fourth stadium. By that stage, the larvae had been irreversibly committed to the non-diapause pattern. On the other hand, larvae that were reared under the short-day photoperiod would be diapause-determined unless transferred to long daylengths sometime during larval growth. Diapause determination could be reversed by long-day exposure at any stage up to the beginning of the fifth stadium, but not after that point.

Diapause determination may occur in prelarval stages. The horn fly, *Haemotobia irritans*, for example, was found to be committed to a pupal diapause in response to short-day photoperiods experienced by the female progenitor (Depner, 1962). A most interesting and significant effect of prelarval influence has been reported in *Heliothis zea* (Wellso and Adkisson, 1966). Pupal diapause is determined by the daylengths to which the larvae are exposed, but the nature of the response is influenced by the photoperiods experienced by the eggs and their parents. Moths and eggs that had been exposed to short-day photoperiods (10L:14D) gave rise to larvae that would not enter pupal diapause when reared under the same short-day schedule. When the moths

200

and eggs had been exposed to somewhat longer daylength (14L:10D) and the larvae were reared under the short-day photoperiod, a high incidence of pupal diapause was induced.

IMAGINAL DIAPAUSE

Diapause in the adult (imaginal) insect is manifested primarily as a suppression of reproductive function, and for this reason is frequently referred to as *reproductive diapause* or *gonotropic dissociation*. The diapausing insects may show a number of behavioral and metabolic characteristics in addition to cessation of reproductive functions, as will be discussed in subsequent paragraphs. The effect of photoperiod in controlling the induction and termination of adult diapause is thought to be principally on the neuroendocrine system. The behavioral and metabolic characteristics have generally been considered to be secondary aspects of a gonadotropic hormone deficiency syndrome. Instances of photoperiodically controlled imaginal diapause have been compiled as Table XVII.

Behavioral Characteristics

As the insect enters the diapause state, its behavior may undergo marked changes. Feeding, locomotion, and tactic responses may all be quite different during diapause, as compared to either prediapause or postdiapause behavior. Newly emerged adults of the Colorado potato beetle, *Leptinotarsa decemlineata*, for example, are positively phototactic and are active feeders. At the beginning of diapause, they cease to feed, react negatively to light, and leave their host plants to bury themselves in the soil. The digging behavior, which results in the beetles being buried under several inches of soil, has been used as a criterion for the onset of diapause (de Wilde, 1960, 1962b; de Wilde and de Boer, 1961; LeBerre, 1965). A number of other beetle species tend to migrate from host plants to hibernation sites at the beginning of diapause; examples of this behavior include the alfalfa weevil, *Hypera postica* (Huggans and Blickenstaff, 1964), and the boll weevil, *Anthonomus grandis* (Brazzel and Newsom, 1959). Coccinellid beetles migrate to mountainous regions for hibernation, and these beetles have been shown to be in a state of reproductive diapause (Hodek and Cerkasov, 1960, 1961a,b, 1963).

Physiological Characteristics

Adult diapause involves a rather well-defined pattern in respect to metabolic processes. The rates of oxygen consumption are generally

TABLE XVII

Examples of Adult Diapause in Which Photoperiodic Control
(Induction or Termination) Has Been Demonstrated or Reasonably Inferred

Order and family	Genus and species	References
LEPIDOPTERA		
Noctuidae	*Chorizagrotis auxiliaris* (Grote)	Jacobson (1960)
Tortricidae	*Acalla fimbriana* Thnbg.	Danilevskii (1961)
Nymphalidae	*Vanessa io* L.	Danilevskii (1961)
DIPTERA		
Culicidae	*Anopheles maculipennis messeae* Fall.	Vinogradova (1960)
	Anopheles maculipennis atroparvus Thiel	Vinogradova (1960)
	Anopheles superpictus Gr.	Vinogradova (1960)
	Culex pipiens pipiens (L.)	Vinogradova (1960), Eldridge (1966)
Calliphoridae	*Protophormia terraenovae* R.D.	Danilevskii (1961)
COLEOPTERA		
Chrysomelidae	*Leptinotarsa decemlineata* Say	de Wilde (1953, 1954)
	Chrysomela fastuosa Scud.	Danilevskii (1961)
	Haltica saliceti Ws.	Danilevskii (1961)
	Psylliodes chrysocephala	Ankersmit (1964)
Coccinellidae	*Coccinella septempunctata* L.	Hodek and Cerkasov (1960), Hodek (1962)
	Semiadalia undecimnotata Schneid.	Hodek and Cerkasov (1958)
Curculionidae	*Anthonomus grandis* Boheman	Earle and Newsom (1964)
	Sitona cylindricollis Fah.	Hans (1961)
	Hypera postica (Gyll.)	Guerra and Bishop (1962), Huggans and Blickenstaff (1964)
	Ceuthorhynchus assimilis (Pay.)	Ankersmit (1964)
	Ceuthorhynchus pleurostigma	Ankersmit (1964)
HOMOPTERA		
Aphididae	*Drepanosiphum platanoides*	Dixon (1963)
Psyllidae	*Psylla pyri* L.	Bonnemaison and Missonier (1955)
	Psylla peregrina Foes.	Missonier (1956)
Delphacidae	*Stenocranus minutus*	Müller (1958, 1960a)
HEMIPTERA		
Miridae	*Lygus hesperus* Knight	Beards and Strong (1966), Leigh (1966)
ORTHOPTERA		
Tetrigidae	*Acrydium arenosum*	Sabrosky *et al.* (1933)
Acrididae	*Nomadacris septemfasciata* Serv.	Norris (1958, 1959)
	Anacridium aegyptium L.	Norris (1958)

202

TABLE XVII (*Continued*)

Order and family	Genus and species	References
TRICHOPTERA		
Limnephilidae	*Limnephilus* spp.	Novak and Sehnal (1963)
ACARINA		
Tetranychidae	*Tetranychus urticae* Koch	Bondarenko and Hai-Yuan (1958), Nuber (1961)
Ixodidae	*Dermacentor marginatus*	Belozerov (1963)

lower than in comparable nondiapause forms, although the suppression of respiratory metabolism is by no means as extreme as in pupal diapause (Lees, 1955, 1956; Hodek and Cerkasov, 1963; Davey, 1956; Belozerov, 1966; Cunningham and Tombes, 1966). The diapausing insects typically show a relatively low water content and an increased fat content. In many cases the fat bodies are hypertrophied, and the deposition of fat body reserves is quite extensive (de Wilde, 1961; Lees, 1956; Hodek and Cerkasov, 1962, 1963; Harwood and Halfhill, 1964; Takahashi and Harwood, 1964; Tombes, 1964b, 1966; Harwood and Takata, 1965). The glycogen content of the fat bodies may also be relatively high during diapause. Some of these reserves may be metabolized during diapause, because there is no intake of food. At the termination of the diapause state and the resumption of gametogenesis and egg production, reserves of glycogen and lipids are usually mobilized and rapidly utilized. Takahashi and Harwood (1964) found that adult mosquitoes (*Culex tarsalis*) displayed rhythmic changes in glycogen levels. These rhythms appeared to be of a circadian type, with glycogen depletion occurring during the scotophase and glycogen accumulation taking place during the late scotophase and the photophase.

Comparisons have been made of the fatty acid composition of diapause and nondiapause adult insects. Adult forms of the alfalfa weevil, *Hypera postica*, were found to contain seven different fatty acids: myristic, palmitic, palmitoleic, stearic, oleic, linoleic, and linolenic. With the onset of diapause, there was a decline in the concentrations of oleic acid and the saturated fatty acids and an increase in the relative concentrations of the polyunsaturated fatty acids (Tombes, 1966). Females of *C. tarsalis* that had been reared under a short-day photoperiod were found to have a lipid content containing 62% unsaturated fatty acids; whereas long-day forms showed unsaturated fatty acids to the extent of only

52% of the total extractable lipids (Harwood and Takata, 1965). The fatty acids found in boll weevil adults were shown to depend mainly on the insects' diet, but diapausing individuals tended to have a slightly higher concentration of oleic acid than did nondiapausing weevils. During postdiapause reproductive activity, the beetle's content of mono-unsaturated fatty acids tended to decline, but the levels of 18-carbon polyunsaturated fatty acids increased (Lambremont *et al.*, 1964).

The state of the insect's gonadal development during diapause has been investigated in several species. Male development is usually far more advanced and is less affected by diapause than is the case for the female. Male insects are usually near sexual maturity at the time of emergence, and may be sexually active prior to the onset of reproductive diapause. Diapause in the male is usually less intense, and less well defined than in the female. Spermatogenesis does not occur during diapause, but the male system frequently contains viable sperm cells during diapause (Hodek and Cerkasov, 1958; Brazzel and Newsom, 1959; Hodek, 1962). For these reasons, most investigations of adult diapause have been concentrated on the female system. The ensuing discussion pertains only to the reproductive diapause of the female insect.

The prediapause reproductive system of the newly emerged insect is usually in an early stage of development. Ovarioles are small and narrow, and the few oocytes that have formed have not yet entered the active phases of vitellogenesis. In many beetles, flies, and mosquitoes, the ovarioles remain relatively undeveloped until the insect has done some feeding; where diapause occurs, the ovarioles remain undeveloped during the diapause period, and active oogenesis and vitellogenesis are postdiapause phenomena. Some exceptions occur, however, suggesting that diapause may be less intense in some species than in others. For example, Joly (1945) observed that a limited amount of vitellogenesis occurred during the diapause of some aquatic beetles (*Dytiscus marginalis*) so that some oocytes were nearly mature at the termination of diapause. An interesting situation has been reported in the diamond-back moth, *Plutella maculipennis*, where photoperiod exerts an influence on reproduction but does not induce a state of diapause. Harcourt and Cass (1966) observed that early summer generations of these moths laid more eggs per moth than did the late summer generations. When they reared the larvae under controlled conditions, they found that larvae reared under long-day conditions (16L:8D) gave rise to moths

204

that laid an average of 74 eggs. Moths from short-day reared (12L:12D) larvae produced only one half as many eggs (37/moth). These investigators suggested that the effect of the short-day was to induce an incipient diapause.

Development of the female reproductive system and the deposition of yolk in the oocytes is under endocrine control. A gonadotropic hormone from the corpora allata plays a major role in reproductive physiology, and this hormone is apparently identical to JH (Wigglesworth, 1964). The role of the corpus allatum in the induction and termination of diapause has been investigated by several workers. The early work of Joly (1945) showed that reproductive diapause in *D. marginalis* involved a suppression of corpus allatum function; the implantation of active corpora allata would stimulate oocyte development in diapausing beetles. Gonadotropic activity of the corpora allata has been shown to be dependent upon factors originating in the brain and transmitted via the corpora cardiaca, however. Grison (1949) observed that the implantation of brains from nondiapausing Colorado potato beetles would stimulate oocyte development in diapausing beetles of the same species, suggesting a brain-produced factor acting as a stimulant for hormone production by the corpora allata. These results were confirmed by de Wilde and co-workers (1965), by the finding that diathermic destruction of the medial neurosecretory cells of nondiapausing potato beetles induced a diapause state. Research on another chrysomelid beetle (*Galeruca tanaceti*) has also demonstrated the dependence of the corpus allatum on neurosecretory functions of the brain (Siew, 1965a,b,c).

J. de Wilde and his co-workers have published an extensive series of studies on the role of the corpora allata in diapause of the adult Colorado potato beetle (de Wilde and de Boer, 1961; de Wilde, 1960, 1962b, 1963, 1965). Extirpation of the corpora allata from nondiapause beetles was found to induce the behavioral, metabolic, and gonadal effects characteristic of the diapause state. The implantation of active corpora into such operated insects caused the termination of the diapause state. Implantation of from 1 to 12 pairs of corpora allata into naturally diapausing beetles did not terminate the diapause condition, however, suggesting that diapause was naturally induced and maintained by factors other than corpora allata function alone. No evidence was obtained that suggested the presence of a "diapause hormone" as postulated by Schroder (1957). De Wilde has interpreted these results as indicating that diapause was caused by a cessation of corpus allatum function, but implanted corpora were unable to restore gonadal development because the implanted organs had been surgically separated from the required neurosecretory supporting system. The effect of photoperiod is thought to be primarily on the brain and neurosecretory system of the beetle, and via this system the photoperiod exerts a controlling influence on the secretion of gonadotropic hormone by the corpora allata. This general hypothesis was supported by the experimental results of Bowers and Blickenstaff (1966) in a study of diapause in the alfalfa weevil. Topical applications of a synthetic corpus allatum hormone (10,11-epoxyfarnesenic acid methyl ester) had the effect of terminating diapause. The synthetic hormone did not activate the beetles corpora allata, however, leading these investigators to postulate that the corpora allata are inhibited during diapause.

Diapause Determination

Reproductive diapause may be of either the estival or hibernal type. In species showing estivation, the adults emerge during the late spring, estivate through the summer, and deposit their eggs in the late summer and autumn. The alfalfa weevil, *Hypera postica,* is an example of this type (Guerra and Bishop, 1962; Tombes, 1964a). In the case of hibernal, or winter, diapause, the adult forms usually emerge in the late summer and autumn, enter diapause, and reproduce during the following spring. Diapause in the Colorado potato beetle is of the hibernal type, and is induced by short-day photoperiods to which the newly emerged adult beetles are exposed, although the photoperiods experienced by the larval stages may have a modifying effect (de Wilde *et al.,* 1959). Diapause may also be induced in older potato beetles that have already actively reproduced, so that a small percentage of the population may diapause and overwinter a second time (Ushatinskaya, 1961). Adult diapause in the cotton boll weevil, *Anthonomus grandis,* was found to be determined by short-day photoperiods experienced by the larval stages, with the adult form being insensitive to daylength (Earle and Newsom, 1964). Similarly, diapause of the imagoes of some mosquitoes was found to be determined by photoperiods to which the larval stages had been exposed (Vinogradova, 1960; McCrary and Jenner, 1965). On the other hand, only the young adults of the coccinellid beetle *Coccinella septempunctata* were found to be responsive to photoperiod, and the determination of adult diapause was quite unaffected by photoperiods occurring during larval development (Hodek and Cerkasov, 1961a,b).

206

A complex photoperiodic response was demonstrated in the tropical locust, *Nomadacris septemfasciata*. In its normal environment near the equator, the yearly daylength cycle is from 11 hours 40 minutes to 12 hours 30 minutes. Even within this very narrow range, daylength was found to control the insect's reproductive diapause, according to the studies of Norris (1958, 1959, 1962, 1965). The critical daylength was found to be about 12 hours, but the intensity of diapause was dependent upon the photoperiod under which the nymphs were reared; so that the adult photoperiodic responses were modified in accord with the nymphal experience. If the nymphs were reared under a 12-hour daylength, adult diapause was of relatively short duration. But if the nymphs were reared under a 13-hour daylength, the adult diapause induced by a subsequent 12-hour daylength was found to be of several months duration.

Reproductive diapause in the homopteron *Stenocranus minutus* was also found to be rather complex in terms of the photoperiodic effects (Müller, 1958, 1960a). When this insect was reared under long-day photoperiods, a reproductive diapause occurred in the adult stage. This diapause could be terminated by exposing the insects to short-day conditions for about 4 weeks. However, if the nymphs were reared under short-day conditions, an adult diapause was also manifested. In this case the diapause could be terminated by exposing the insects to several weeks of long daylengths followed by a return to short-day photoperiods. Although under photoperiodic control, the diapause was induced by either short- or long-day conditions; but its termination required an alternation of daylengths.

9 □ Photoperiodism and Ecological Adaptation

Photoperiodism plays an important role in the complex ecological adaptations of insects. As an environmental factor, photoperiod differs from physical forces such as temperature, moisture, radiation, air currents, and pressure, and also from chemical factors as represented by nutritious and deleterious substances that are found in the environment. These several physical and chemical factors may pose either threats or opportunities for the continued survival of a species, by their direct action on the biological system. Photoperiod, however, exerts no directly beneficial or harmful effects on the organism, but provides an adaptive opportunity as a source of temporal information. Its dawn and dusk signals, and the time interval between them, are available for utilization as informational inputs from the environment. The insect's adaptations to photoperiod have evolved as ordered responses to these stimuli as presaging the occurrence of environmental conditions to which the insect must display different adaptive ordered responses if it is to survive. Photoperiodic determination of polymorphic forms of aphids, for example, represents an important adaptive response. Its ecological significance, however, lies in the resulting phenological synchrony between the biology of the aphid, the biology of the aphid's host plants, and the seasonal climatic cycle of the environment, rather than in any direct physical effects that daylight and darkness might be postulated to have exerted on the aphid itself.

Photoperiodic adaptations involve the reception of light-on and light-off stimuli as an input of bits of environmental information. These token stimuli influence the internal temporal organization of the insect by virtue of their phase-setting effects on physiological rhythms. Genetically determined behavioral and developmental alternatives are probably implemented in accord with the temporal organization of the living system. Thus, the insect's responses to photoperiod may become an integral part of from one to several of the organism's ecological adaptations.

Photoperiodic responses that subserve important ecological adaptations may be manifested in terms of immediate daily responses or as long-term seasonal effects. The behavioral aspects of photoperiodism belong in the former category, and include photoperiodic control of locomotor and flight patterns, eclosion and swarming rhythms, and feeding and ovipositional rhythms. Seasonal effects include the photoperiodic control of polymorphism, diapause, and synchrony of insect with environmental phenology.

Many insect species have wide geographical distributions, in which broad ranges of environmental conditions are to be found. The ecological adaptations required for the survival and perpetuation of the species will differ in different parts of the geographical distribution. It is not surprising, therefore, that within a single species, geographical populations have evolved. These geographical populations may differ greatly in their specific ecological adaptations, and consequently in their photoperiodism. These several aspects of the subject will be discussed in subsequent sections of this chapter.

PHOTOPERIODISM AND WATER CONSERVATION

Terrestrial animals have evolved complex physiological mechanisms for the conservation of body water. Because the transpiration of water is essentially a surface phenomenon, small animals are placed at a disadvantage by virtue of their relatively high surface:volume ratios. The problem of water conservation becomes of acute biological importance among insects and other small terrestrial arthropods. Insects have solved this problem through the evolution of a number of morphological, physiological, and behavioral adaptations. These adaptations include a very complex relatively impermeable cuticular structure, precise control mechanisms governing gaseous exchange through the spiracles and tracheal system, and a number of tactical behavioral responses to light, temperature, and moisture. Photoperiodism has been shown to play a role in some of these adaptations.

The diel photoperiod is accompanied by cyclic temperature and humidity changes. As the light intensity declines during sunset and evening twilight, air temperature also tends to fall and the relative humidity rises. During morning twilight and dawn, temperatures tend to be at the daily minimum and relative humidity at the maximum. Transpiration rates tend to increase with rising temperatures but to vary inversely with relative humidity (or directly with saturation deficiency). Photoperiod and changes in light intensity may be utilized as token stimuli associated with behavioral adaptations for the minimizing of water loss.

This point is well illustrated by the results of studies of the ecological adaptations and behavioral patterns of small isopod crustaceans known as wood lice. Cloudsley-Thompson (1952) found that these little animals had a daily activity rhythm that was regulated by photoperiod. They moved about actively during the night, at which time the temperatures were relatively low and the humidity was relatively high. The wood lice tended to respond negatively to light and positively to moisture, so that during daylight hours they remained secluded in relatively dark, damp sites. When the wood lice were in the daytime phase of the activity rhythm, they displayed a strongly negative phototaxis and a strongly positive humidity response. During the nighttime phase of the activity rhythm, the response to humidity was less well defined, but they still displayed a negative response to light. Under conditions of very low relative humidity, however, a weakly positive phototactic response was observed, but after the wood lice had been held in the dark for several hours, the light response was always negative. These several behavioral characteristics can be correlated quite nicely with the animal's nocturnal habits and its adaptations for water conservation (Cloudsley-Thompson, 1960a). Because the humidity response is weaker during the night phase of activity, the wood lice can move about in dry places that they would never frequent during the day. The increased photonegative response after dark exposure tends to insure that the wood lice will go into hiding immediately upon the advent of daylight. If their daytime habitat should dry up, however, the tendency toward positive phototaxis permits the wood lice to wander about in the daylight until another dark damp hiding place is encountered. Although the activity rhythm has been shown to be regulated by photoperiod rather than by temperature and humidity cycles, the behavioral responses that are entrained to the photoperiodic response play an important role in the control of transpiration in the wood louse.

The role of photoperiodism in body water conservation has been partially elucidated by the studies of Pittendrigh (1958a) on the ecological adaptations of two closely related species of *Drosophila*. Both *D. pseudo-obscura* and *D. persimilis* are found in forest environments, but *D. persimilis* is an upland form that occupies somewhat cooler and wetter habitats than does *D. pseudoobscura*. Water conservation is of great importance to both species, of course, but *D. pseudoobscura* lives under greater stress than does *D. persimilis* in regard to the dangers of excessive transpiration. Measurements of transpiration rates showed *D. persimilis* to lose water more readily than does *D. pseudoobscura*. Two important differences in behavioral responses were also demonstrated. Under experimental choice-test conditions, adults of both species responded positively to humidity gradients; *D. pseudoobscura* reacted more sharply than did *D. persimilis*, however, indicating a greater sensitivity and more efficient response to moisture. The fly from the drier environment, *D. pseudoobscura*, was found to display a negative phototaxis; whereas *D. persimilis* showed a weakly positive phototactic reaction.

The two *Drosophila* species were found to display a significant difference in their photoperiodic reactions. As was discussed in Chapter 3, *Drosophila* populations show a photoperiodically controlled circadian rhythm of adult emergence. Adult emergence tends to occur almost exclusively at dawn and during a few hours following dawn. This rhythmic phenomenon has been shown to be, at least in part, an adaptation for the conservation of body moisture. The newly emerged adult fly is quite susceptible to desiccation; its integument is neither fully "waterproofed" nor sclerotized upon emergence from the pupa. If partial desiccation should occur, the fly would be unable to expand its wings properly. The tendency to emerge at about dawn is an adaptation to minimize the dangers attending this crucial developmental event. Environmental temperatures tend to be low and relative humidity high at this time of the day. The adult emergence rhythm of *Drosophila pseudoobscura* was found to show an emergence peak very shortly after dawn, taking full advantage of the temperature and humidity conditions prevailing. However, the *D. persimilis* emergence rhythm showed a later peak, with adult emergence occurring mainly at about 4 hours after dawn. Because of its drier natural environment, *D. pseudoobscura* evolved an emergence rhythm more closely entrained to the light-on photoperiodic stimulus than was necessary for *D. persimilis*.

Drosophila adults and many other insects display daily activity rhythms that are regulated by photoperiod, and in which the principal times of locomotor activity occur during periods of low light intensity — dawn and dusk. Such crepuscular activity patterns may frequently be associated with the insect's ecological adaptations, particularly in respect to the conservation of water. This point may be illustrated by examples of flight and biting activity of a number of forest-inhabiting mosquito species (Pittendrigh, 1958a; Haddow, 1964). Although the daily rhythm of activity appears to be controlled by photoperiod, actual flight and feeding occurs only within a relatively narrow range of light intensities. The vertical distribution of the mosquitoes in a forest canopy is apparently determined by light intensity and relative humidity. The insects tend to confine their activities to a zone of optimum light and humidity. The position of the optimal zone will be different at different times of the day. Mosquito flight and feeding activity tends to move upward toward sunset, and downward after dawn, as the optimum zone moves along the vertical profile of the canopy.

Estival diapause is a physiological and developmental adaptation for increasing the probability of survival during periods of high temperatures and comparative dryness. Although its ecological significance includes its role in adaptations pertaining to seasonal development, phenology, and geographical distribution, diapause may also be viewed as playing a significant part in the insect's adaptations for the conservation of water. The diapausing terrestrial insect, whether egg, larva, pupa, or adult, is almost invariably highly resistant to desiccation. A highly developed impervious cuticle (or chorion) and a greatly suppressed metabolic rate are the principal mechanisms underlying the efficient husbanding of body moisture by the organism. By virtue of a photoperiodically induced state of diapause, many insect species are enabled to survive seasons of heat and dryness to which nondiapause forms of the same species would quickly succumb.

PHOTOPERIODISM AND REPRODUCTION

The perpetuation of a population of any given insect species requires that male and female members of the population come into contact with each other for the purpose of mating and reproduction. This obvious biological requirement has to be met through the behavioral patterns and attending physiological states of the individual members of the population. A high degree of synchrony between adult males and females in respect to seasonal development, adult emergence, locomotor behavior, and sexual responsiveness — including the production of and response to sex pheromones — would appear to be necessary. The propinquity of individuals needed for efficient reproduction could not be

213

accomplished on the basis of randomly distributed development and behavior, except perhaps in populations of extremely high density.

Photoperiodism may frequently be involved in the adaptations promoting mating and reproduction. Photoperiodically regulated rhythms of locomotor activity tend to insure that large numbers of the population will be moving about simultaneously and displaying similar tactic reactions to light, moisture, and other environmental factors. Such behavior certainly will increase the probability of contact between the sexes. Probability of contact is further enhanced by photoperiodic synchrony of flight or walking activity with the production of sex pheromones by one sex and responsiveness to the pheromones by the other sex. Daily rhythms of pheromone production and response have been demonstrated in the cabbage looper, *Trichoplusia ni* (Shorey, 1966), and have been at least implicated in several other species (see Chapter 2, p. 35).

Mosquitoes, midges, and other nematocerous flies may display swarming behavior (discussed in Chapter 3), which is controlled by underlying circadian rhythms but expressed in response to light intensity. In the case of mosquitoes, the swarms are made up of only males, and are not mating flights. Mating may be associated with the swarming, however, in that females may fly into the swarm and then leave the swarm with a male. Swarming in many species of Chironomidae is associated with adult emergence and mating. Whether mating occurs in the swarm or outside of it, swarming is a rhythmic activity that is of significance as an adaptation that promotes mating and reproduction.

The emergence, swarming, mating, and oviposition of tidal zone marine midges, such as *Clunio marinus*, is controlled by photoperiod, and has particular significance from an ecological standpoint (Neumann, 1962, 1966). The role of photoperiod in these rhythmic behavioral patterns was discussed in Chapter 3. The reproductive life of the females of *C. marinus* is extremely short. Emergence, mating, and egg deposition all occur within a 2-hour period that must coincide with low tide. The midges deposit their eggs in clumps of seaweed that are exposed only during times of maximum low tide. The synchrony of emergence and reproduction with the 15-day tidal cycle appears to involve adaptations to both photoperiod and the lunar cycle.

PHOTOPERIOD AND THE ACQUISITION OF FOOD

Quite apart from long-term effects associated with phenology and seasonal development, the day-to-day feeding activities of insects may

214

be strongly influenced by photoperiod. Thus, despite the physiological advantages of a nocturnal or crepuscular way of life from the standpoint of water conservation, many insects are diurnal because of their food habits. Whether phytophagous or predatory, the insect may be obliged to adapt its food-getting activities to coordinate with the biological periodism of its food source. The foraging flights of honeybees are known to be a daily rhythmic activity, and are coordinated with the times of day when blossoms are open and nectar is available. Although the role of photoperiod in bee behavior has not been fully elucidated, a strong circadian component is detectable (Lindauer, 1960, 1963). The daily flight and feeding patterns of strong flying diurnal insects that rely on visual acuity to find their food also display a circadian component that coordinates their activities; these include insects such as sphingids, asilids, odonatans, and many others. The relationships between daily activity and food habits appear to be relatively simple and obvious, but there has been little experimental work done on this phase of periodism.

PHOTOPERIODISM AND SEASONAL DEVELOPMENT

Of the several biologically important aspects of insect photoperiodism, phenology and seasonal development have been investigated the most intensively. Photoperiod plays a central role in ecological adaptations related to the beginning of insect growth and activity in the spring, form determination, host plant sequences, the determination of both estival and hibernal diapause, voltinism (the number of generations per year), and winter survival. The 1961 monograph of A. S. Danilevskii, "Photoperiodism and Seasonal Development of Insects," was devoted almost exclusively to this one aspect of photoperiodism. Photoperiodic control of diapause is probably the most important aspect of the seasonal development phenomena.

Seasonal cycles of daylength are different at different latitudes. In areas of high latitude, daylength changes are relatively extreme, with late spring and summer daylengths being very long (see Chapter 1, Table I). Temperatures during the growing season are relatively low, and the growing season itself is comparatively short. Areas of lower latitudes, on the other hand, show relatively shorter days during the relatively longer and warmer growing season. These seasonal differences between areas of different latitudes suggest that insect populations of high latitudes must adapt to quite different conditions than those con-

215

fronting insect populations inhabiting low latitude environments. One might expect, therefore, that the northern populations of a widely distributed insect species might differ from southern populations in regard to the ecological adaptations related to daylength and temperature. Such geographical population differences within species have been demonstrated in a large number of instances (Table XVIII). Population differences have been observed in many aspects of photoperiodism, as will be apparent in several of the subsequent sections of this chapter.

In addition to the genetic mechanisms that must underlie any adaptive process within a biological population, there are at least five characteristics of an insect population that are of great importance to its adaptations to seasonal changes. These characteristics are (1) the critical daylength for diapause (or form) determination; (2) the growth stage at which diapause (or form) is determined; (3) the growth stage at which the response is manifested; (4) the effect of temperature on the critical daylength; and (5) the temperature characteristics of the insect's growth (developmental temperature threshold and required day-degree accumulation).

The complexity of different combinations of the above characteristics precludes any sweeping generalization concerning photoperiodism and seasonal development. Different insect species, inhabiting the same geographical area and subjected to the same climatic conditions, may show quite different photoperiodic adaptations because of differences in these several response characteristics. This point is illustrated by the following considerations of specific examples that have been worked out in good detail. The ecological adaptations related to photoperiodism and seasonal development have been elucidated for several European and Asian species. A great deal of such research needs to be carried out on North American forms, particularly those of economic importance.

TABLE XVIII

Insect Species in Which Geographical
Populations Have Been Shown to Differ in Photoperiodism

Order and family	Genus and species	References
LEPIDOPTERA		
Noctuidae	*Mamestra brassicae* (L.)	Masaki (1956), Masaki and Sakai (1956)
	Acronycta rumicis L.	Danilevskii (1961)

TABLE XVIII (*Continued*)

Order and family	Genus and species	References
	Acronycta leporina L.	Danilevskii (1961)
	Acronycta megacephala (Fabr.)	Danilevskii (1961)
	Chloridea obsoleta Fabr.	Danilevskii (1961)
	Demas coryli L.	Danilevskii (1961)
Bombycidae	*Bombyx mori* L.	Morohoshi (1957)
Phycitidae	*Plodia interpunctella* (Hübner)	Tzanakakis (1959)
Pyraustidae	*Ostrinia nubilalis* (Hübner)	Beck and Apple (1961)
Lymantridae	*Dasychira pudibunda* L.	Geyspitz and Zarankina (1963)
	Stilpnotia salicis (L.)	Danilevskii (1961)
Crambidae	*Chilo suppressalis* (Walker)	Inouye and Kamano (1957)
Arctiidae	*Spilosoma menthastri* Esp.	Danilevskii (1961)
	Hylophila prasinama L.	Danilevskii (1961)
Geometridae	*Abraxas miranda* Butler	Masaki (1959)
Lasiocampidae	*Dendrolimus pini* L.	Danilevskii (1961)
Sphingidae	*Smerinthus populi* L.	Danilevskii (1961)
Tortricidae	*Pandemis ribeana* Hübner	Danilevskii (1961)
	Capua reticulana Hübner	Danilevskii (1961)
Pieridae	*Pieris napi* L.	Lees (1955)
	Pieris rapae (L.)	Danilevskii (1961)
	Pieris brassicae L.	Danilevskii (1961)
COLEOPTERA		
Curculionidae	*Ceuthorhynchus pleurostigma* Marsh	Ankersmit (1964, 1965)
DIPTERA		
Culicidae	*Anopheles freeborni* Aitken	Depner and Harwood (1966)
	Anopheles maculipennis	Vinogradova (1960)
Chironomidae	*Clunio marinus* Hal.	Neumann (1962, 1966)
HYMENOPTERA		
Braconidae	*Apanteles glomeratus* L.	Danilevskii (1961)
Diprionidae	*Neodiprion sertifer* (Geoff.)	Wallace and Sullivan (1966)
HEMIPTERA		
Miridae	*Adelphocoris linoleatus* (Goeze)	Ewen (1966)
HOMOPTERA		
Cicadellidae	*Nephotettix bipunctatus cincticeps*	Masaki (1961)
Aphididae	*Brevicoryne brassicae* (L.)	Cognetti and Pagliai (1963)
ACARINA		
Tetranychidae	*Tetranychus urticae* Koch	Bondarenko and Hai-Yuan (1958)
	Tetranychus telarius (L.)	Bondarenko (1950)
	Metatetranychus ulmi	Danilevskii (1961)

217

Short-Day and Long-Day Adaptations

As was pointed out in an earlier discussion (Chapter 7), insects of some species develop without diapause under long-day conditions, but experience a diapause if the daylengths are short. Because growth is continuous under long-day conditions, such species are known as "long-day" forms. Other species show an opposite reaction to photoperiod, and diapause is induced by long-day but not by short-day photoperiods; such species are "short-day" forms. These two types of photoperiodic adaptations should not be viewed as indicating the existence of radically different physiological mechanisms controlling growth and diapause. They are, instead, differences related to species characteristics in regard to critical daylength, growth stage at which diapause is determined, and growth stage at which diapause is manifested (characteristics 1, 2, and 3, above).

The commercial silkworm, *Bombyx mori*, is a so-called "short-day" species. Under field conditions, this species diapauses as an egg. The eggs hatch in the early spring, at which time daylengths are still relatively short. Diapause determination of the next generation is dependent on the photoperiods experienced by the late embryonic and early larval stages of the parental generation. These are short-day photoperiods in the case of eggs that have overwintered in diapause. The adult moths of this generation emerge in the early summer and lay eggs that develop without diapause. Daylengths are long during the late embryonic and early larval development of this generation, however, and the diapause determination is made. The moths emerge in the autumn and deposit eggs that pass the winter in diapause. The over-all phenological adaptation functions to synchronize the biology of the insect with that of its host plant and with the seasonal climatic cycle. But the ecological adaptation can be seen to involve the evolution of three specific components: (1) the sensitivity of embryonic and young larval stages to photoperiods; (2) the occurrence of diapause in the early embryonic stages; and (3) the utilization of photoperiodic stimuli in the control of developmental programming, with diapause being determined in response to long daylengths. As might be expected with this type of adaptation, low environmental temperatures tend to decrease the incidence of diapause, as compared to the effects of higher temperatures.

The photoperiodic adaptations of a "short-day" insect such as *B. mori* would appear to be in sharp contrast to those of a "long-day" form that also overwinters in an embryonic diapause. The red spider mite, *Metatetranychus ulmi*, shows an embryonic diapause that is determined by photoperiods experienced by the female parent. The mite, however, is a "long-day" species, and diapause is induced in response to relatively short daylengths (Lees, 1950, 1953a,b). Daylengths experienced during the deutonymphal stage and the early part of adult life determine whether or not the eggs produced will be of the diapausing type. The photoperiodic adaptations result in a synchronizing of the biology of the mite with that of its host and the seasonal cycle of climate. The spring-time mite population reaches maturity in the late spring, at which time the daylengths are very long, and the eggs laid are of the nondiapause type. Mites that reach the deutonymphal and early adult stage in the late summer and autumn are exposed to short days, and their eggs are determined for diapause. In terms of specific adaptive reactions, the mite differs from the silkworm in two ways. First, the growth stage that is sensitive to photoperiod occurs late in development, rather than early. Second, the determination of diapause is effected by short-day rather than long-day photoperiods. Even though the specific adaptations are quite different in the two arthropods, in each case the specific components operate as a unified system contributing to the phenological adaptations of the species.

The so-called "long-day" type of response, in which diapause is not induced if the sensitive stages experience only long-day photoperiods, has at least one advantage over the "short-day" type. Long-day forms have the potential of producing an indefinite number of generations during a growing season. The short-day forms, on the other hand, are limited to two generations per year, because the long summer days have the effect of committing the next generation to a state of diapause.

Photoperiodic determination of diapause may involve a third type of photoperiodic response, which was called the "short-day"–"long-day" response type in a previous chapter (see Fig. 40, type III). With insects showing this pattern of response, diapause is not induced by either the very long or the very short daylengths, but only by daylengths of intermediate length. The European corn borer, *Ostrinia nubilalis*, is an example of this type, and daylengths shorter than 8 hours or longer than 16 hours induced larval development without diapause. Daylengths longer than 8 hours but shorter than 16 hours induced very high incidences of diapause (Beck, 1962a). The ecological significance of this type of response pattern is not clear. The corn borer under field conditions could experience days with less than 8 hours of photophase only during the middle of the winter, at which time the insects would already be in diapause and environmental temperatures would tend to prohibit growth. Insects showing this type of photoperiodic response are usually classed as "long-day" forms, and the laboratory-produced effects of extremely short daylengths are dismissed as being of no ecological significance.

The converse of the above type of response is that which was called the "long-day–short-day" response (Fig. 40, type IV). In this response pattern, the insects are diapause determined by exposure to either short or very long daylengths, and diapause is averted only by a narrow range of relatively long days. This type of response has been reported in but very few insects, all of which were found in far northern latitudes. The ecological significance of the diapause-determinative power of the extremely long photophases is not at all clear, and these insects are also generally considered to be "long-day" forms.

An alternation of daylengths has been found to play a part in the determination of diapause in some species. As was discussed in the previous chapter, such effects have been shown to influence the termination of adult diapause in *Stenocranus minutus* (Müller, 1958, 1960a,b) and *Nomadacris septemfasciata* (Norris, 1965), and the induction of pupal diapause in *Heliothis zea* (Wellso and Adkisson, 1966). This type of response pattern may also play a part in the alternation of generations in aphids, particularly as related to the "interval timer" effects related to ovipara production (Lees, 1966). The requirement for an alternation of daylengths probably plays a part in the seasonal biology of the species. The alternation of daylengths would be from short days to long days during the early part of the growing season. The seasonal progression during the late summer and autumn would be in the opposite direction, and long days would precede short days. The ability of the insects to respond differentially to these sequences would provide a basis for distinguishing vernal from autumnal seasonal changes in daylength.

Estival and Hibernal Diapauses

Summer season, or estival, diapause involves the same set of five response characteristics as enumerated above. Obviously the specific adaptations must differ from those leading to winter diapause. Estival diapause involving photoperiodic responses has been shown in adults of a few species of beetles and in the pupae of some lepidopterous forms. Estivation is to be observed in many insect forms, but the role of photoperiod has been demonstrated in but a few.

The general features of estival diapause may be illustrated by the observations of Ankersmit (1964, 1965) on the photoperiodism and

220

seasonal development of the cabbage gall weevil, *Ceutorhynchus pleuro-stigma*. This weevil feeds on a number of cruciferous plants. The eggs are deposited in the root collar region of the plant, and the larvae live in galls; the adult weevils are leaf feeders. There are two races of the insect in Western Europe; both races are present in the Netherlands, where they were studied by Ankersmit. The two races are of interest because they differ in their photoperiodism, diapause characteristics, phenology, and host plant relationships. One race is known as the *spring race*, because eggs are deposited and the larvae become established on the host plants during the spring. The adult weevils of the spring race emerge during the late summer (August). They do not produce eggs at this time, but they hide in the soil in a state of hibernal diapause. These diapausing adults overwinter, and become reproductive in the spring (May). Ankersmit could detect no effects of photoperiod on the behavior or ovarian development of the young adults of the spring race. He concluded that adult diapause was obligatory and was not determined by the photoperiods to which the adults were exposed. However, he did not investigate the effects of photoperiod on the larval stages.

The second race of the cabbage gall weevil is known as the *autumn race*. Overwintering is accomplished in the form of larvae, presumably in diapause. These larvae complete their development in the spring, and the adult weevils emerge in the early summer (June). The weevils then go into an estivation type of diapause until late summer or early autumn (late August, early September). The maturation of eggs is a postdiapause event, and eggs are deposited in September. In this race, photoperiod plays an important part in the imaginal diapause. The photoperiod-sensitive stage is the newly emerged adult weevil, and the photoperiods experienced during larval development were found to be without effect on the adult. If the young beetles were exposed to long-day photoperiods and relatively high temperatures, they went into diapause. The critical daylength was not sharply definable, but was apparently between 14 and 16 hours. Temperatures above 21°C tended to promote the determination of the estival diapause. Diapause termination was found to be enhanced by daylengths shorter than the critical value and by environmental temperatures between 17° and 21°C.

The differences between the spring and autumn races of the cabbage gall weevil are largely attributable to their different photoperiodic responses. These differences in photoperiodism have some important consequences in regard to other aspects of the insect's seasonal biology, however. Gall formation and larval growth tend to be far more successful on young rapidly growing plants than on older plants. Because the two races reproduce at distinctly different times of the year, their host plant relationships must also necessarily differ. In the northern areas of the Netherlands, both races are present, and the principal host plant is rutabaga (swedes); cabbage is rarely infested. In areas farther to the south (Wageningen), the autumn race is found on cabbage and winter-rape, because these plants are in a suitable vegetative stage of growth during the early autumn. The spring race in this area is found to infest a cruciferous weed, *Sinapis arvensis*, and is only rarely encountered on other hosts. *Sinapis arvensis* is in a suitably juvenile stage of growth during the spring at the time that the weevils deposit their eggs, and suitable cabbage is not available at that time. In other parts of the Netherlands, the seasonal phenology of host plants is such that the spring race infests cabbage as the preferred host, and *S. arvensis* is seldom attacked.

The autumn and spring races of the cabbage gall weevil are not separate species; they are indistinguishable morphologically, and fertile hybrids have been produced under laboratory conditions. The two races are also sympatric, but because of their photoperiodic adaptations, they are reproductively isolated from each other. The spring race mates and reproduces in the spring, and the autumn race reaches the reproductive stage many months later. Their reproductive isolation is a phenological phenomenon. The differences in the photoperiodism of the two races have resulted in differences in phenology and host plant specificity, and have produced a separation of the species gene pool. The latter effect may easily be involved in the evolutionary process of speciation.

Facultative diapause of the estival and hibernal types may occur within a species without involving a division of the species into distinct races. An example is the cabbage moth, *Mamestra* (=*Barathra*) *brassicae*, a noctuid with a facultative pupal diapause (Masaki, 1956, 1957a,b; Masaki and Sakai, 1965). This insect overwinters in a pupal diapause that was induced by short-day photoperiods. Diapause has been shown to be determined in the larval stages, with the critical daylength being between 13 and 14 hours, depending on the temperature and also on the geographical population under observation. Nondiapausing pupae of the spring generation were found to require from 13 to 18 days for adult development and emergence. Using 8°C as the developmental threshold, nondiapausing pupae were found to require from 200 to 350 day-degrees of temperature accumulation for adult moth emergence. However, Masaki and co-workers observed that when newly pupated individuals were exposed to daylengths of 16 hours or more

222

with concurrent high temperatures (ca. 30°C), many of them required from 50 to 100 days for adult emergence. In these cases the required temperature accumulations were from 900 to 1200 day-degrees. Such a delayed pupal development was interpreted as constituting an estival diapause.

Estivation of the cabbage moth pupae was found to be determined by the photoperiod and temperature conditions experienced during the first few days after pupation. The suppression of development was not the result of heat injury caused by the relatively high temperatures. If newly formed pupae were exposed to low temperatures (15°–20°C) for the first few days, subsequent 30°C temperatures did not induce the estival diapause. The duration of the diapause was shortened by environmental temperatures between 15° and 20°C. Such incubation temperatures had the effect of reducing both the duration of the diapause and the day-degree accumulation required for the completion of development. Pupae in winter diapause, on the other hand, were unaffected by exposure to such gentle chilling; they required more drastic low temperature treatment in order to terminate the diapause state.

In respect to diapause induction, the cabbage moth appears to be both a long-day and a short-day species, although high temperature plays a major role in the determination of the estival diapause. Both estival and hibernal diapauses are important adaptations in the ecology of the species. The occurrence of estival diapause was found to be partly a phenotypic response, but genetic factors were also involved. Masaki (1961) tested different geographical populations of the cabbage moth in respect to the incidence of estivation. Using a 16-hour daylength and 25°C, he found that populations from different parts of the Japanese archipelago differed markedly in their responses (Fig. 53).

Cabbage moth populations inhabiting the northern parts of Japan (45°N) are normally subjected to a relatively cool growing season with long daylengths. Spring emergence of adults from the overwintering pupae does not occur until June. The first generation of larvae matures in late July and early August. Some of these first generation pupae go into winter diapause, and no estivation occurs. All of the pupae of the second generation are committed to diapause.

In the middle part of the archipelago (about 40°N), the spring moth emergence occurs in late May. There is a midsummer moth flight of the adults of the first generation. Some of the first generation pupae may undergo a relatively short estival diapause, and the moths from these pupae make up a small late summer flight. All pupae of the second

223

generation enter hibernal diapause. If estivation should occur under conditions of a relatively short summer season or in a cooler than average year, the progeny of the estivating individuals will not have time to reach maturity before the onset of unfavorable weather conditions. These progeny will perish, and their genes will be eliminated from the population's gene pool. The selection pressure against estivation will tend to be rather intense in northern and relatively cool areas.

Southern areas of Japan (35°N) have cabbage moth populations that show an early May spring flight of overwintered individuals. The first generation of progeny reach pupation in June, and nearly all of them enter estival diapause in response to the high temperatures and long daylengths that prevail. There is, therefore, little or no midsummer

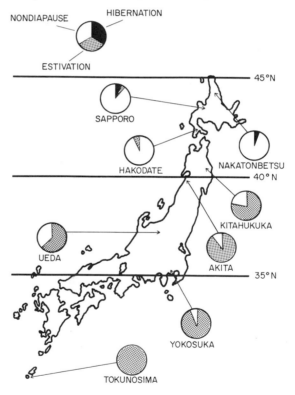

Fig. 53. Incidence of estival and hibernal diapause in different geographical populations of the cabbage moth, Mamestra brassicae, in Japan, when tested at 25°C and 16L:8D. [Adapted from Masaki (1961).]

224

moth flight. The estivating pupae complete their development and the moths emerge in late summer—late August and early September—and the progeny of these moths enter a pupal diapause of the hibernal type.

Photoperiodism in Univoltine Insects

The importance of photoperiodism in the seasonal development and ecological adaptations of univoltine species is little appreciated, and has been investigated in very few forms. It is an aspect of ecology and physiology that merits much detailed investigation, however. Univoltine insects are usually considered to have an obligatory diapause at one or another growth stage. Although the concept of "obligatory diapause" may be of dubious value, in some species diapause occurs in every individual of each generation under the natural conditions to which the insect is adapted. The seasonal biology of the insect and the time at which diapause occurs may, nevertheless, be strongly influenced by photoperiod. These effects are illustrated by the specific examples discussed below.

Dasychira pudibunda is an Asiatic tussock moth whose seasonal development was studied by Geyspitz and co-workers (Geyspitz, 1953; Geyspitz and Zarankina, 1963). The caterpillars of this species pupate in the autumn, and the winter is passed in a pupal diapause. Field observations on the insect's seasonal biology indicated that northern populations completed one generation during the relatively short, cool growing season. Southern populations were also found to have but one generation per year, despite the longer growing season and higher prevailing temperatures. Experimental rearings of the larvae disclosed some unusual adaptations. Larvae that were reared under relatively low temperatures and short-day photoperiods grew more rapidly and pupated sooner than did larvae that were reared under high temperature, long-day conditions (Table XIX). The temperature threshold for development was found to be about 8°C, and the required day-degree accumulations were found to be higher at high temperatures than at low temperatures. At 25°C and continuous illumination, the required day-degree accumulation was nearly 7 times that required by insects reared at 15°C under a 10-hour daylength. This effect was accounted for, at least in large part, by the finding that the number of larval instars was variable, depending upon both temperature and daylength. Under a short-day photoperiod and 15°C, the larval development was completed in either 5 or 6 instars; whereas under high temperature and continuous light, up to 11

TABLE XIX

Effect of Daylength and Temperature on
Larval Development of *Dasychira pudibunda* L.[a]

Rearing temperatures:	15°C	20°	25°
Continuous illumination			
Larval development (days):	91	113	121
Larval instars (no.):	5–7	7–9	9–11
Temperature accumulation (day-degrees):	638	1315	2950
Average pupal weight (mg):	664	835	726
Short-day (10L:14D)			
Larval development (days):	63	73	117
Larval instars (no.):	5–6	7–8	7–9
Temperature accumulation (day-degrees):	430	878	2883
Average pupal weight (mg):	441	816	640

[a]Based on data of Geyspitz and Zarankina (1963).

instars occurred before the larvae pupated. Measurements of growth rates displayed by the individual larval instars disclosed that instars 1 through 6 showed positive temperature coefficients, but the so-called "supernumerary" instars 7 through 11 grew more slowly at the relatively higher temperatures. The overall effect of these two adaptations to daylength and temperature (supernumerary larval instars and temperature inhibition of growth) was to prolong larval development during the middle of the summer and to synchronize pupation and diapause with the onset of the short, cool days of autumn. Different geographical populations were observed to differ somewhat in the effects of daylength and temperature on larval development.

The pine moths *Dendrolimus pini* and *Dendrolimus sibiricus* are semivoltine insects; that is, they normally require two growing seasons to complete their life cycles. They overwinter as larvae in diapause; the first winter is usually spent as young larvae (about third instar) and the second as nearly mature larvae (fifth to eighth instar). Pupation occurs following the ninth larval instar. Experimental rearings of the larvae have shown that larval diapause is determined by photoperiod. No diapause occurred when the larvae were reared under continuous illumination, but diapause occurred in response to any other photoperiodic schedule. Photoperiod was also found to influence the time (instar) of diapause occurrence; the shorter the daylength, the younger the larvae at the onset of diapause (Table XX) (Geyspitz, 1965). At 20°C, a 12-hour daylength induced diapause in *D. pini* after 36 photoperiodic cycles (days), and the larvae were all of the third instar. A 16-hour day-length required twice as many inductive cycles (73 days), and the dia-pausing larvae were in the fourth to sixth instars. The critical daylength for both species was considered to be between 16 and 17 hours, based on the observation that the diapause induction period was greatly pro-longed when the photophase was 17 hours or longer (Table XX). Larval growth rate was not influenced by photoperiod; so a long dia-pause induction time was always associated with the occurrence of diapause in the later instars.

The duration of diapause in the two pine moth species was also found to be controlled by photoperiod. Short-day induced diapause tended to be of shorter duration than did long-day induced diapause, although the duration was also temperature sensitive in both cases. The duration of the diapause tended to be inversely proportional to the rearing temperature.

Larval diapause in *Dendrolimus* may be induced more than once. For example, when larvae were reared at 12.5°C and a 12-hour photoperiod, all of them went into diapause. They remained in diapause for about 50 days in the case of *D. pini* and about 37 days in the case of *D. sibiricus*, after which diapause was terminated. The larvae then actively fed and grew for a period of from 3 to 4 weeks, after which about half of them again diapaused. The second diapause was of relatively short duration, lasting only about 3 weeks. When pine moth larvae were reared under longer daylengths and higher temperatures, the delay between the first and second larval diapause was greatly prolonged, so that the second diapause occurred in the more advanced larval instars. Not all of the larvae experienced two periods of diapause, and under suitable condi-tions of long-day photoperiod and optimal temperatures, development was most frequently completed without the second diapause.

Under the conditions of their natural environment, the pine moths usually show a 2-year life cycle. The life cycle has been observed to be

TABLE XX
Effect of Photoperiod on the Characteristics of
Larval Diapause in the Pine Moth *Dendrolimus pini* at 20°C[a]

Daylength (hr):	12	14	15	16	17	18	20	24
Diapause incidence (%):	100	100	100	100	100	100	85	0
Diapause induction (days):	36	37	44	73	177	174	180	—
Diapause instar:	3	3-4	3-5	4-6	7-8	7-8	7-9	—

[a]Based on data of Geyspitz (1953, 1965).

completed in but 1 year, but only when two exceptionally warm summers occurred consecutively. In such a case, the high summer temperatures during the first year allowed rapid larval growth, and the larvae entered the winter diapause in a relatively advanced developmental stage. Larval development could then be completed during the following summer, but only in those years when the temperatures were sufficiently high to permit the insects to pupate before the daylengths decreased to a point below the critical daylength of about 16.5 hours.

Diapause apparently occurs in every generation of the cricket *Gryllus campestris*, but the rate of nymphal growth and the duration of diapause have been shown to be determined by environmental factors (Fuzeau-Braesch, 1965, 1966). Short-day photoperiods tended to hasten growth and shorten the duration of diapause, in comparison to the effects of long days. The immature stages of some dragonfly species (*Tetragoneuria cynosura, Enallagma divagans, Enallagma traviatum*, and *Ischnura posita*) have been shown to respond to daylengths in terms of the rate of seasonal development (Corbet, 1963). In these insects, growth rates tended to be higher under long-day than under short-day conditions. Corbet (1963) suggested that such rate effects of daylength may play an important role in synchronizing adult emergence under field conditions. From 50 to 75% of the annual adult emergence of a dragonfly species may occur over a period of only 3 to 4 days.

GEOGRAPHICAL POPULATIONS

Latitude and Critical Daylength

Measurements of critical daylengths for the induction of diapause have been made on different geographical populations of a number of species. Northern forms tend to show a much longer critical daylength than do southern forms of the same species. This latitudinal effect has been reported in many insect species, and is typified by the latitudinal adaptation of *Acronycta rumicis*, as depicted in Fig. 54 (Danilevskii, 1961). Populations of the cabbage gall weevil, *Ceutorhynchus pleurostigma*, from the Netherlands (latitude 52°N) showed a critical daylength of about 15 hours; the same species from France at a latitude of 43°N had a critical daylength of about 14 hours (Ankersmit, 1964). Similarly, the critical daylength for diapause determination in the mite *Tetranychus urticae* was found to be 17 hours in a population from 60°N, 12.5 hours in a population at 45°N, and only 12 hours in a 41°N population (Bondarenko and Hai-Yuan, 1958). In general, it is thought that critical day-

228

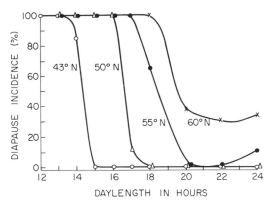

Fig. 54. Effect of photoperiod on the incidence of diapause in Acronycta rumicis populations from different northern latitudes. [Adapted from Danilevskii (1961).]

length for diapause determination tends to increase from 1.0 to 1.5 hours for every 5° increase in the latitude of the insect population's origin.

As was discussed in Chapter 7, the critical daylength tends to be influenced by environmental temperatures. High ambient temperatures tend to increase and low temperatures tend to decrease the critical daylength. Geographical populations have been found to vary in the effects of temperature, however. Although northern populations tend to display a longer critical daylength than do southern forms of the same species, the effect of relatively high temperatures is usually somewhat less on northern than on southern populations. In the case of the Russian populations of *A. rumicis*, for example, short-day induction of diapause could be averted by rearing temperatures of from 28° to 30°C in a population originating at 43°N. With the geographical population found at 60°N, however, short-day induction of diapause could not be averted, even with temperatures as high as 32°C. When the larvae were reared under long-day conditions or under continuous illumination, a higher environmental temperature was required to avert diapause induction among the northern forms than among the southern forms (Danilevskii, 1960, 1961). Many species or races that show a relatively short critical daylength will be entirely free from diapause under continuous illumination, regardless of temperature.

Temperature Accumulation and Seasonal Development

The seasonal development of an insect population may be predicted from year to year on the basis of summations of day-degrees. This tech-

TABLE XXI

Day-Degree Summations above 10°C Required during
the Development of Different Populations of *Acronycta rumicis*[a]

Population	Day-degrees required			Total day-degrees
	Eggs	Larvae	Pupae	
Leningrad (60°N)	76	245	197	518
Belgorod (50°N)	72	243	199	514
Sukhumi (43°N)	69	267	208	544

[a]From Danilevskii (1961).

nique is based on an accurate measurement of the temperature threshold for growth and development of the species, and on accurate records of the daily mean temperature of the insect's environment. The difference, in degrees, between the developmental threshold and the daily mean temperature represents the day-degree accumulation for any given day. Although this method of predicting phenological events contains some inherent sources of error, it has been employed as a useful approximation of seasonal development.

The day-degree temperature accumulations required for the development of many species have been determined. The accumulation required for the completion of the entire life cycle, or of any given part, has usually been considered to be reasonably constant for the species. The investigations of A. S. Danilevskii and his research group have shown that, of the several species investigated, geographical populations did not differ significantly in the cumulative day-degrees required for seasonal development. The total day-degrees required for the development of *Acronycta rumicis* from egg to adult, for example, was found to be quite similar among widely separated geographical populations (Table XXI). This would imply that at any given rearing temperature in the laboratory, the developmental rates of the different individuals of different geographical origin should be quite similar. Such has been shown to be the case with *Acronycta rumicis, Spilosoma menthastri, Pieris brassicae, Lymantria dispar,* and *Euproctis chrysorrhoea* (Danilevskii, 1957, 1960, 1961).

Bondarenko and Hai-Yuan (1958) observed, however, that northern populations of the mite *Tetranychus urticae* grew more rapidly at a given temperature than did mites of a southern origin. Although they did not determine day-degree requirements, the observation would imply that the northern mites displayed either a lower developmental temperature threshold or a lower temperature accumulation requirement. Population differences in the day-degree totals required for larval development (hatching to pupation) were demonstrated by Beck and Apple (1961) in the European corn borer, *Ostrinia nubilalis.* This study did not encompass a wide range of latitudes, since it involved borer populations from only the United States and southern Canada. Although population differences in day-degree requirements were found, the differences did not appear to be correlated with the latitude of the population origin. The data of Table XXII show that the cumulative day-degrees required by a corn borer population originating at 45°N was not significantly different from the number required by the most southern population studied (37°N). The lowest temperature accumulation was required by a Massachusetts population located at 42°30'N. Critical daylength were not determined precisely, but the most northern population had a critical daylength for diapause determination that was in excess of 15 hours, and the most southern population showed a critical daylength of about 14.5 hours. The Massachusetts population displayed the shortest critical daylength, which was under 14.5 hours. In this insect, at least, it is apparent that adaptation to local conditions in respect to day-degree summation required for growth is separate from adaptations related to photoperiodic responses.

Adaptations of geographical populations in respect to critical daylength for diapause determination and day-degree temperature requirements for seasonal growth are both involved in determining the number of generations produced per year. The relationships between these two adaptations have not been worked out in detail for any in-

TABLE XXII

Temperature Accumulations Required for
Larval Development in Different Geographical Populations of
the European Corn Borer, *Ostrinia nubilalis* (Temperature Threshold 50°F, 10°C)[a]

Population source		Total day-degrees	
Area	Latitude	°F	°C
Wisconsin	45°N	540	300
Wisconsin	43°N	645	358
Ontario	43°N	555	308
Massachusetts	42.5°N	480	266
Iowa	42°N	620	345
Kansas	39°N	655	364
Missouri	37°N	580	322

[a]Based on Beck and Apple (1961).

231

sect species, but something of how they might interact may be seen by considering the seasonal development of two populations of the European corn borer. The normal seasonal temperature accumulation in day-degrees above a base of 10°C is approximately similar in Wisconsin at a latitude of 45°N and in Massachusetts at a latitude of 42.5°N, despite the difference in latitude. However, the Wisconsin borer population shows a critical daylength of more than 15 hours and a seasonal day-degree requirement of 722 (from oviposition to pupation). The Massachusetts population has a critical daylength of less than 14.5 hours and a seasonal temperature requirement of only 605 day-degrees. Whereas the Wisconsin population is consistently univoltine, the rapid growth and low critical daylength of the Massachusetts population result in its being consistently bivoltine. With either a longer critical daylength or a higher day-degree requirement, the Massachusetts borer population could not complete the development of two generations per summer season (Beck and Apple, 1961; Beck, 1963).

Adult Emergence Rhythms

The marine midge, *Clunio marinus*, shows a well-defined circadian rhythm of adult emergence, and this rhythm has been shown to be phase-regulated by photoperiod (Neumann, 1962). The female midges live for only a few hours, within which mating and oviposition occurs. Oviposition is usually confined to masses of seaweed that are exposed and accessible for egg deposition only at low water times of the semi-monthly spring tide. Spring tides occur during 1 or 2 days after the full and new moons. At a given locality, the ebb spring tides will occur at the same times of day once every 15 days. To effect perpetuation of the midge population, reproductive females must be present during the 1 or 2 days of the spring tide and at the local time of ebb tide. The biological synchrony required is, therefore, extremely demanding. *Clunio* has met this challenge, however, and displays a 15-day lunar-regulated adult emergence cycle as well as a circadian emergence rhythm (Neumann, 1965, 1966). The tidal patterns differ among different coastal areas, however, calling for adaptations of the local midge populations in respect to both the days of the synodical cycle and the local time of day at which the adult midges emerge. Neumann (1966) studied the adaptations of six western European and Mediterranean geographical populations of *Clunio marinus*, and demonstrated that each population has evolved an adult emergence pattern that was well adapted to its local tidal schedule.

232

GENETICS OF PHOTOPERIODISM

Genetic mechanisms for transmitting photoperiodic response characteristics from one generation to the next have been tacitly assumed by biologists who have investigated any of the various aspects of photoperiodism. Whether the observed response is in the form of a daily rhythm of locomotor behavior, adult emergence, metabolic activity, or diapause determination, genetic control of rhythmic functions would appear to be a necessary component of the biological system. The genetic aspects of photoperiodism are of particular interest in connection with ecological adaptations and the evolution of geographical populations.

Diapause Determination

One of the earliest studies of the genetics of diapause was that of Arbuthnot (1944), who investigated the so-called "univoltine" and "bivoltine" races of the European corn borer, *Ostrinia nubilalis*. Arbuthnot demonstrated that the voltinism of this species was controlled by multiple genetic factors. An apparently homozygous univoltine strain was selected, but he was unable to develop a purely bivoltine genetic line. Hybridization between the two genetic lines was difficult but could be accomplished. The diapause characteristics of the hybrids appeared to be intermediate between those of the parental lines. Because photoperiod was not controlled, and the published report contained no account of the lighting conditions under which the borers were reared, the results are now difficult to interpret. The role of photoperiod in the voltinism and seasonal development of the European corn borer was not demonstrated until long after this genetic study.

Selection for diapause induction by long-day photoperiods was carried out by Tanaka (1951), using the Chinese oak silkworm, *Antheraea pernyi*. This species is usually considered to be multivoltine with a pupal diapause that is induced by short-day photoperiods. Tanaka exposed the growing caterpillars to long daylengths, and selected only the diapausing individuals for perpetuation of the culture. By such selection, a strain was developed that would consistently diapause under long-day conditions. In its natural environment, such a strain would be univoltine.

Selection in the converse direction was accomplished by Harvey (1957), working with the spruce budworm, *Choristoneura fumiferana*. This species is univoltine, or even semi-voltine in some geographical populations (Harvey, 1961). The larvae normally display what was called an "obligatory diapause" in the second larval instar, but Harvey observed that an occasional larva would spin the usual hibernaculum and then emerge from it, to wander about attempting to feed. In its normal forest habitat, such an unconventional larva would perish upon the onset of cold weather. Laboratory rearing of such larvae and the careful selection of genetic lines resulted in a genetic strain of spruce budworm that would develop without diapause under long-day conditions. Harvey concluded that the ability to develop without diapause was determined by multiple genes that were not sex linked.

The pink bollworm, *Pectinophora gossypiella*, has a facultative prepupal diapause that is induced by short-day photoperiods. Laboratory rearings under a 12-hour daylength and 28°C temperature result in a diapause incidence approaching 100%. However, the few individuals that did not diapause under such conditions were selected and perpetuated by Barry and Adkisson (1966). After 23 generations of such selection, a genetic line of pink bollworm was produced in which diapause rarely occurred. Again, multiple genetic factors that were not sex linked appeared to control the diapause-nondiapause characteristics.

The commercial silkworm, *Bombyx mori*, has been subjected to much genetic study, and a large number of different genetic strains have been developed (Lees, 1955; Morohoshi, 1957). Some of the genetic lines differ in their tendency to produce diapause-determined eggs under different temperature and light conditions. Voltinism is apparently controlled by six genetic alleles; three of the alleles are sex linked and three are autosomal dominants. Epistasis is shown by the sex-linked genes, but the autosomal genes are simply cumulative. A wide range of diapause tendencies is possible with such a multiplicity of genetic factors.

Geographical Populations

Geographical populations of a given species may show quite different photoperiodic adaptations, particularly in respect to the critical daylength for diapause determination. Cross-breeding experiments between members of two such populations have been performed in a number of instances. As discussed above, univoltine and multivoltine populations of the European corn borer were hybridized, and the progeny showed an intermediate tendency toward diapause (Arbuthnot, 1944). Ankersmit (1965) crossed the "autumn" and "spring" races of the cabbage gall weevil, *Ceutorhynchus pleurostigma*, and obtained fertile offspring that also showed diapause characteristics that were inter-

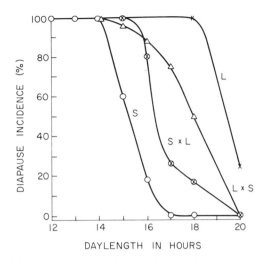

Fig. 55. *Effects of daylength on the incidence of diapause in Leningrad (L) and Sukhumi (S) populations of Acronycta rumicis, and their F₁ hybrids. [Adapted from Danilevskii (1961).]*

mediate between those of the parental lines. The most detailed research on critical daylength for diapause induction was reported by Danilevskii (1961), in which geographical races of several species were studied by means of both crosses and backcrosses. Danilevskii and co-workers studied the following species: *Acronycta rumicis, Spilosoma menthastri, Pieris brassicae, Leucoma salicis, Ostrinia nubilalis, Apanteles glomeratus, Culex pipiens, Dendrolimus pini*, and *Dendrolimus sibiricus*.

Geographical populations from the area of Leningrad (60°N) were compared with those from the region of Sukhumi, which is on the shores of the Black Sea at a latitude of about 43°N. The noctuid *Acronycta rumicis* has a pupal diapause that is induced by short-day photoperiods. The Leningrad population (L) is characterized by a critical daylength of about 19 hours; whereas the Sukhumi (S) population has a critical daylength of only 15 hours. Crosses between members of the two populations produced progeny with intermediate critical daylengths, but with the critical daylength values being somewhat more dependent on the origin of the female parent than that of the male (Fig. 55). In this figure, the origin symbol (L or S) for the female is followed by that of the male; thus the designation L × S means that a Leningrad female was crossed with a Sukhumi male. The F₂ generations of such crosses showed a critical daylength of 17 hours in the case of both LS × LS and SL × SL. A number of backcrosses were made with the LS hybrids, and the

TABLE XXIII

Diapause Incidence in the Progeny of Backcrosses of L x S
Hybrids and the Parent Lines of *Acronycta rumicis* (Photoperiod: 17L:7D)[a]

Hybrid female x male	Diapause incidence (%)
LS x LS	45
L x LS	100
LS x L	99
S x LS	32
LS x S	2

[a]Based on data of Danilevskii (1961).

progeny were reared under a 17L:7D photoperiod. The incidences of
diapause among the progeny of these crosses are shown in Table XXIII.
Backcross to the Leningrad stock caused the greatest increase in the
incidence of diapause, suggesting that these progeny had the longest
critical daylength. Conversely, backcrosses to the Sukhumi line resulted
in a lowered incidence of diapause.

The results of the experiments with *Acronycta* strongly suggest that
photoperiodic determination of diapause is controlled by multiple
genetic factors. The critical daylength of the progeny appears consistently to be intermediate between those of the parental lines, depending on the ratio of factors inherited from each. Essentially similar
results were obtained by Danilevskii in each of the several species studied. An insect species with wide latitudinal geographical distribution
will tend to evolve into geographical populations displaying adaptive
photoperiodic response characteristics. Sympatric populations may
hybridize, with the progeny showing photoperiodism that will be intermediate between those characteristics of the parents. Thus, a latitudinal
gradation of photoperiodic reactions will be produced as the result of
continuous interbreeding among locally adapted forms. Because of
constant intense selective pressure, a north-south continuum of adaptive
photoperiodic responses will be maintained in the species population as
a whole.

Adult emergence rhythms in the marine midge *Clunio marinus* were
found to differ widely among geographical populations of the species.
Neumann (1965, 1966) studied the genetics of these population characteristics. The circadian time of maximum adult emergence was found
to be controlled by several genes. As shown in Fig. 56, F_1 and F_2 generations showed adult emergence peaks that were temporally intermediate

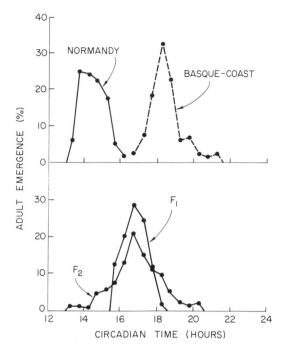

Fig. 56. Circadian times of adult emergence in two populations of Clunio marinus and their progeny. [Adapted from Neumann (1965).]

between those of the parental lines. The F_2 generation showed a broader distribution of emergence times than did the F_1, but the extremes did not exceed extremes of the parental lines. From these experiments, as well as the results of a series of backcrosses, Neumann concluded that the emergence rhythm was under polygenic control, but that the number of genes involved was relatively small.

Evolutionary Trends in Voltinism

Most of the work on geographical populations has been done on old, well-established populations that were probably in reasonably stable equilibria with their environments. The European corn borer is an exception, however, because it represents a 20th century introduction. Most borer populations are probably still in the process of becoming adapted to local seasonal conditions.

The first European corn borers in North America were found in 1917, in Massachusetts. A short time later, a second infestation was reported in New York. The two infestations apparently were separate introductions, and they were found to differ in their seasonal development. The New York population was typically univoltine; whereas the Massachusetts borers were bivoltine (Caffrey and Worthley, 1927). Massachusetts borers were experimentally reared in a field insectary located in New York, and they were found to persist in their bivoltinism. The two populations could interbreed, and it was concluded that they represented two separate geographical populations of European origin.

The life history charts compiled by Caffrey and Worthley (1927) showed that a small per cent of the bivoltine Massachusetts population was univoltine. Similarly, Barber (1925) observed a variable degree of bivoltinism in the typically univoltine New York population. By 1921, the corn borer had spread westward into Ohio and Michigan, where it appeared to produce but one generation per year. The insect invaded Indiana in 1926 and Wisconsin in 1931; in these states it also tended to be univoltine. It was first found in Illinois in 1939, where it showed a mixed voltinism in which about half of the early summer generation would go into diapause. The borer was found in Iowa in 1941, where it was typically bivoltine. By 1950, the European corn borer had spread westward into Oklahoma and Colorado, and southward to the Gulf of Mexico.

Of particular interest to the present discussion is the well-documented tendency for the supposedly univoltine corn borer populations of Michigan, Ohio, Indiana, Ontario, and southern Wisconsin to display a distinct trend toward multivoltinism. The initial characteristic of univoltinism in these populations is thought to be the result of their originating from the New York infestation. In southern areas, such as Missouri and Mississippi, there has been a trend toward three borer generations per growing season.

The demonstration of a genetic basis for voltinism (Arbuthnot, 1944) led to an attempt to account for geographical population differences in voltinism on the basis of areal differences in annual mean temperatures and precipitation records (Arbuthnot, 1949). This was not successful, because daylength was not taken into account, and because it was based on the assumption that local populations could not evolve adaptations to local climatic conditions. With the refinement of the day-degree accumulation technique for following the insect's seasonal development (Apple, 1952) and the demonstration of the role of photoperiod in diapause, a better understanding of the factors underlying voltinism was possible. Using an Ontario borer population, Mutchmor (1959) found that voltinism could be predicted approximately on the basis of the development of the larvae prior to the occurrence of the critical daylength of 14.5 hours. Any borer attaining maturity while the daylengths exceeded 14.5 hours would go on to pupate; whereas those maturing after the daylengths were below the critical value would diapause. Apple and Beck (1961), in a study of a southern Wisconsin population, found that if the seasonal day-degree accumulation exceeded 972 day-degrees (°C) (or 1750 day-degrees °F) before the daylength had decreased to 14.75 hours (July 25), a second generation of corn borers could be expected. Smaller seasonal temperature accumulations prior to the critical daylength would result in a greater prevalence of univoltinism, and a seasonal day-degree accumulation of less than 722 (°C) (or 1300 day-degrees °F) resulted in virtual univoltine development. The finding that different geographical populations of the corn borer differ in their temperature and photoperiod adaptations means that criteria for predicting seasonal development must be determined for each local population of interest. Only a continuing study of carefully chosen local borer populations will provide the information needed on the evolutionary processes involved in the development of stable geographical populations. A recent study of geographical populations of the European corn borer in the midwestern United States has shown that such populations may differ from each other in several characteristics in addition to their developmental and photoperiodic responses (Sparks *et al.*, 1966a,b).

□ □ References

Adkisson, P. L. (1961). Effect of larval diet on the seasonal occurrence of diapause in the pink bollworm. *J. Econ. Entomol.* **54**, 1107-1112.

Adkisson, P. L. (1963). Time measurement in the photoperiodic induction of diapause in the pink bollworm, *Texas Agr. Expt. Sta. Progr. Rept.* **2274**.

Adkisson, P. L. (1964). Action of photoperiod in controlling insect diapause. *Am. Naturalist* **98**, 357-374.

Adkisson, P. L. (1965). Light-dark reactions involved in insect diapause. *In* "Circadian Clocks" (J. Aschoff, ed.), pp. 344-350. North-Holland Publ., Amsterdam.

Adkisson, P. L. (1966). Internal clocks and insect diapause. *Science* **154**, 234-241.

Adkisson, P. L., R. A. Bell, and S. G. Wellso (1963). Environmental factors controlling the induction of diapause in the pink bollworm, *Pectinophora gossypiella* (Saunders). *J. Insect Physiol.* **9**, 299-310.

Albrecht, F. and P. Cassier (1965). Influence de la photopériode et de la température sur les élevages de *Locusta migratoria migratorioides* phase grégaire. *Compt. Rend. Acad. Sci.* **260**, 6449-6451.

Allard, H. A. (1931). The photoperiodism of the firefly *Photinus pyralis* Linn. Its relation to the evening twilight and other conditions. *Proc. Entomol. Soc. Wash.* **33**, 49-58.

Allen, N., W. S. Kinard, and M. Jacobson (1962). Procedure used to recover a sex attractant for the male tobacco hornworm. *J. Econ. Entomol.* **55**, 347-351.

Anderson, N. H. (1966). Depressant effect of moonlight on activity of aquatic insects. *Nature* **209**, 319-320.

Andrewartha, H. G. (1952). Diapause in relation to the ecology of insects. *Biol. Rev. Cambridge Phil. Soc.* **27**, 50-107.

Ankersmit, G. W. (1964). Voltinism and its determination in some beetles of cruciferous crops. *Mededel Landbouwhogeschool Wageningen* **64**(8), 1-60.

Ankersmit, G. W. (1965). Over enkele consequenties van de fotoperiodieke reactie van *Ceuthorhynchus pleurostigma. Entomol. Ber.* **25**, 16-17.

Apple, J. W. (1952). Corn borer development and control on canning corn in relation to temperature accumulation. *J. Econ. Entomol.* **45**, 877-879.

Apple, J. W. and S. D. Beck (1961). Prediction of midsummer European corn borer pupation. *Proc. N. Central Branch Entomol. Soc. Am.* **16**, 42-43.

Arbuthnot, K. D. (1944). Strains of the European corn borer in the United States. *U. S. Dept. Agr. Tech. Bull.* **869**.

Arbuthnot, K. D. (1949). Temperature and precipitation in relation to the number of generations of European corn borer in the United States. *U.S. Dept. Agr. Tech. Bull.* **987**.

Aschoff, J. (1958). Tierische Periodik unter dem Einfluss von Zeitgebern. *Z. Tierpsychol.* **15**, 1-30.

Aschoff, J. (1960). Exogenous and endogenous components in circadian rhythms. *Cold Spring Harbor Symp. Quant. Biol.* **25**, 11-26.

Aschoff, J. (1965). Circadian rhythms in man. *Science* **148**, 1427-1432.

Aschoff, J. (1966). Circadian activity pattern with two peaks. *Ecology* **74**, 657-661.

Babcock, K. W. (1924). Environmental studies on the European corn borer, *Pyrausta nubilalis* Hubn. *J. Econ. Entomol.* **17**, 120-125.

Babcock, K. W. (1927). The European corn borer, *Pyrausta nubilalis* Hübn. I. A discussion of its dormant period. *Ecology* **8**, 45-59.

Baker, F. C. (1935). The effect of photoperiodism on resting treehole mosquito larvae. *Can. Entomologist* **67**, 149-153.

240

Bakker, K. and F. X. Nelissen (1963). On the relations between the duration of the larval and pupal period, weight and diurnal rhythm in emergence in *Drosophila melanogaster*. *Entomol. Exptl. Appl.* **6**, 37-52.

Ball, H. J. (1958). The effect of visible spectrum irradiation on growth and development in several species of insects. *J. Econ. Entomol.* **51**, 573-578.

Ball, H. J. (1961). The response of *Oncopeltus fasciatus* to limited areas of the electromagnetic spectrum. *Ann. Entomol. Soc. Am.* **54**, 534-536.

Ball, H. J. (1965). Photosensitivity in the terminal abdominal ganglion of *Periplaneta americana* (L.). *J. Insect Physiol.* **11**, 1311-1315.

Banerjee, A. C. and G. C. Decker (1966a). Studies on sod webworms. I. Emergence rhythm, mating, and oviposition behavior under natural conditions. *J. Econ. Entomol.* **59**, 1237-1244.

Banerjee, A. C. and G. C. Decker (1966b). Studies on sod webworms. II. Oviposition behavior of *Crambus trisectus* under regulated light conditions in the laboratory. *J. Econ. Entomol.* **59**, 1245-1248.

Barber, G. W. (1925). Remarks on the number of generations of the European corn borer in America. *J. Econ. Entomol.* **18**, 496-502.

Barker, R. J. (1963). Inhibition of diapause in *Pieris rapae* L. by supplementary photophases. *Experientia* **19**, 185.

Barker, R. J., A. Mayer, and C. F. Cohen (1963). Photoperiod effects in *Pieris rapae*. *Ann. Entomol. Soc. Am.* **56**, 292-294.

Barker, R. J., C. F. Cohen, and A. Mayer (1964). Photoflashes: A potential new tool for control of insect populations. *Science* **145**, 1195-1197.

Barry, B. D. and P. L. Adkisson (1966). Certain aspects of the genetic factors involved in the control of larval diapause of the pink bollworm. *Ann. Entomol. Soc. Am.* **59**, 122-125.

Bateman, M. A. (1955). The effect of light and temperature on the rhythm of pupal ecdysis in the Queensland fruit fly. *Dacus (Strumeta) tryoni* (Frogg). *Australian J. Zool.* **3**, 22-33.

Bates, M. (1941). Laboratory observations on the sexual behavior of anopheline mosquitoes. *J. Exptl. Zool.* **86**, 153-173.

Beards, G. W. and F. E. Strong (1966). Photoperiod in relation to diapause in *Lygus hesperus* Knight. *Hilgardia* **37**, 345-362.

Beck, S. D. (1962a). Photoperiodic induction of diapause in an insect. *Biol. Bull.* **122**, 1-12.

Beck, S. D. (1962b). Temperature effects on insects: Relation to periodism. *Proc. N. Central Branch, Entomol. Soc. Am.* **17**, 18-19.

Beck, S. D. (1963). Physiology and ecology of photoperiodism. *Bull. Entomol. Soc. Am.* **9**, 8-16.

Beck, S. D. (1964). Time-measurement in insect photoperiodism. *Am. Naturalist* **98**, 329-346.

Beck, S. D. (1967). Water intake and the termination of diapause in the European corn borer, *Ostrinia nubilalis*. *J. Insect Physiol.* **13**, 739-750.

Beck, S. D. (1968). Environmental photoperiod and the programming of insect development. *In* "Evolution and Environment." Yale Univ. Press, New Haven, Connecticut. In press.

Beck, S. D. and N. Alexander (1964a). Chemically and photoperiodically induced diapause development in the European corn borer, *Ostrinia nubilalis*. *Biol. Bull.* **126**, 175-184.

Beck, S. D. and N. Alexander (1964b). Hormonal activation of the insect brain. *Science* **143**, 478-479.

Beck, S. D. and N. Alexander (1964c). Proctodone, an insect developmental hormone. *Biol. Bull.* **126**, 185-198.

Beck, S. D. and J. W. Apple (1961). Effects of temperature and photoperiod on voltinism of geographical populations of the European corn borer, *Pyrausta nubilalis* (Hbn). *J. Econ. Entomol.* **54**, 550-558.

Beck, S. D. and W. Hanec (1960). Diapause in the European corn borer, *Pyrausta nubilalis* (Hbn.). *J. Insect Physiol.* **4**, 304-318.

Beck, S. D., N. M. Bilstad, and J. H. Lilly (1950). Prepupal changes in the ventricular epithelium of the European corn borer, *Pyrausta nubilalis* (Hbn.). *Ann. Entomol. Soc. Am.* **43**, 305-310.

Beck, S. D., C. A. Edwards, and J. T. Medler (1958). Feeding and nutrition of the milkweed bug *Oncopeltus fasciatus* (Dallas). *Ann. Entomol. Soc. Am.* **51**, 283-288.

Beck, S. D., E. J. Cloutier, and D. G. R. McLeod (1963). Photoperiod and insect development. *Proc. 23rd Biol. Colloq. Oregon State Univ., 1962* pp. 43-64.

Beck, S. D., I. B. Colvin, and D. E. Swinton (1965a). Photoperiodic control of a physiological rhythm. *Biol. Bull.* **128**, 177-188.

Beck, S. D., J. L. Shane, and I. B. Colvin (1965b). Proctodone production in the European corn borer, *Ostrinia nubilalis*. *J. Insect Physiol.* **11**, 297-303.

Beling, L. (1929). Über das Zeitgedächtnis der Bienen. *Z. Vergleich. Physiol.* **9**, 259-338.

Bell, R. A. and P. L. Adkisson (1964). Photoperiodic reversibility of diapause induction in an insect. *Science* **144**, 1149-1151.

Belozerov, V. N. (1963). Day length as a factor determining the delay of egg-laying of females of *Dermacentor marginalis* (Sulz.). *Mockba* **5**, 521-526.

Belozerov, V. N. (1964). Larval diapause in the tick *Ixodes ricinus* L. and its relation to external conditions. *Rev. Entomol. USSR* **43**, 1626-1637.

Belozerov, V. N. (1966). The dynamics of the respiratory metabolism during development of ixodid ticks. II. Respiration of imagoes. *Rev. Entomol. USSR* **45**, 509-522.

Bentley, E. W., D. L. Gunn, and D. W. Ewer (1941). The biology and behavior of *Ptinus tectus*, a pest of stored products. I. The daily rhythm of locomotor activity, especially in relation to light and temperature. *J. Exptl. Biol.* **18**, 182.

Blake, G. M. (1959). Control of diapause by an 'internal clock' in *Anthrenus verbasci* (L.). *Nature* **183**, 126-127.

Blake, G. M. (1960). Decreasing photoperiod inhibiting metamorphosis in an insect. *Nature* **188**, 168-169.

Blake, G. M. (1963). Shortening of a diapause-controlled life cycle by means of increasing photoperiod. *Nature* **198**, 462-463.

Bliss, D. E. (1962). Neuroendocrine control of locomotor activity in land crab, *Gecarcinus lateralis*. *In* "Neurosecretion" (H. Heller and R. B. Clark, eds.), pp. 391-410. Academic Press, New York.

Bode, V. C., R. DeSa, and J. W. Hastings (1963). Daily rhythm of luciferin activity in *Gonyaulax polyedra*. *Science* **141**, 913-915.

Bondarenko, N. V. (1950). The influence of short days on the annual cycle of development of the common spider mite. *Compt. Rend. Acad. Sci., USSR* **70**, 1077-1080.

Bondarenko, N. V. and K. Hai-Yuan (1958). The peculiarities of the appearance of diapause in different geographical populations of the spider mite. *Dokl. Akad. Nauk SSSR* **119**, 295-298 (transl. for Am. Inst. Biol. Sci.).

Bonnemaison, L. (1951). Contribution a l'étude des facteurs provoquant l'apparition des formes ailées et sexuées les Aphidinae. *Ann. Epiphyties* **2**, 1-380.

242

Bonnemaison, L. (1956). Determinisme de l'apparition des larves estivales de *Periphyllus* (Aphidinae). *Compt. Rend. Acad. Sci.* **243**, 1166-1168.

Bonnemaison, L. (1958). Facteurs d'apparition des formes sexupares ou sexuées chez le puceron cendre du pommier (*Sappaphis plantaginea* Pass.). *Ann. Epiphyties* (C) **3**, 331-355.

Bonnemaison, L. (1964). Action combinée de la photopériode et de l'effet de groupe sur l'apparition des sexupares ailés de *Dysaphis plantaginea* Pass. *Compt. Rend. Acad. Sci.* **259**, 1663-1665.

Bonnemaison, L. (1965a). Action d'une photopériode de durée croissante ou décroissante sur l'apparition des formes sexuées de *Dysaphis plantaginea* Pass. *Compt. Rend. Acad. Sci.* **260**, 5138-5140.

Bonnemaison, L. (1965b). Facteurs conditionnant l'apparition des mâles chez l'Aphide *Dysaphis plantaginea*. *Compt. Rend. Acad. Sci.* **260**, 318-319.

Bonnemaison, L. (1966a). Action de l'alternance de scotophases de 12 h et de longues photophases sur la production des sexupares de *Dysaphis plantaginea*. *Compt. Rend. Acad. Sci.* **262**, 2609-2611.

Bonnemaison, L. (1966b). Combinasion de photophases et de scotophases avec des températures élevées ou basses sur la production des sexupares de *Dysaphis plantaginea*. *Compt. Rend. Acad. Sci.* **263**, 177-179.

Bonnemaison, L. (1966c). Action de l'alternance de scotophase et de photophases dans un cycle de 24-h sur la production des sexupares de *Dysaphis plantaginea*. *Compt. Rend. Acad. Sci.* **262**, 2498-2501.

Bonnemaison, L. and J. Missonnier (1955). Influence de photopériodisme sur le déterminisme des formes estivales ou hivernales et de la diapause chez *Psylla pyri* L. (Homopteres). *Compt. Rend. Acad. Sci.* **240**, 1277-1279.

Borthwick, H. A. and S. B. Hendricks (1960). Photoperiodism in plants. *Science* **132**, 1223-1228.

Bowers, W. S. and C. C. Blickenstaff (1966). Hormonal termination of diapause in the alfalfa weevil. *Science* **154**, 1673-1674.

Brazzel, J. R. and L. D. Newsom (1959). Diapause in *Anthonomus grandis* Boh. *J. Econ. Entomol.* **52**, 603-611.

Bremer, H. (1926). Über die tageszeitliche Konstanz im Schlupftermine der Imagines einiger Insekten und ihre experimentelle Beeinflussbarkeit. *Z. Wiss. Insektenbiol.* **21**, 209-216.

Brett, W. J. (1955). Persistent diurnal rhythmicity in *Drosophila* emergence. *Ann. Entomol. Soc. Am.* **48**, 119-131.

Brown, F. A. (1959). Living clocks. *Science* **130**, 1535-1544.

Brown, F. A. (1965). A unified theory for biological rhythms. *In* "Circadian Clocks" (J. Aschoff, ed.), pp. 231-261. North-Holland Publ., Amsterdam.

Brown, F. A. and H. M. Webb. (1948). Temperature relations of an endogenous daily rhythmicity of the fiddler crab, *Uca. Physiol. Zool.* **21**, 371-381.

Brown, F. A., M. Fingerman, and M. N. Hines (1954). A study of the mechanism involved in shifting of the phases of the endogenous daily rhythm by light stimuli. *Biol. Bull.* **106**, 308-317.

Brown, R. H. J. and J. E. Harker (1960). A method of controlling the temperature of insect neurosecretory cells *in situ*. *Nature* **185**, 392.

Bruce, V. G. and C. S. Pittendrigh (1957). Endogenous rhythms in insects and microorganisms. *Am. Naturalist* **91**, 179-195.

Buck, J. B. (1937). Studies on the firefly. I. The effects of light and other agents on flashing in *Photinus pyralis*, with special reference to periodicity and diurnal rhythm. *Physiol. Zool.* **10**, 45-58.

Bull, D. L. and P. L. Adkisson (1960). Certain factors influencing diapause in the pink bollworm, *Pectinophora gossypiella*. *J. Econ. Entomol.* **53**, 793-798.

Bull, D. L. and P. L. Adkisson (1962). Fat content of the larval diet as a factor influencing diapause and growth rate of the pink bollworm. *Ann. Entomol. Soc. Am.* **55**, 499-502.

Bull, D. L. and D. A. Lindquist (1965). A comparative study of insecticide metabolism in photoperiod-entrained and unentrained bollworm larvae *Heliothis zea* (Boddie). *Comp. Biochem. Physiol.* **16**, 321-325.

Bünning, E. (1935). Zur Kenntnis der endogenen Tagesrhythmik bei Insekten und Pflanzen. *Ber. Deut. Botan. Ges.* **53**, 594-623.

Bünning, E. (1958). Über den Temperatureinfluss auf die endogenen Tagesrhythmik besonders bei *Periplaneta americana*. *Biol. Zentr.* **77**, 141-152.

Bünning, E. (1960a). Biological clocks. *Cold Spring Harbor Symp. Quant. Biol.* **25**, 1-9.

Bünning, E. (1960b). Circadian rhythms and the time measurement in photoperiodism. *Cold Spring Harbor Symp. Quant. Biol.* **25**, 249-256.

Bünning, E. (1964). "The Physiological Clock," 2nd ed. Academic Press, New York.

Bünning, E. and G. Joerrens (1960). Tagesperiodische antagonistische Schwankungen der Blau-violett- und Gelbrot-Empfindlichkeit als Grundlage der photoperiodischen Diapause-Induktion bei *Pieris brassicae*. *Z. Naturforsch.* **15**, 205-213.

Bünning, E. and G. Joerrens (1962). Versuche uber den Zeitmessorgang bei der photoperiodischen Diapause-Induktion von *Pieris brassicae*. *Z. Naturforsch.* **17**, 57.

Burges, H. D. (1960). Studies on the dermestid beetle *Trogoderma granarium* Everts. IV. Feeding, growth, and respiration with particular reference to diapause larvae. *J. Insect Physiol.* **5**, 317-334.

Burges, H. D. (1962). Diapause, pest status and control of the khapra beetle, *Trogoderma granarium* Everts. *Ann. Appl. Biol.* **50**, 614-617.

Caffrey, D. J. and L. H. Worthley (1927). A progress report on the investigations of the European corn borer. *U. S. Dept. Agr. Bull.* **1476**.

Callahan, P. S. (1958). Behavior of the imago of the corn earworm, *Heliothis zea* (Boddie), with special reference to emergence and reproduction. *Ann. Entomol. Soc. Am.* **51**, 271-283.

Callahan, P. S. (1965a). An infrared electromagnetic theory of diapause inducement and control in insects. *Ann. Entomol. Soc. Am.* **58**, 561-564.

Callahan, P. S. (1965b). Intermediate and far infrared sensing of nocturnal insects. I. Evidence for a far infrared (FIR) electromagnetic theory of communication and sensing in moths and its relationship to the limiting biosphere of the corn earworm. *Ann. Entomol. Soc. Am.* **58**, 727-745.

Cambournac, F. J. C. and R. B. Hill (1940). Observations on the swarming of *Anopheles maculipennis* var. *atroparvus*. *Am. J. Trop. Med. Hyg.* **20**, 133-140.

Campbell, B. O. (1964). Solar and lunar periodicities in oxygen consumption by the mealworm, *Tenebrio molitor*. Ph.D. Thesis, Northwestern Univ. *Dissertation Abstr. 64-12262*.

Caspers, H. (1951). Rhythmische Erscheinungen in der Fortpflanzung von *Clunio marinus* und das Problem der lunaren Periodizitat bei Organisme. *Arch. Hydrobiol. Suppl.* **18**, 415-594.

Chippendale, G. M. and S. D. Beck (1966). Hemolymph proteins of *Ostrinia nubilalis* during diapause and prepupal differentiation. *J. Insect Physiol.* **12**, 1629-1638.

Church, N. S. (1955a). Hormones and the termination and reinduction of diapause in *Cephus cinctus* (Nort.). *Can. J. Zool.* **33**, 339-369.

Church, N. S. (1955b). Moisture and diapause in the wheat stem sawfly, *Cephus cinctus* Nort. *Can. Entomologist* **87**, 85-97.

Claret, J. (1966a). Mise en évidence du rôle photorécepteur du cerveau dans l'induction de la diapause, chez *Pieris brassicae. Ann. Endocrinol. (Paris)* **27**, 311-320.

Claret, J. (1966b). Recherche du centre photorécepteur lors de l'induction de la diapause chez *Pieris brassicae. Compt. Rend. Acad. Sci.* **262**, 1464-1465.

Clarke, K. U. and P. A. Langley (1963a). Studies on the initiation of growth and moulting in *Locusta migratoria migratorioides* R & F. III. The role of the frontal ganglion. *J. Insect Physiol.* **9**, 411-421.

Clarke, K. U. and P. A. Langley (1963b). Studies on the initiation of growth and moulting in *Locusta migratoria migratorioides* R & F. IV. The relationship between the stomato-gastric nervous system and neurosecretion. *J. Insect Physiol.* **9**, 423-430.

Clements, A. N. (1963). "The Physiology of Mosquitoes." Macmillan, New York.

Clever, U. and P. Karlson (1960). Induktion von Puff-veränderungen in den Speichel-drüsenchromosomen von *Chironomus tentans* durch Ecdyson. *Exptl. Cell Res.* **20**, 623-626.

Cloudsley-Thompson, J. L. (1952). Studies in diurnal rhythms. II. Changes in the physio-logical responses of the wood louse *Oniscus asellus* (L.) to environmental stimuli. *J. Exptl. Biol.* **29**, 295-303.

Cloudsley-Thompson, J. L. (1958). Studies in diurnal rhythms. VIII. The endogenous chronometer in *Gryllus campestris. J. Insect Physiol.* **2**, 275-280.

Cloudsley-Thompson, J. L. (1960a). Adaptive functions of circadian rhythms. *Cold Spring Harbor Symp. Quant. Biol.* **25**, 345-354.

Cloudsley-Thompson, J. L. (1960b). Studies in diurnal rhythms. X. Synchronization of the endogenous chronometer in *Blaberus giganteus* (L.) (Dictyoptera: Blattaria) and in *Gryllus campestris* L. (Orthoptera: Gryllidae). *Entomologist* **3**, 121-127.

Cloutier, E. J. and S. D. Beck (1963). Spermatogenesis and diapause in the European corn borer, *Ostrinia nubilalis. Ann. Entomol. Soc. Am.* **56**, 253-255.

Cloutier, E. J., S. D. Beck, D. G. R. McLeod, and D. L. Silhacek (1962). Neural transplants and insect diapause. *Nature* **195**, 1222-1224.

Cognetti, G. and A. Pagliai (1963). Razze sessuali in *Brevicoryne brassicae* L. *Arch. Zool. Ital.* **48**, 329-337.

Cole, C. L. and P. L. Adkisson (1964). Daily rhythm in the susceptibility of an insect to a toxic agent. *Science* **144**, 1148-1149.

Cole, C. L. and P. L. Adkisson (1965). A circadian rhythm in the susceptibility of an insect to an insecticide. *In* "Circadian Clocks" (J. Aschoff, ed.), pp. 309-313. North-Holland Publ., Amsterdam.

Corbet, P. S. (1956). Environmental factors influencing the induction and termination of diapause in the emperor dragonfly, *Anax imperator* Leach. *J. Exptl. Biol.* **33**, 1-14.

Corbet, P. S. (1957). The life history of the emperor dragonfly, *Anax imperator* Leach. *J. Animal Ecol.* **26**, 1-69.

Corbet, P. S. (1960). Patterns of circadian rhythms in insects. *Cold Spring Harbor Symp. Quant. Biol.* **25**, 357-360.

Corbet, P. S. (1963). "A Biology of Dragonflies." Quadrangle Books, Chicago, Illinois.

Corbet, P. S. (1965). Asymmetry in eocrepuscular diel periodicities of insects. *Can. Ento-mologist* **97**, 878-880.

Corbet, P. S. (1966a). Diel patterns of mosquito activity in a high arctic locality: Hazen Camp, Ellesmere Island, N. W. T. *Can. Entomologist* **98**, 1238-1252.

Corbet, P. S. (1966b). The role of rhythms in insect behaviour. *Symp. Roy. Entomol. Soc., London* **3**, 13-28.

Cothran, W. R. and G. G. Gyrisco (1966). A modified photoperiod control device. *J. Econ. Entomol.* **59**, 236-238.

Crawford, C. S. (1966). Photoperiod-dependent oviposition rhythm in *Crambus teterrellus* (Lepidoptera: Pyralidae: Crambinae). *Ann. Entomol. Soc. Am.* **59**, 1285-1288.

Cunningham, R. K. and A. S. Tombes (1966). Succinate oxidase system in the alfalfa weevil, *Hypera postica*, during aestivation (summer diapause). *Comp. Biochem. Physiol.* **18**, 725-733.

Danilevskii, A. S. (1957). Photoperiodism as a factor in the formation of geographical races in insects. *Entomol. Obozrenie* **36**, 5-27 (in Russian).

Danilevskii, A. S. (1960). Intraspecific physiological adaptations of insects toward zonal-geographic peculiarities of climate. *In* "The Ontogeny of Insects" (I. Hrdý, ed.), pp. 293-296. Academic Press, New York.

Danilevskii, A. S. (1961). "Photoperiodism and Seasonal Development of Insects," English translation, 1965. Oliver & Boyd, Edinburgh and London.

Davey, K. G. (1956). The physiology of dormancy in the sweet clover weevil. *Can. J. Zool.* **34**, 86-98.

Davey, K. G. (1961a). Substances controlling the rate of beating of the heart of *Periplaneta*. *Nature* **192**, 284.

Davey, K. G. (1961b). The mode of action of the heart accelerating factor from the corpus cardiacum of insects. *Gen. Comp. Endocrinol.* **1**, 24-29.

Davey, K. G. (1962a). The nervous pathway involved in the release by feeding of a pharmacologically active factor from the corpus cardiacum of *Periplaneta*. *J. Insect Physiol.* **8**, 579-583.

Davey, K. G. (1962b). The mode of action of the corpus cardiacum on the hind gut in *Periplaneta americana*. *J. Exptl. Biol.* **39**, 319-324.

Davidson, J. (1929). On the occurrence of the parthenogenetic and sexual forms of *Aphis rumicis* L. with special reference to the influence of environmental factors. *Ann. Appl. Biol.* **16**, 104-134.

Davis, R. (1966). Daily rhythm in flight and development of the corn leaf aphid, *Rhopalosiphum maidis*. *Ann. Entomol. Soc. Am.* **59**, 82-85.

deFluiter, H. J. (1950). De invloed van de daglengte en temperatur op het optreden van de geslachtsdieren bij *Aphis fabae* Scop., de zwarte bonenluis. *Tijdschr. Plantenziekten* **56**, 265-285.

Depner, K. R. (1962). Effects of photoperiod and of ultraviolet radiation on the incidence of diapause in the horn fly, *Haematobia irritans* (L.). *Intern. J. Bioclimatol. Biometeorol.* **5**, 68-71.

Depner, K. R. and R. F. Harwood (1966). Photoperiodic responses of two latitudinally diverse groups of *Anopheles freeborni*. *Ann. Entomol. Soc. Am.* **59**, 7-11.

Dethier, V. G. (1963). "The Physiology of Insect Senses." Wiley, New York.

de Wilde, J. (1953). Diapause in the Colorado potato beetle. *Acta Physiol. Pharmacol. Neerl.* **3**, 141.

de Wilde, J. (1954). Aspects of diapause in adult insects with special regard to the Colorado beetle, *Leptinotarsa decemlineata*. *Arch. Neerl. Zool.* **10**, 375-385.

de Wilde, J. (1958). Perception of the photoperiod by the Colorado potato beetle (*Leptinotarsa decemlineata* Say). *Proc. 10th Intern. Congr. Entomol., Montreal, 1956* **2**, 213-218.

de Wilde, J. (1960). Diapause in the Colorado beetle (*Leptinotarsa decemlineata* Say) as an endocrine deficiency syndrome of the corpora allata. *In* "The Ontogeny of Insects" (I. Hrdy, ed.), pp 226-230. Academic Press, New York.

de Wilde, J. (1961). Extrinsic control of endocrine functions in insects. *Bull. Res. Council Israel* **10B**, 36-52.

de Wilde, J. (1962a). Photoperiodism in insects and mites. *Ann. Rev. Entomol.* **7**, 1-26.

de Wilde, J. (1962b). Analysis of the diapause syndrome in the Colorado potato beetle (*Leptinotarsa decemlineata* Say): Behaviour and reproduction. *Acta Physiol. Pharmacol. Neerl.* **11**, 525.

de Wilde, J. (1963). Photoperiodic control of corpus allatum activity in the Colorado beetle. *Acta Physiol. Pharmacol. Neerl.* **12**, 344.

de Wilde, J. (1965). Photoperiodic control of endocrines in insects. *Arch. Anat. Microscop. Morphol. Exptl.* **54**, 547-564.

de Wilde, J. and J. A. de Boer (1961). Physiology of diapause in the adult Colorado beetle. II. Diapause as a case of pseudoallatectomy. *J. Insect Physiol.* **6**, 152-161.

de Wilde, J. and H. Bonga (1958). Observations on threshold intensity to different wave lengths of photoperiodic responses in the Colorado beetle (*Leptinotarsa decemlineata* Say). *Entomol. Exptl. Appl.* **1**, 301-307.

de Wilde, J., C. S. Duintjer, and L. Mook (1959). Physiology of diapause in the adult Colorado beetle (*Leptinotarsa decemlineata* Say). I. The photoperiod as a controlling factor. *J. Insect Physiol.* **3**, 75-85.

de Wilde, J., B. M. Bier, and J. A. de Boer (1965). Hersenoperaties bij de Coloradokever. *Entomol. Ber.* **25**, 18-19.

Dickson, R. C. (1949). Factors governing the induction of diapause in the oriental fruit moth. *Ann. Entomol. Soc. Am.* **42**, 511-537.

Dickson, R. C. and E. Sanders (1945). Factors inducing diapause in the oriental fruit moth. *J. Econ. Entomol.* **38**, 605-606.

Dixon, A. F. G. (1963). Reproductive activity of the sycamore aphid, *Drepanosiphum platanoides* (Schr.). *J. Animal Ecol.* **32**, 33-38.

Downes, J. A. (1965). Adaptations of insects in the arctic. *Ann. Rev. Entomol.* **10**, 257-274.

Dubynina, T. S. (1966). Onset of diapause and reactivation in *Tetranychus urticae* (Koch). *Entomol. Rev.* **44**, 159-161 (transl. for Entomol. Soc. Am.).

Dunnung, R. A. (1956). A diurnal rhythm in the emergence of *Pegomyia betae* Curtis from the puparium. *Bull. Entomol. Res.* **47**, 645-653.

Dutky, S. R., M. S. Schechter, and W. N. Sullivan (1962). A lard can device for experiments in photoperiodism. *J. Econ. Entomol.* **55**, 575.

Earle, N. W. and L. D. Newsom (1964). Initiation of diapause in the boll weevil. *J. Insect Physiol.* **10**, 131-139.

Edwards, D. K. (1960). A method for continuous determination of displacement activity in a group of flying insects. *Can. J. Zool.* **38**, 1021-1025.

Edwards, D. K. (1962). Laboratory determinations of the daily flight times of separate sexes of some moths in naturally changing light. *Can. J. Zool.* **40**, 511-530.

Edwards, D. K. (1964a). Activity rhythms of lepidopterous defoliators. I. Techniques for recording activity, eclosion, and emergence. *Can. J. Zool.* **42**, 923-937.

Edwards, D. K. (1964b). Activity rhythms of lepidopterous defoliators. II. *Halisidota argentata* Pack. (Arctiidae) and *Nepytia phantasmaria* Stkr. *Can. J. Zool.* **42**, 939-958.

Edwards, D. K. (1965). Activity rhythms of lepidopterous defoliators. III. The Douglas fir tussock moth, *Orgyia pseudotsugata* (McDunnough) (Liparidae). *Can. J. Zool.* **43**, 673-681.

Edwards, J. S. (1966). Neural control of metamorphosis in *Galleria mellonella*. *J. Insect Physiol.* **12**, 1423-1433.

Eidmann, H. (1956). Über rhythmische Erscheinungen bei der Stabhleuschrecke *Carausius morosus. Z. Vergleich. Physiol.* **28**, 370-390.

Eldridge, B. F. (1966). Environmental control of ovarian development in mosquitoes of the *Culex pipiens* complex. *Science* **151**, 826-828.

Engelmann, F. (1957). Die Steuerung der Ovarfunktion bei der ovoviviparen Schabe *Leucophaea maderae* (Fabr.). *J. Insect Physiol.* **1**, 257-278.

Engelmann, W. (1966). Effect of light and dark pulses on the emergence rhythm of *Drosophila pseudoobscura. Experientia* **22**, 606-608.

Engelmann, W. and D. G. Shappirio (1965). Photoperiodic control of the maintenance and termination of larval diapause in *Chironomus tentans. Nature* **207**, 548-549.

Evans, W. G. and G. G. Gyrisco (1958). The influence of light intensity on the nocturnal emergence of the European chafer. *Ecology* **39**, 761-763.

Ewen, A. B. (1966). A possible endocrine mechanism for inducing diapause in the eggs of *Adelphocoris lineolatus* (Goeze). *Experientia* **22**, 470.

Fernandez, A. T. and N. M. Randolph (1966). The susceptibility of houseflies reared under various photoperiods to insecticide residues. *J. Econ. Entomol.* **59**, 37-39.

Fingerman, M., H. Lago, and M. Lowe (1958). Rhythms of locomotor activity and O_2-consumption of the grasshopper *Romalea microptera. Am. Midland Naturalist* **59**, 58-66.

Fiske, V. M. (1964). Serotonin rhythm in the pineal organ: Control by the sympathetic nervous system. *Science* **146**, 253-254.

Flitters, N. E. (1964). The effect of photoperiod, light intensity, and temperature on copulation, oviposition, and fertility of the Mexican fruit fly. *J. Econ. Entomol.* **57**, 811-813.

Forel, A. (1910). "Das Sinnenleben der Insekten." Munchen.

Fowler, D. J. and C. J. Goodnight (1966). Neurosecretory cells: Daily rhythmicity in *Leiobunum longipes. Science* **152**, 1078-1080.

Fukaya, M. and J. Mitsuhashi (1961). Larval diapause in the rice stem borer with special reference to its hormonal mechanism. *Nogyo Cijutsu Kenkyusho Hokoku Byori Konchu (Bull. Natl. Inst. Agr. Sci. Japan)* **13**, 1-32.

Fukuda, S. (1951). Factors determining the production of non-diapause eggs in the silkworm. *Proc. Japan. Acad.* **27**, 582-586.

Fukuda, S. (1952). Function of the pupal brain and suboesophageal ganglion in the production of non-diapause and diapause eggs in the silkworm. *Annotationes Zool. Japon.* **25**, 149.

Fukuda, S. (1953a). Determination of voltinism in the multivoltine silkworm. *Proc. Japan. Acad.* **29**, 385-388.

Fukuda, S. (1953b). Alteration of voltinism in the silkworm following transection of pupal oesophageal connectives. *Proc. Japan. Acad.* **29**, 389-391.

Fuzeau-Braesch, S. (1965). Hibernation de *Gryllus campestris* L. (Orthopteres:Gryllidae): Analyse de la stabilite et des exigences de la diapause. *Compt. Rend. Soc. Biol.* **159**, 1048-1052.

Fuzeau-Braesch, S. (1966). Étude de la diapause de *Gryllus campestris. J. Insect Physiol.* **12**, 449-455.

Garner, W. W. and H. A. Allard (1920). Effect of relative length of day and night and other factors on growth and reproduction in plants. *J. Agr. Res.* **18**, 553-606.

Geyspitz, K. F. (1953). Reactions of monovoltine butterflies to prolongation of day length. *Entomol. Obozrenie* **33**, 17-31.

Geyspitz, K. F. (1965). Photoperiodic and temperature reactions affecting the seasonal development of the pine moths *Dendrolimus pini* L. and *D. sibiricus* Tschetw. *Entomol. Rev.* **44**, 316-325 (transl. for Entomol. Soc. Am.).

248

Geyspitz, K. F. and A. I. Zarankina (1963). Some features of the photoperiodic reaction of *Dasychira pudibunda* L. (Lepidoptera, Orgyidae). *Entomol. Rev.* **42**, 14-19 (transl. for Entomol. Soc. Am.).

Gillett, J. D. (1961). Cyclic feeding activity in colonized mosquitoes. *Nature* **190**, 881-883.

Gillett, J. D. and A. J. Haddow (1957). Laboratory observations on the oviposition cycle in the mosquito *Aedes (Stegomyia) africanus* (Theobald). *Ann. Trop. Med. Parasitol.* **51**, 170-174.

Gillett, J. D., A. J. Haddow, and P. S. Corbet (1959). Observations on the oviposition cycle of *Aedes (Stegomyia) aegypti* (L.) *Ann. Trop. Med. Parasitol.* **53**, 35-41.

Gilmour, D. (1965). "The Metabolism of Insects." Freeman, San Francisco, California.

Glass, E. H. (1963). A pre-diapause arrested development period in the red-banded leafroller *Argyrotaenia velutinana. J. Econ. Entomol.* **56**, 634-635.

Goryshin, N. I. (1958). An ecological analysis of the seasonal cycle of the cotton bollworm (*Chloridea obsoleta* F.) in the northern areas of its range. *Sci. Mem. Lenin. State Univ.* **240**, 3-20.

Goryshin, N. I. (1963). Light-dark periodicity and the photoperiodic reaction in insects. *Entomol. Rev.* **42**, 10-13 (transl. for Am. Inst. Biol. Sci.).

Goryshin, N. I. (1964). The influence of diurnal light and temperature rhythms on diapause in Lepidoptera. *Entomol. Rev.* **43**, 43-46 (transl. for Entomol. Soc. Am.).

Greenslade, P. J. M. (1963). Daily rhythms of locomotor activity in some Carabidae (Coleoptera). *Entomol. Exptl. Appl.* **6**, 171-180.

Grison, P. (1949). Effects d'implantation de cerveaux chez le Doryphore (*Leptinotarsa decemlineata* Say) en diapause. *Compt. Rend. Acad. Sci.* **228**, 428-430.

Guerra, A. A. and J. L. Bishop (1962). The effect of aestivation on sexual maturation in the female alfalfa weevil (*Hypera postica). J. Econ. Entomol.* **55**, 747-749.

Haddow, A. J. (1945). The mosquitoes of Bwamba County Uganda. II. Biting activity with special reference to the influence of microclimate. *Bull. Entomol. Res.* **36**, 33-73.

Haddow, A. J. (1954). Studies on the biting habits of African mosquitoes. An appraisal of methods employed with special reference to the twenty-four hour catch. *Bull. Entomol. Res.* **45**, 199-242.

Haddow, A. J. (1956). Rhythmic biting activity of certain east African mosquites. *Nature* **177**, 531.

Haddow, A. J. (1961). Entomological studies from a high tower in Mpanga Forest, Uganda. VII. The biting behaviour of mosquitoes and Tabanids. *Trans. Roy. Entomol. Soc., London* **113**, 315-335.

Haddow, A. J. (1964). Observations on the biting habits of mosquitoes in the forest canopy at Zike, Uganda, with special reference to the crepuscular period. *Bull. Entomol. Res.* **55**, 589-608.

Haddow, A. J. and J. D. Gillett (1957). Observations on the oviposition cycle of *Aedes (Stegomyia) aegypti. Ann. Trop. Med. Parasitol.* **51**, 159-169.

Haddow, A. J. and J. D. Gillett (1958). Laboratory observations on the oviposition cycle in the mosquito *Taeniorhynchus (Coquillettidia) fuscopennatus* Theobald. *Ann. Trop. Med. Parasitol.* **52**, 320-325.

Haddow, A. J., P. S. Corbet, and J. D. Gillett (1960). Laboratory observations on the oviposition cycle in the mosquito *Aedes (Stegomyia) apicoargenteus* Theobald. *Ann. Trop. Med. Parasitol.* **54**, 392-396.

Halberg, F. (1960). Temporal coordination of physiologic function. *Cold Spring Harbor Symp. Quant. Biol.* **25**, 289-308.

Halberg, F., E. Halberg, C. P. Barnum, and J. J. Bittner (1959). Physiologic 24-hour periodicity in human beings and mice, the lighting regimen and daily routine. *Am. Assoc. Advance Soc. Publ.* **55**, 803-878.

Hamner, K. C. (1965). Photoperiodism in plants as related to circadian system. *In* "Circadian Clocks" (J. Aschoff, ed.), pp. 331-332. North-Holland Publ., Amsterdam.

Handel, E. V. and A. O. Lea (1965). Medial neurosecretory cells as regulators of glycogen and triglyceride synthesis. *Science* **149**, 298-300.

Hanec, W. and S. D. Beck (1960). Cold hardiness in the European corn borer, *Pyrausta nubilalis. J. Insect Physiol.* **5**, 169-180.

Hans, H. (1961). Termination of diapause and continuous laboratory rearing of the sweet clover weevil, *Sitona cylindricollis* Fahr. *Entomol. Exptl. Appl.* **4**, 41-46.

Harcourt, D. G. and L. M. Cass (1966). Photoperiodism and fecundity in *Plutella maculipennis* (Curt.). *Nature* **210**, 217-218.

Harker, J. E. (1953). The diurnal rhythm of activity of mayfly nymphs. *J. Exptl. Biol.* **30**, 525-533.

Harker, J. E. (1954). Diurnal rhythms in *Periplaneta americana. Nature* **173**, 689-690.

Harker, J. E. (1955). Control of diurnal rhythms of activity in *Periplaneta americana* L. *Nature* **175**, 733.

Harker, J. E. (1956). Factors controlling the diurnal rhythm of activity of *Periplaneta americana. J. Exptl. Biol.* **33**, 224-234.

Harker, J. E. (1958). Diurnal rhythms in the animal kingdom. *Biol. Rev.* **33**, 1-52.

Harker, J. E. (1960a). The effect of perturbations in the environmental cycle on the diurnal rhythm of activity of *Periplaneta americana* L. *J. Exptl. Biol.* **37**, 154-163.

Harker, J. E. (1960b). Internal factors controlling the suboesophageal ganglion neurosecretory cycle in *Periplaneta americana* L. *J. Exptl. Biol.* **37**, 164-170.

Harker, J. E. (1960c). Endocrine and nervous factors in insect circadian rhythms. *Cold Spring Harbor Symp. Quant. Biol.* **25**, 279-286.

Harker, J. E. (1961). Diurnal rhythms. *Ann. Rev. Entomol.* **6**, 131-146.

Harker, J. E. (1964). "The Physiology of Diurnal Rhythms." Cambridge Univ. Press, London and New York.

Harker, J. E. (1965a). The effect of a biological clock on the development rate of *Drosophila* pupae. *J. Exptl. Biol.* **42**, 323-337.

Harker, J. E. (1965b). The effect of photoperiod on the developmental rate of *Drosophila* pupae. *J. Exptl. Biol.* **43**, 411-423.

Harvey, G. T. (1957). The occurrence and nature of diapause-free development in the spruce budworm, *Choristoneura fumiferana* (Clem.). *Can. J. Zool.* **35**, 549-572.

Harvey, G. T. (1958). A relationship between photoperiod and cold storage treatment in the spruce budworm. *Science* **128**, 1205-1206.

Harvey, G. T. (1961). Second diapause in spruce budworm from eastern Canada. *Can. Entomol.* **93**, 594-602.

Harwood, R. F. (1964). Physiological factors associated with male swarming of the mosquito *Culex tarsalis* Coq. *Mosquito News* **24**, 320-325.

Harwood, R. F. and E. Halfhill (1964). The effect of photoperiod on fat body and ovarian development of *Culex tarsalis. Ann. Entomol. Soc. Am.* **57**, 596-600.

Harwood, R. F. and N. Takata (1965). Effect of photoperiod and temperature on fatty acid composition of the mosquito *Culex tarsalis. J. Insect Physiol.* **11**, 711-716.

Hasegawa, K. (1952). Studies on the voltinism of the silkworm, *Bombyx mori* L., with special reference to the organs concerning determination of voltinism. *J. Fac. Agric. Tottori Univ.* **1**, 83-124.

Hasegawa, K. (1957). The diapause hormone of the silkworm, *Bombyx mori. Nature* **179**, 1300-1301.

Hasegawa, K. (1963). Studies on the mode of action of the diapause hormone in the silkworm, *Bombyx mori* L. I. The action of diapause hormone injected into pupae of different ages. *J. Exptl. Biol.* **40**, 517-529.

Hasegawa, K. (1964). Studies on the mode of action of the diapause hormone in the silkworm, *Bombyx mori* L. II. Content of diapause hormone in the suboesophageal ganglion. *J. Exptl. Biol.* **41**, 855-863.

Hasegawa, K. and O. Yamashita (1965). Studies on the mode of action of the diapause hormone in the silkworm, *Bombyx mori* L. VI. The target organ of the diapause hormone. *J. Exptl. Biol.* **43**, 271-277.

Hastings, J. W. and V. C. Bode (1962). Biochemistry of rhythmic systems. *Ann. N. Y. Acad. Sci.* **98**, 876-889.

Hastings, J. W. and A. Keynan (1965). Molecular aspects of circadian systems. *In* "Circadian Clocks" (J. Aschoff, ed.) pp. 167-182. North-Holland Publ., Amsterdam.

Hastings, J. W. and B. M. Sweeney (1958). A persistent diurnal rhythm of luminescence in *Gonyaulax polyedra*. *Biol. Bull.* **115**, 440-458.

Hastings, J. W. and B. M. Sweeney (1959). The *Gonyaulax* clock. *Am. Assoc. Advance. Sci. Publ.* **55**, 567-584.

Highnam, K. C. and P. T. Haskell (1964). The endocrine system of isolated and crowded *Locusta* and *Schistocerca* in relation to oocyte growth, and the effects of flying on maturation. *J. Insect Physiol.* **10**, 849-864.

Hilsenhoff, W. L. (1966). The biology of *Chironomus plumosus* (Diptera: Chironomidae) in Lake Winnebago, Wisconsin. *Ann. Entomol. Soc. Am.* **59**, 465-473.

Hinton, H. E. (1957). Some aspects of diapause. *Sci. Progr.* **178**, 307-320.

Hodek, I. (1962). Experimental influencing of the imaginal diapause in *Coccinella septempunctata* L. *Acta Soc. Entomol. Cech.* **59**, 297-313.

Hodek, I. and J. Cerkasov (1958). A study of the imaginal hibernation of *Semiadalia undecimnotata* Schneid. in the open. *Acta Soc. Zool. Bohem.* **22**, 180-192.

Hodek, I. and J. Cerkasov (1960). Prevention and artificial induction of the imaginal diapause in *Coccinella 7-punctata* L. *Nature* **187**, 345.

Hodek, I. and J. Cerkasov (1961a). Experimental influencing of the imaginal diapause in *Coccinella septempunctata* L. *Acta Soc. Zool. Bohem.* **24**, 70-90.

Hodek, I. and J. Cerkasov (1961b). Prevention and artificial induction of imaginal diapause in *Coccinella septempunctata* L. *Entomol. Exptl. Appl.* **4**, 179-190.

Hodek, I. and J. Cerkasov (1962). Three problems in the study of diapause in Coccinellidae. *Proc. 11th Intern. Congr. Entomol. Vienna, (1960)* **1**, 773-774.

Hodek, I. and J. Cerkasov (1963). Imaginal dormancy in *Semiadalia undecimnotata* Schneid. II. Changes in water, fat, and glycogen content. *Acta Soc. Zool. Bohem.* **27**, 298-318.

Hodek, I. and J. Cerkasov (1965). Biochemical changes in *Semiadalia undecimnotata* (Schneider) adults during diapause. *Nature* **205**, 925-926.

Hodgson, E. S. (1955). An ecological study of the behavior of the leaf-cutting ant *Atta cephalotes. Ecology* **36**, 293-304.

Hodson, A. C. (1937). Some aspects of the role of water in insect hibernation. *Ecol. Monographs.* **7**, 271-315.

Hogan, T. W. (1961). The action of urea on diapause in eggs of *Acheta commodus* (Walk.). *Australian J. Biol. Sci.***14**, 419-426.

Hogan, T. W. (1962). The effect of ammonia on the rate of termination of diapause in eggs of *Acheta commodus* (Walk). *Australian J. Biol. Sci.* **15**, 538-542.

Huggans, J. L. and C. C. Blickenstaff (1964). Effects of photoperiod on sexual development in the alfalfa weevil. *J. Econ. Entomol.* **57**, 167-168.

251

Hughes, R. D. (1960). Induction of diapause in *Erioschia brassicae* Bouche. *J. Exptl. Biol.* **37**, 218-223.

Inouye, H. and S. Kamano (1957). The effects of photoperiod and temperature on the induction of diapause in the rice stem borer, *Chilo suppressalis. Nippon Oyo Dobutsu Konchu Gaku Zasshi (Japan. J. Appl. Entomol. Zool.).* **1**, 100-105.

Jacobson, L. A. (1960). Influence of photoperiod on oviposition by the army cutworm, *Chorizagrotis auxiliaris* (Lepidoptera: Noctuidae) in an insectary. *Ann. Entomol. Soc. Am.* **53**, 474-475.

Jahn, T. L. and F. Crescitelli (1940). Diurnal changes in the electrical response of the compound eye. *Biol. Bull.* **78**, 42-52.

Jahn, T. L. and V. J. Wolff (1943). Electrical aspects of a diurnal rhythm in the eye of *Dytiscus fasciuentris. Physiol. Zool.* **16**, 101-109.

Jermy, T. and G. Saringer (1955). Die Rolle der Photoperiode in der Auslösung der Diapause des Kartoffelkäfers (*Leptinotarsa decemlineata* Say) und des Amerikanischen weissen Bärenspinners (*Hyphantria cunea* Drury). *Acta Agron. Acad. Sci. Hung.* **5**, 419-440.

Johnson, B. (1963). A histological study of neurosecretion in aphids. *J. Insect Physiol.* **9**, 727-739.

Johnson, B. and P. R. Birks (1960). Studies on wing polymorphism in aphids. I. The developmental process involved in the production of different forms. *Entomol. Exptl. Appl.* **3**, 327-339.

Johnson, B. and B. Bowers (1963). Transport of neurohormones from the corpora cardiaca in insects. *Science* **141**, 264-266.

Johnson, C. G. and L. R. Taylor (1957). Periodism and energy summation with special reference to flight rhythms in aphids. *J. Exptl. Biol.* **34**, 209-221.

Johnson, C. G., L. R. Taylor, and E. Haine (1957). The analysis and reconstruction of diurnal flight curves in aliencolae of *Aphis fabae* Scop. *Ann. Appl. Biol.* **45**, 682-701.

Joly, P. (1945). La fonction ovarienne et son controle humorale chez les Dytiscides. *Arch. Zool. Exptl. Gen.* **84**, 49-164.

Jones, M. D. R., M. G. Ford, and J. D. Gillett (1966). Light-on and light-off effects on the circadian flight activity in the mosquito *Anopheles gambiae. Nature* **211**, 871-872.

Kalmus, H. (1934). Über die Natur des Zeitgedächtnisses der Bienen. *Z. Vergleich. Physiol.* **20**, 405-419.

Kalmus, H. (1935). Periodizität und Autochronie (Ideochronie) als zeitregelnde Eigenschaften der Organismen. *Biol. Gen.* **11**, 93-114.

Kappus, K. D. (1965). The photoperiodic induction of diapause in eggs of *Aedes triseriatus* (Say). Ph.D. Thesis, Ohio State Univ. *Dissertation Abstr. 65-5650.*

Karakashian, M. W. and J. W. Hastings (1962). The inhibition of a biological clock by Actinomycin D. *Proc. Natl. Acad. Sci. U. S.* **48**, 2130-2136.

Karakashian, M. W. and J. W. Hastings (1963). The effects of inhibitors of macromolecular biosynthesis upon the persistent rhythm of luminescence in *Gonyaulax. J. Gen. Physiol.* **47**, 1-12.

Katiyar, K. P. and W. H. Long (1961). Diapause in the sugarcane borer, *Diatraea saccharalis. J. Econ. Entomol.* **54** 285-287.

Kennedy, D. (1958). Responses from the crayfish caudal photoreceptor. *Am. J. Ophthalmol.* **46**, 19-26.

Kennedy, D. (1963). Physiology of photoreceptor neurons in the abdominal nerve cord of the crayfish. *J. Gen. Physiol.* **46**, 551-572.

Kennedy, J. S. and H. L. G. Stroyan (1959). Biology of aphids. *Ann. Rev. Entomol.* **4**, 139-160.

Kenten, J. (1955). The effect of photoperiod and temperature on reproduction in *Acyrthosiphon pisum* (Harris) and on the forms produced. *Bull. Entomol. Res.* **46**, 599-624.

Kiesel, A. (1894). Untersuchungen zur Physiologie des facettierten Augen. *Sitzber. Akad. Wiss. Wien* **103**, 97-139.

Kind, T. V. (1965). Neurosecretion and voltinism in *Orgyia antigua* L. *Entomol. Rev.* **44**: 326-327 (transl. for Entomol. Soc. Am.).

King, L. L. and D. M. Benjamin (1965). The effect of photoperiod and temperature on the development of multivoltine populations of *Neodiprion rugifrons* Middleton. *Proc. N. Central Branch Entomol. Soc. Am.* **20**, 129-140.

Kisimoto, R. (1956). Effect of diapause in the fourth larval instar on the determination of wing-form in the adult of the small brown planthopper, *Delphacodes striatella* Fallen. *Nippon Oyo Dobutsu Konchu Gaku Zasshi (Japan. J. Appl. Entomol. Zool.).* **12**, 202-210.

Kisimoto, R. (1959). Studies on the diapause in the planthoppers and leafhoppers. III. Sensitivity of various larval stages to photoperiod and the forms of ensuing adults in the green rice leafhopper. *Nephotettix cincticeps. Nippon Oyo Dobutsu Konchu Gaku Zasshi (Japan. J. Appl. Entomol. Zool.)* **3**, 200-207.

Klug, H. (1958). Histo-physiologische Untersuchungen über die Aktivitätsperiodik bei Carabiden. *Wiss. Z. Humboldt-Univ. Berlin, Math.-Naturw. Reihe.* **8**, 405-434.

Kobayashi, M. and Y. Ishitoya (1964). Hormonal system on the control of the egg diapause in the silkworm, *Bombyx mori* L. *Nippon Sanshiga Ku Zasshi (J. Sericult. Sci. Japan).* **33**, 111-114.

Kogure, M. (1933). The influence of light and temperature on certain characters of the silkworm, *Bombyx mori. J. Dept. Agr. Kyushu Univ.* **4**, 1-93.

Koidsumi, K. (1952). Water content and the hormone center for the pupation of hibernating larvae of *Chilo simplex* Butler. *Annotationes Zool. Japon.* **25**, 156-167.

Kuznetsova, I. A. (1962). Factors producing the onset of diapause in *Pectinophora malvella* (Hb). *Entomol. Rev.* **41**, 313-316 (transl. for Am. Inst. Biol. Sci.).

Lambremont, E. N., M. S. Blum, and R. M. Schrader (1964). Storage and fatty acid composition of triglycerides during adult diapause of the boll weevil. *Ann. Entomol. Soc. Am.* **57**, 526-532.

Larczenko, K. (1957). Feeding and diapause of the Colorado potato beetle. *Roczniki Nauk Rolniczych* **74**, 287-314.

Larsen, J. R. (1958). Hormone-induced ovarian development in mosquitoes. *Science* **127**, 587-588.

Larsen, J. R. and D. Bodenstein (1959). The humoral control of egg maturation in the mosquito. *J. Exptl. Zool.* **140**, 343-381.

LeBerre, J. R. (1965). Quelques considerations d'ordre écologique et physiologique sur la diapause du Doryphore *Leptinotarsa decemlineata* Say. *Compt. Rend. Soc. Biol.* **159**, 2131-2135.

Lees, A. D. (1950). Diapause and photoperiodism in the fruit tree red spider mite (*Metatetranychus ulmi* Koch). *Nature* **166**, 874.

Lees, A. D. (1952). The physiology of diapause in the fruit tree red spider mite. *Proc. 9th Intern. Congr. Entomol. Amsterdam, 1952* **1**, 351-354.

Lees, A. D. (1953a). Environmental factors controlling the evocation and termination of diapause in the fruit tree red spider mite *Metatetranychus ulmi* Koch. *Ann. Appl. Biol.* **40**, 449-486.

Lees, A. D. (1953b). The significance of the light and dark phases in the photoperiodic control of diapause in *Metatetranychus ulmi. Ann. Appl. Biol.* **40**, 487-497.

Lees, A. D. (1954). Photoperiodism in arthropods. *Proc. 1st Intern. Photobiol. Congr., Amsterdam 1954 pp. 36.45.*

Lees, A. D. (1955). "The Physiology of Diapause in Arthropods." Cambridge Univ. Press, London and New York.

Lees, A. D. (1956). The physiology and biochemistry of diapause. *Ann. Rev. Entomol.* **1**, 1-16.

Lees, A. D. (1959a). The role of photoperiod and temperature in the determination of parthenogenetic and sexual forms in the aphid *Megoura viciae* Buckton. I. The influence of these factors on apterous virginoparae and their progeny. *J. Insect Physiol.* **3**, 92-117.

Lees, A. D. (1959b). Photoperiodism in insects and mites. *Am. Assoc. Advance Soc. Publ.* **55**, 585-600.

Lees, A. D. (1960a). Some aspects of animal photoperiodism. *Cold Spring Harbor Symp. Quant. Biol.* **25**, 261-268.

Lees, A. D. (1960b). The role of photoperiod and temperature in the determination of parthenogenetic and sexual forms in the aphid *Megoura viciae* Buckton. II. The operation of the 'interval timer' in young clones. *J. Insect Physiol.* **4**, 154-175.

Lees, A. D. (1961). Clonal polymorphism in aphids. *Symp. Roy. Entomol. Soc. London* **1**, 68-79.

Lees, A. D. (1963). The role of photoperiod and temperature in the determination of parthenogenetic and sexual forms in the aphid *Megoura viciae* Buckton. III. Further properties of the maternal switching mechanism in apterous aphids. *J. Insect Physiol.* **9**, 153-164.

Lees, A. D. (1964). The location of the photoperiodic receptors in the aphid *Megoura viciae* Buckton. *J. Exptl. Biol.* **41**, 119-133.

Lees, A. D. (1965). Is there a circadian component in the megoura photoperiodic clock? *In* "Circadian Clocks" (J. Aschoff, ed.), pp. 351-356. North-Holland Publ., Amsterdam.

Lees, A. D. (1966). The control of polymorphism in aphids. *Advan. Insect Physiol.* **3**, 207-277.

Leigh, T. F. (1966). A reproductive diapause in *Lygus hesperus* Knight. *J. Econ. Entomol.* **59**, 1280-1281.

Leuthold, R. (1966). Die Bewegungsaktivität der Weiblichen Schabe *Leucophaea maderae* (F.) im Laufe des Fortpflanzungszyklus und ihre experimentelle Beeinflussung. *J. Insect Physiol.* **12**, 1303-1331.

Lewis, C. B. and J. D. Bletchly (1943). The emergence rhythm of the dung-fly *Scopeuma* (=*Scatophaga*) *stercoraria* (L.). *J. Am. Ecol.* **12**, 11-18.

Lindauer, M. (1960). Time-compensated sun orientation in bees. *Cold Spring Harbor Symp. Quant. Biol.* **25**, 371-377.

Lindauer, M. (1963). Time sense of bees. *Proc. 16th Intern. Congr. Zool.* **4**, 351-354.

Logen, D. and R. F. Harwood (1965). Oviposition of the mosquito *Culex tarsalis* in response to light cues. *Mosquito News* **25**, 462-465.

Love, G. J. and J. G. Whelchel (1955). Photoperiodism and the development of *Aedes triseriatus. Ecology* **36**, 340-342.

Lukefahr, M. J., L. W. Noble, and D. F. Martin (1964). Factors inducing diapause in the pink bollworm. *U. S. Dept. Agr. Tech. Bull.* **1304**.

Lutz, F. E. (1932). Experiments with Orthoptera concerning diurnal rhythms. *Am. Museum Novitates* **550**, 1-24.

Lutz, P. E. (1961). Pattern of emergence in the dragonfly *Tetragoneuria cynosura. J. Elisha Mitchell Sci. Soc.* **77**, 114-115.

Lutz, P. E. and C. E. Jenner (1960). Relationship between oxygen consumption and photo-periodic induction of the termination of diapause in nymphs of the dragonfly *Tetragoneuria cynosura*. *J. Elisha Mitchell Sci. Soc.* **76**, 192-193.

Lutz, P. E. and C. E. Jenner (1964). Life-history and photoperiodic responses of nymphs of *Tetragoneuria cynosura* (Say). *Biol. Bull.* **127**, 304-316.

MacGillvary, M. E. and G. B. Anderson (1964). The effect of photoperiod and temperature on the production of gamic and agamic forms in *Macrosiphum euphorbiae* (Thomas). *Can. J. Zool.* **42**, 491-510.

McCluskey, E. S. (1958). Daily rhythms in male harvester and Argentine ants. *Science* **128**, 536.

McCluskey, E. S. (1963). Rhythms and clocks in harvester and Argentine ants. *Physiol. Zool.* **36**, 273-292.

McCluskey, E. S. (1965). Circadiam rhythms in male ants in five diverse species. *Science* **150**, 1037-1039.

McCrary, A. B. and C. E. Jenner (1965). Influence of day length on sex ratio in the giant mosquito, *Toxorhynchites rutilus*, in nature. *Am. Zool.* **5**, 206.

McElroy, W. D. (1964). Insect bioluminescence. *In* "The Physiology of Insecta" (M. Rockstein, ed.), Vol. 1, pp. 463-508. Academic Press, New York.

McFarlane, J. E. (1964). Factors affecting growth and wing polymorphism in *Gryllodes sigillatus* (Walk.): Dietary protein level and a possible effect of photoperiod. *Can. J. Zool.* **42**, 767-771.

McLeod, D. G. R. (1963). Physiology of diapause in the European corn borer, *Ostrinia nubilalis*. Ph.D. thesis, Univ. of Wisconsin, Madison, Wisconsin.

McLeod, D. G. R. (1964). Diapause in *Euxesta notata* (Weidemann). *Proc. Entomol. Soc. Ontario* **94**, 61-62.

McLeod, D. G. R. and S. D. Beck (1963a). The anatomy of the neuroendocrine complex of the European corn borer, *Ostrinia nubilalis*, and its relation to diapause. *Ann. Entomol. Soc. Am.* **56**, 723-727.

McLeod, D. G. R. and S. D. Beck (1963b). Photoperiodic termination of diapause in an insect. *Biol. Bull.* **124**, 84-96.

Mansingh, A. and B. N. Smallman (1966). Photoperiod control of an 'obligatory' pupal diapause. *Can. Entomol.* **98**, 613-616.

Marcovitch, S. (1923). Plant lice and light exposure. *Science* **58**, 537-538.

Marcovitch, S. (1924). The migration of the Aphididae and the appearance of the sexual forms as affected by the relative length of daily light exposure. *J. Agr. Res.* **27**, 513-522.

Masaki, S. (1956). The local variation in the diapause pattern of the cabbage moth. *Barathra brassicae* Linne, with particular reference to the aestival diapause. *Mie Daigaku Nagakubo Gakujutsu Hokoku (Bull. Fac. Agr. Mie Univ.)* **13**, 29-46.

Masaki, S. (1957a). Larval sensitive stage for the action of external factors controlling the occurrence of diapause in the cabbage moth pupa, *Barathra brassicae* Linne. *J. Fac. Agr. Hokkaido Univ.* **50**, 197-210.

Masaki, S. (1957b). Further experiments on the thermal relations of the diapause development in the cabbage moth pupa, *Barathra brassicae* Linne. *J. Fac. Agr. Hokkaido Univ.* **50**, 211-224.

Masaki, S. (1959). Seasonal changes in the mode of diapause in the pupae of *Abraxas miranda* (Butler). *Hirosaki Daigaku Nogakuku Gakujutsu Hokoku (Bull. Fac. Agr. Hirosaki Univ)*, **5**, 14-27.

Masaki, S. (1961). Geographic variation of diapause in insects. *Hirosaki Daigaku Nogakuku Gakujutsu Hokoku (Bull. Fac. Agr. Hirosaki Univ.)* **7**, 66-98.

Masaki, S. and N. Oyama (1963). Photoperiodic control of growth and wing-form in *Nemobius yezoensis* Shiraki. *Kontyu* **31**, 16-26 *(Entomology)*.

Masaki, S. and T. Sakai (1965). Summer diapause in the seasonal cycle of *Mamestra brassicae* Linne. *Nippon Oyu Dobutsu Konchu Gaku Zasshi (Japan. J. Appl. Entomol. Zool.)* **9**, 191-205.

Masleninkova, V. A. (1961). Effect of the host's hormones on the diapause of *Pteromalus puparum* L. *Dokl. Biol. Sci. Sect. (Engl. Transl.)* **139**, 654-656 (transl. for Am. Inst. Biol. Sci.).

Mellanby, K. (1958). Water drinking by the larva of the European corn borer. *J. Econ. Entomol.* **51**, 744-745.

Menaker, M. and A. Eskin (1966). Entrainment of circadian rhythms by sound in *Passer domesticus. Science* **154**, 1579-1581.

Menaker, M. and G. Gross (1965). Effect of fluctuating temperature on diapause induction in the pink bollworm. *J. Insect Physiol.* **11**, 911-914.

Messenger, P. S. (1964). The influence of rhythmically fluctuating temperatures on the development and reproduction of the spotted alfalfa aphid, *Therioaphis maculata. J. Econ. Entomol.* **57**, 71-76.

Michal, K. (1931). Oszillation im Sauerstoffverbrauch der Mehlwurmlarven *(Tenebrio molitor). Zool. Anz.* **95**, 65-75.

Mills, J. N. (1966). Human circadian rhythms. *Physiol. Rev.* **46**, 128-171.

Minis, D. H. (1965). Parallel peculiarities in the entrainment of a circadian rhythm and photoperiodic induction in the pink bollworm *(Pectinophora gossypiella). In* "Circadian Clocks" (J. Aschoff, ed.), pp. 333-343. North-Holland Publ., Amsterdam.

Missionier, J. (1956). Note sur la biologie du psylle de l'aubepine *(Psylla peregrina* Foerster). *Ann. Epiphyties* **7**, 253-262.

Mochida, O. and M. Yoshimeki (1962). Relations with development of the gonads, dimensional changes of the corpora allata, and duration of postdiapause period in hibernating larvae of the rice stem borer. *Nippon Oyu Dobutsu Konchu Gaku Zasshi (Japan. J. Appl. Entomol. Zool.)* **6**, 114-123.

Monchadskii, A. S. (1935). On the role of contact moisture after the winter dormant period (diapause) in the corn borer larva. *Plant Protect. (Leningr.)* **1935**, 39-50.

Montgomery, B. E. and J. M. Macklin (1962). Rates of development in the later instars of *Neotetrum pulchellum* (Drury). *Proc. N. Central Branch Entomol. Soc. Am.* **17**, 21-23.

Mori, S. (1944). Daily frequency of activities of *Cavernularia obesa valenciennes.* III. Effect of light intensity. *Dobutsugaka Zasshi (Zool. Mag.).* **56**, 1-17.

Moriarty, F. (1959). The 24-hour rhythm of emergence of *Ephestia kuhniella* Zell. from the pupa. *J. Insect Physiol.* **3**, 357-366.

Moroshi, S. (1957). "Physiogenetical Studies on Moltinism and Voltinism in *Bombyx mori:* A New Hormonal Antagonistic Balance Theory on the Growth." Japan. Soc. Promotion of Science, Tokyo.

Moroshi, S. (1959). Hormonal studies on the diapause and nondiapause eggs of the silkworm, *Bombyx mori* L. *J. Insect Physiol.* **3**, 28-40.

Müller, H. J. (1954). Der Saisondimorphismus bei Zikaden der Gattung *Euscelis* Brulle. *Beitr. Entomol.* **4**, 1-56.

Müller, H. J. (1955). Die Saisonformenbildung von *Arachnia levana*, ein photoperiodisch gesteuter Diapause-effect. *Naturwissenschaften* **42**, 134-135.

Müller, H. J. (1957). Die Wirkung exogener Faktoren auf die Zyklische Formenbildung der Insekten, inbesondere der Gattung *Euscelis*. *Zool. Jahrb.* **85**, 317-430.

Müller, H. J. (1958). Über den Einfluss der Photoperiode auf Diapause und Körpergrosse der Delphacide *Stenocranus minutus* Fabr. *Zool. Anz.* **160**, 294-311.

Müller, H. J. (1960a). Die Bedeutung der Photoperiode im Lebensablauf der Insekten. *Z. Angew. Entomol.* **47**, 7-24.

Müller, H. J. (1960b). Über photoperiodisch bedingte Ökomorphosen bei Insekten. *In* "The Ontogeny of Insects" (I. Hrdý, ed.), pp. 297-304. Academic Press, New York.

Müller, H. J. (1961). Erster Nachweis einer Eidiapause bei den Jassiden *Euscelis plebejus* Fall. und *lineolatus* Brulle. *Z. Angew. Entomol.* **48**, 233-241.

Müller, H. J. (1962a). Über den Saisondimorphen entwicklungszyklus und die Aufhebung der Diapause bei *Aleurochiton complanatus* (Baerensprung). *Entomol. Exptl. Appl.* **5**, 124-138.

Müller, H. J. (1962b). Zur Biologie und Morphologie der Saisonformen von *Aleurochiton complanatus* (Baerensprung). *Z. Morphol. Oekol. Tiere* **51**, 345-374.

Müller, H. J. (1962c). Über die Induktion der Diapause und der Ausbildung der Saisonformen bei *Aleurochiton complanatus* (Baerensprung). *Z. Morphol. Oekol. Tiere* **51**, 575-610.

Müller, H. J. (1965). Zur weiteren Analyse der Ökomorphosen von *Euscelis plebejus* Fall. I. Die Wirkung der natürlichen Photoperioden, insbesondere der Kontinuierlichen Änderung der Tageslänge. *Zool. Beitr.* **11**, 151-182.

Mutchmor, J. A. (1959). Some factors influencing the occurrence and size of the midsummer flight of the European corn borer, *Ostrinia nubilalis* (Hbn), in southwestern Ontario. *Can. Entomol.* **91**, 798-806.

Mutchmor, J. A. and W. E. Beckel (1958). Importance of photoperiod and temperature in inducing diapause in the European corn borer, *Pyrausta nubilalis* (Hubn.). *Nature* **181**, 204.

Mutchmor, J. A. and W. E. Beckel (1959). Some factors affecting diapause in the European corn borer, *Ostrinia nubilalis* (Hubn.). *Can. J. Zool.* **37**, 161-168.

Myers, K. (1952). Rhythms in emergence and other aspects of behaviour of the Queensland fruit fly (*Dacus (Strumeta) tryoni* Frogg) and the solanum fruit fly (*Dacus (Strumeta) cacuminatus* Hering). *Australian J. Sci.* **15**, 101-102.

Nayar, K. K. (1958). Studies on the neurosecretory system of *Iphita limbata* Stal. V. Probable endocrine basis of oviposition in the female insect. *Proc. Indian Acad. Sci. Sect. B* **47**, 233-251.

Neumann, D. (1962). Über die Steuerung der lunaren Schwärmperiodik der Mücke *Clunio marinus*. *Verhandl. Deut. Zool. Ges.* **1962**, 275-285.

Neumann, D. (1965). Die intraspezifische Variabilitat der lunaren und täglichen Schlupfzeiten von *Clunio marinus*. *Verhandl. Deut. Zool. Ges.* **1965**, 223-233.

Neumann, D. (1966). Die lunare und tägliche Schlüpfperiodik der Mücke *Clunio*. Steuerubg und Abstimmung auf die Gezeitenperiodik. *Z. Vergleich. Physiol.* **53**, 1-61.

Neville, A. C. (1963). Daily growth layers in locust rubber-like cuticle influenced by an external rhythm. *J. Insect Physiol.* **9**, 177-186.

Neville, A. C. (1965). Circadian organization of chitin in some insect skeletons. *Quart J. Microscop. Sci.* **106**, 315-325.

Nielsen, E. T. (1961). Twilight and the "crep" unit. *Nature* **190**, 878-879.

Nielsen, E. T. (1963). Illumination at twilight. *Oikos* **14**, 9-21.

Nielsen, H. T. and E. T. Nielsen (1962). Swarming of mosquitoes. Laboratory experiments under controlled conditions. *Entomol. Exptl. Appl.* **5**, 14-32.

Norris, M. J. (1958). Influence of photoperiod on imaginal diapause in Acridids. *Nature* **181**, 58.

Norris, M. J. (1959). The influence of day length on imaginal diapause in the red locust, *Nomadacris septemfasciata* (Serv.) *Entomol. Exptl. Appl.* **2**, 154-168.

Norris, M. J. (1962). Diapause induced by photoperiod in a tropical locust, *Nomadacris septemfasciata* (Serv.). *Ann. Appl. Biol.* **50**, 600-603.

Norris, M. J. (1965). The influence of constant and changing photoperiods on imaginal diapause in the red locust (*Nomadacris septemfasciata* Serv.). *J. Insect Physiol.* **11**, 1105-1119.

Novak, K. and F. Sehnal (1963). The development cycle of some species of the genus *Limnephilus* (Trichoptera). *Acta Soc. Entomol. Cech.* **60**, 67-80.

Nowosielski, J. W. and R. L. Patton (1963). Studies on circadian rhythms of the house cricket, *Gryllus domesticus* L. *J. Insect Physiol.* **9**, 401-410.

Nowosielski, J. W. and R. L. Patton (1964). Daily fluctuations in the blood sugar concentration of the house cricket, *Gryllus domesticus* L. *Science* **144**, 180-181.

Nowosielski, J. W., R. L. Patton, and J. A. Naegele (1964). Daily rhythm of narcotic sensitivity in the house cricket, *Gryllus domesticus* L., and the two-spotted spider mite, *Tetranychus urticae* Koch. *J. Cellular Comp. Physiol.* **63**, 393-398.

Nuber, K. (1961). Overwintering of the red spider mite, *Tetranychus urticae* Koch, in hop gardens. *Hoefchen Briefe* **14**, 6-15.

Nuorteva, P. (1965). The flying activity of *Helina binotata* Zett. in subarctic conditions. *Ann. Entomol. Fennicae* **31**, 117-131.

Odhiambo, T. R. (1966). The metabolic effects of the corpus allatum hormone in the male desert locust. II. Spontaneous locomotor activity. *J. Exptl. Biol.* **45**, 51-63.

Oka, H. and H. Hashimoto (1959). Lunare Periodizitat in der Fortpflanzung einer pazifichen Art von *Clunio. Biol. Zentr.* **78**, 545-559.

Otuka, M. and H. Santa (1955). Studies on the diapause in the cabbage armyworm, *Barathra brassicae* L. III. The effect of the rhythm of light and darkness on the induction of diapause. *Nogyo Gijutsu Kenkyusho Hokoku Byori Konchu (Bull, Natl. Inst. Agr. Sci.).* pp. 49-56.

Palmen, E. (1955). Diel periodicity of pupal emergence in natural populations of some chironomids (Diptera). *Ann. Zool. Soc. Zool. Botan. Fennicae Vonamo* **17**, 1-30.

Palmen, E. (1956). Periodic emergence in some chironomids—an adaptation to nocturnalism. *In* "Bertil Hanstrom Zoological Papers," pp. 248-256. Zoological Institute, Lund, Sweden.

Palmen, E. (1958). Diel periodicity of pupal emergence of some north European chironomids. *Proc. 10th Intern. Congr. Entomol., Montreal, 1956* **2**, 219-224.

Pammer, E. (1965). Spinnverhalten und Diapauseinduktion bei *Philosamia cynthia. Naturwissenschaften* **52**, 649.

Papillon, M. (1965). Influence de la photopériode et de la température sur les élevages de *Schistocerca gregaria* phase grégaire. *Compt. Rend. Acad. Sci.* **260**, 6446-6448.

Paris, O. H. and C. E. Jenner (1959). Photoperiodic control of diapause in the pitcher-plant midge, *Metriocnemus knabi. Am. Assoc. Advance Soc. Publ.* **55**, 601-624.

Park, O. and J. G. Keller (1932). Studies in nocturnal ecology. II. Preliminary analysis of activity rhythms in nocturnal forest insects. *Ecology* **13**, 335-346.

Pease, R. W. (1962). Factors causing seasonal forms in *Ascia monuste* (Lepidoptera). *Science* **137**, 987-988.

Pepper, J. H. (1937). Breaking the dormancy in the sugar-beet webworm, *Loxostege sticticalis* L, by means of chemicals. *J. Econ. Entomol.* **30**, 380.

Phillips, J. R. and L. D. Newsom (1966). Diapause in *Heliothis zea* and *Heliothis virescens*. *Ann. Entomol. Soc. Am.* **59**, 154-159.

Pittendrigh, C. S. (1954). On temperature independence in the clock system controlling emergence time in *Drosophila*. *Proc. Natl. Acad. Sci. U. S.* **40**, 1018-1029.

Pittendrigh, C. S. (1958a). Adaptation, natural selection, and behavior. *In* "Behavior and Evolution" (A. Roe and G. G. Simpson, eds.), pp. 390-416. Yale Univ. Press, New Haven, Connecticut.

Pittendrigh, C. S. (1958b). Perspectives in the study of biological clocks. *In* "Symposium on Perspectives in Marine Biology," pp. 239-268. Univ. of California Press, Berkeley, California.

Pittendrigh, C. S. (1960). Circadian rhythms and circadian organization of living systems. *Cold Spring Harbor Symp. Quant. Biol.* **25**, 159-182.

Pittendrigh, C. S. (1961). On temporal organization in living systems. *Harvey Lectures Ser.* **56**, 93-125.

Pittendrigh, C. S. (1965). On the mechanism of the entrainment of a circadian rhythm by light cycles. *In* "Circadian Clocks" (J. Aschoff, ed.), pp. 277-297. North-Holland Publ., Amsterdam.

Pittendrigh, C. S. and V. G. Bruce (1957). An oscillator model for biological clocks. *In* "Rhythmic and Synthetic Processes in Growth" (D. Rudnick, ed.), pp. 75-109. Princeton Univ. Press, Princeton, New Jersey.

Pittendrigh, C. S. and V. G. Bruce (1959). Daily rhythms as coupled oscillator systems and their relation to thermoperiodism and photoperiodism. *Am. Assoc. Advance Soc. Publ.* **55**, 475-505.

Pittendrigh, C. S. and D. H. Minis (1964). The entrainment of circadian oscillations by light and their role as photoperiodic clocks. *Am. Naturalist* **98**, 261-294.

Pittendrigh, C. S., V. G. Bruce, and P. Kaus (1958). On the significance of transients in daily rhythms. *Proc. Natl. Acad. Sci., U.S.* **44**, 965-973.

Polick, B., J. W. Nowosielski, and J. A. Naegele (1964). Daily sensitivity rhythm of the two-spotted spider mite, *Tetranychus urticae*, to DDVP. *Science* **145**, 405.

Polick, B., J. W. Nowosielski, and J. A. Naegele (1965). Daily rhythm of oviposition in the two-spotted spider mite. *J. Econ. Entomol.* **58**, 467-469.

Prat, H. (1956a). Regimes de la thermogenese chez la blatte Americaine. *Rev. Can. Biol.* **14**, 360-398.

Prat, H. (1956b). Analyse micro-calorimetrique des variations de la thermogenese chez divers insectes. *Can. J. Zool.* **32**, 172-197.

Prosser, C. L. (1934). Action potentials in the nervous system of the crayfish. I. Responses to illumination of the eye and caudal ganglion. *J. Cellular Comp. Physiol.* **4**, 363-377.

Raabe, M. (1963). Mise en evidence, chez des insectes d'ordres varies, d'elements neurosecreteurs tritocerebaux. *Compt. Rend. Acad. Sci.* **257**, 1171.

Rabb, R. L. (1966). Diapause in *Protoparce sexta* (Lepidoptera: Sphingidae). *Ann. Entomol. Soc. Am.* **59**, 160-165.

Remmert, H. (1955a). Untersuchungen über das Tageszeitlich gebundene Schlüpfen von *Pseudomittia arenaria*. *Z. Vergleich. Physiol.* **37**, 338-354.

Remmert, H. (1955b). Tageszeitlich gebundenes Schlüpfen bei *Pseudomittia arenaria*. *Naturwissenschaften* **42**, 261.

Renner, M. (1956). Ein Transozeanversuch zum Zeitsinn der Honigbiene. *Naturwissenschaften* **42**, 540.

Renner, M. (1960). The contribution of the honey bee to the study of time-sense and astronomical orientation. *Cold Spring Harbor Symp. Quant. Biol.* **25**, 361-367.

Rensing, L. (1964). Daily rhythmicity of corpus allatum and neurosecretory cells in *Drosophila melanogaster* (Meig.). *Science* **144**, 1586-1587.

Rensing, L. (1965a). Ontogenetic timing and circadian rhythms in insects. *In* "Circadian Clocks" (J. Aschoff, ed.), pp. 406-412. North-Holland Publ., Amsterdam.

Rensing, L. (1965b). Circadian rhythms in the course of ontogeny. *In* "Circadian Clocks" (J. Aschoff, ed.), pp. 399-405. North-Holland Publ., Amsterdam.

Rensing, L. (1966). Zur circadianen Rhythmik des Hormonsystems von *Drosophila*. *Z. Zellforsch.* **74**, 539.

Rensing, L., B. Thach, and V. Bruce (1965). Daily rhythms in the endocrine glands of *Drosophila* larvae. *Experientia* **21**, 103-104.

Richards, A. G. and F. Halberg (1964). Oxygen uptake rhythms in a cockroach gauged by variance spectra. *Experientia* **20**, 40.

Roberts, S. K. (1956). "Clock" controlled activity rhythms in the fruit fly. *Science* **124**, 172.

Roberts, S. K. (1960). Circadian activity rhythms in cockroaches. I. The free-running rhythm in steady state. *J. Cellular Comp. Physiol.* **55**, 99-110.

Roberts, S. K. (1962). Circadian activity rhythms in cockroaches. II. Entrainment and phase setting. *J. Cellular Comp. Physiol.* **59**, 175-186.

Roberts, S. K. (1965a). Significance of endocrines and central nervous system in circadian rhythms. *In* "Circadian Clocks" (J. Aschoff, ed.), pp. 198-213. North-Holland Publ., Amsterdam.

Roberts, S. K. (1965b). Photoreception and entrainment of cockroach activity rhythms. *Science* **148**, 958-959.

Roberts, S. K. (1966). Circadian activity rhythms in cockroaches. III. The role of endocrine and neural factors. *J. Cellular Comp. Physiol.* **67**, 473-486.

Rodionova, L. Z. (1962). Experimental regulation of the diapause of the Colorado beetle *(Leptinotarsa decemlineata* Say) by the action of physiologically active substances. *Dokl. Biol. Sci. Sect. (English Transl.)* **145**, 752-754 (transl. for Am. Inst. Biol. Sci.).

Roubaud, E. (1928). L'anhydrobiose reactivante dans le cycle evolutif de la Pyrale du mais. *Compt. Rend. Acad. Sci.* **186**, 792-793.

Ryan, R. B. (1965). Maternal influence on diapause in a parasitic insect, *Coeloides brunneri* Vier. (Hymenoptera: Braconidae) *J. Insect Physiol.* **11**, 1331-1336.

Sabrosky, C. W., I. Larson, and R. K. Nabours (1933). Experiments with light upon reproduction, growth, and diapause in grouse locusts. *Trans. Kansas Acad. Sci.* **36**, 298-300.

Sakai, T. and S. Masaki (1965). Photoperiod as a factor causing seasonal forms in *Lycaena Phlaeas daimio* Seitz (Lepidoptera: Lycaenidae). *Kontyu (Entomology)*, **33**, 275-283.

Salt, R. W. (1961). Principles of insect cold-hardiness. *Ann. Rev. Entomol.* **6**, 55-74.

Saringer, G. (1966). Effect of photoperiod and temperature on the diapause of *Athalia glabricollis* Thomson. *Acta Phytopathol.* **1**, 139-144.

Saunders, D. S. (1962). The effect of age of the female *Nasonia vitripennis* (Walker) (Hymenoptera, Pteromalidae) on the incidence of larval diapause. *J. Insect Physiol.* **8**, 309-318.

Saunders, D. S. (1965a). Larval diapause of maternal origin: Induction of diapause in *Nasonia vitripennis* (Walk.). *J. Exptl. Biol.* **42**, 495-508.

Saunders, D. S. (1965b). Larval diapause induced by a maternally operating photoperiod. *Nature* **206**, 739-740.

Saunders, D. S. (1966a). Larval diapause of maternal origin. II. The effect of photoperiod and temperature on *Nasonia vitripennis*. *J. Insect Physiol.* **12**, 569-581.

Saunders, D. S. (1966b). Larval diapause of maternal origin. III. The effect of host shortage on *Nasonia vitripennis*. *J. Insect Physiol.* **12**, 899-908.

Schaller, F. (1965). Action de la photopériode croissante sur les larves en diapause d'*Aeschna cyanea* Mull. maintenues à basse température. *Compt. Rend. Soc. Biol.* **159**, 846-849.

Scharrer, E. and B. Scharrer (1963). "Neuroendocrinology." Columbia Univ. Press, New York.

Schechter, M. S., S. R. Dutky, and W. N. Sullivan (1963). Recording circadian rhythms of the cockroach with a capacity-sensing device. *J. Econ. Entomol.* **56**, 76-79.

Scheving, L. E. and J. J. Chiakulas (1962). Effect of hypophysectomy on the 24-hour mitotic rhythm of corneal epithelium in urodele larvae. *J. Exptl. Zool.* **149**, 39-43.

Schneider, F. (1950). Die Entwicklung des Syrphidenparasiten *Diplazon fissorius* Grav. *Mitt. Schweiz. Entomol. Ges.* **23**, 155-194.

Schneiderman, H. A. and L. I. Gilbert (1959). The chemistry and physiology of insect growth hormones. *In* "Cell, Organism, and Milieu" (D. Rudnick, ed.), pp. 157-187. Ronald Press, New York.

Schneiderman, H. A. and L. I. Gilbert (1964). Control of growth and development in insects. *Science* **143**, 325-333.

Schneiderman, H. A. and C. M. Williams (1953). The physiology of insect diapause. VII. The respiratory metabolism of the cecropia silkworm during diapause and development. *Biol. Bull.* **105**, 320-324.

Schoonhoven, L. M. (1963). Spontaneous electrical activity in the brains of diapausing insects. *Science* **141**, 173-174.

Schroder, D. (1957). Über die Gewebsatmung des Kartoffelkäfers *Leptinotarsa decemlineata* Say in der Winterruhe und Wachzustand. *J. Insect Physiol.* **1**, 131-142.

Scott, W. N. (1936). An experimental analysis of the factors governing the hour of emergence of adult insects from their pupae. *Trans. Roy. Entomol. Soc., London* **85**, 303-329.

Serfaty, A. (1945). Caractere du rhythme nycthemeral des larves d'Aeschnes. *Bull. Museum Hist. Nat. Paris* **17**, 176.

Shakhbazov, V. G. (1961). The reaction to the length of daylight and the light receptor of the pupa of the Chinese oak silkworm, *Antheraea pernyi* G. *Dokl. Akad. Nauk. SSSR* **140**, 944-946 (transl. for Am. Inst. Biol. Sci.).

Shel'deshova, G. G. (1962). The importance of day length in determining the number of generations and diapause in the apple fruit moth, *Laspeyresia pomonella* L. *Dokl. Akad. Nauk SSSR Biol. Sci. Sect.* **147**, 1287-1289 (transl. for Am. Inst. Biol. Sci.).

Shorey, H. H. (1964). Sex pheromones of noctuid moths. II. Mating behavior of *Trichoplusia ni* with special reference to the role of the sex pheromone. *Ann. Entomol. Soc. Am.* **57**, 371-377.

Shorey, H. H. (1966). The biology of *Trichoplusia ni* (Lepidoptera, Noctuidae). IV. Environmental control of mating. *Ann. Entomol. Soc. Am.* **59**, 502-506.

Shorey, H. H. and L. K. Gaston (1965). Sex pheromones of noctuid moths. V. Circadian rhythm of pheromone-responsiveness in males of *Autographa californica. Heliothis virescens, Spodoptera exigua*, and *Trichoplusia ni. Ann. Entomol. Soc. Am.* **58**, 597-600.

261

Shull, A. F. (1926). Life cycle in aphids affected by duration of light. *Anat. Record* **34**, 168-169.

Shull, A. F. (1928). Duration of light and the wings of the aphid *Macrosiphum solanifolii. Arch. Entwicklungsmech. Organ.* **113**, 210-239.

Shull, A. F. (1929). The effect of intensity and duration of light and of duration of darkness, partly modified by temperature, upon wing production in aphids. *Arch. Entwicklungsmech. Organ.* **115**, 825-851.

Shull, A. F. (1930). Control of gamic and parthenogenetic reproduction in winged aphids by temperature and light. *Z. Induktive Abstammungs-Vererbungslehr,* **55**, 108-126.

Shull, A. F. (1932). An internal but non-genetic character affecting wing production in response to light in an aphid. *Am. Naturalist* **66**, 180-183.

Shull, A. F. (1938). Time of determination and time of differentiation of aphid wings. *Am. Naturalist* **72**, 170-179.

Shull, A. F. (1942). The mechanism through which light and heat influence genetic factors for wing development in aphids. *J. Exptl. Zool.* **89**, 183-195.

Siew, Y. C. (1965a). The endocrine control of adult reproductive diapause in the chrysomelid beetle, *Galeruca tanaceti* (L.). I. *J. Insect Physiol.* **11**, 1-10.

Siew, Y. C. (1965b). The endocrine control of adult reproductive diapause in the chrysomelid beetle *Galeruca tanaceti* (L.). II. *J. Insect Physiol.* **11**, 463-479.

Siew, Y. C. (1965c). The endocrine control of adult reproductive diapause in the chrysomelid beetle *Galeruca tanaceti.* (L.). III. *J. Insect Physiol.* **11**, 973-981.

Slifer, E. H. (1946). The effects of xylol and other solvents on diapause in the grasshopper egg; together with a possible explanation for the action of these agents. *J. Exptl. Zool.* **102**, 333-356.

Smith, O. J. and R. L. Langston (1953). Continuous laboratory propagation of western grape leaf skeletonizer and parasites by prevention of diapause. *J. Econ. Entomol.* **46**, 477-484.

Sparks, A. N. (1966). A microchamber for replicating photophases in diapause studies with the European corn borer. *J. Econ. Entomol.* **59**, 492-493.

Sparks, A. N., T. A. Brindley, and N. D. Penny (1966a). Laboratory and field studies of F1 progenies from reciprocal matings of biotypes of the European corn borer. *J. Econ. Entomol.* **59**, 915-921.

Sparks, A. N., H. C. Chiang, A. J. Keaster, M. L. Fairchild, and T. A. Brindley (1966b). Field studies of European corn borer biotypes in the midwest. *J. Econ. Entomol.* **59**, 922-928.

Squire, F. A. (1939). Observations on the larval diapause of the pink bollworm, *Platyedra gossypiella. Bull. Entomol. Res.* **30**, 475-481.

Stross, R. G. and J. C. Hill. (1965). Diapause induction in *Daphnia* requires two stimuli. *Science* **150**, 1462-1464.

Sullivan, C. R. and D. R. Wallace (1965). Photoperiodism in the development of the European pine sawfly. *Neodiprion sertifer* (Geoff.) *Can. J. Zool.* **43**, 233-245.

Sweeney, B. M. (1965). Do cells have clocks? *Discovery* **26**, 34 *et seq.*

Sweeney, B. M. and J. W. Hastings (1957). Characteristics of the diurnal rhythm of luminescence in *Gonyaulax polyedra. J. Cellular Comp. Physiol.* **49**, 115-128.

Sweeney, B. M. and J. W. Hastings (1960). Effects of temperature upon diurnal rhythms. *Cold Spring Harbor Symp. Quant. Biol.* **25**, 87-103.

Taber, S. (1964). Factors influencing the circadian flight rhythm of drone honey bees. *Ann. Entomol. Soc. Am.* **57**, 769-775.

Takahashi, S. and R. F. Harwood (1964). Glycogen levels of adult *Culex tarsalis* in response to photoperiod. *Ann. Entomol. Soc. Am.* **57**, 621-623.

Takami, T. (1958). *In vitro* cultures of embryos of the silkworm, *Bombyx mori* L. 1. Culture in silkworm extract with special reference to some characteristics of the diapausing egg. *J. Exptl. Biol.* **35**, 286-296.

Takami, T. (1959). Induced growth of diapausing silkworm embryos *in vitro*. *Science* **130**, 98-99.

Tanaka, Y. (1950). Studies on hibernation with special reference to photoperiodicity and breeding of the Chinese Tussar silkworm. II. *Nippon Sanshigaku Zasshi (J. Sericult. Sci. Japan)* **19**, 429-446.

Tanaka, Y. (1951). Studies on hibernation with special reference to photoperiodicity and breeding of the Chinese Tussar silkworm. V. *Nippon Sanshigaku Zasshi (J. Sericult. Sci. Japan)* **20**, 132.

Teesdale, C. (1955). Studies on the bionomics of *Aedes aegypti* (L.) in its natural habitats in a coastal region of Kenya. *Bull. Entomol. Res.* **46**, 711-719.

Thomsen, E. and I. Møller (1963). Influence of neurosecretory cells and of corpus allatum on intestinal protease activity in the adult *Calliphora erythrocephala* Meig *J. Exptl. Biol.* **40**, 301-321.

Tombes, A. S. (1964a). Seasonal changes in the reproductive organs of the alfalfa weevil, *Hypera postica*, in South Carolina. *Ann. Entomol. Soc. Am.* **57**, 422-426.

Tombes, A. S. (1964b). Respiratory and compositional study on the aestivating insect, *Hypera postica* (Gyll.) (Curculionidae). *J. Insect Physiol.* **10**, 997-1003.

Tombes, A. S. (1966). Aestivation (summer diapause) in *Hypera postica* (Coleoptera: Curculionidae). I. Effect of aestivation, photoperiods, and diet on total fatty acids. *Ann. Entomol. Soc. Am.* **59**, 376-380.

Toshima, A. K. Honma, and S. Masaki (1961). Factors influencing the seasonal incidence of diapause in *Carposina niponensis* Walshingham. *Nippon Oyo Dobutsu Konchu Gaku Zasshi (Japan. J. Appl. Entomol. Zool.)*, **5**, 260-269.

Tyshchenko, V. P. (1964). Bioelectric activity of the nervous system in developing and diapausing pupae of Lepidoptera. *Entomol. Rev.* **43**, 59-65 (transl. for Entomol. Soc. Am.).

Tyshchenko, V. P. and J. E. Mandelstam (1965). A study of spontaneous electrical activity and localization of cholinesterase in the nerve ganglia of *Antheraea pernyi* Guer. at different stages of metamorphosis and in pupal diapause. *J. Insect Physiol.* **11**, 1233-1239.

Tzanakakis, M. E. (1959). An ecological study of the Indian meal moth, *Plodia interpunctella* (Hubner), with emphasis on diapause. *Hilgardia* **29**, 205-246.

Ushatinskaya, R. S. (1961). Summer diapause and second wintering of Colorado beetle (*Leptinotarsa decemlineata* Say) in Transcarpathia. *Dokl. Akad. Nauk SSSR* **140**, 804-806 (transl. for Am. Inst. Biol. Sci.).

Van der Kloot, W. G. (1955). The control of neurosecretion and diapause by physiological changes in the brain of the cecropia silkworm. *Biol. Bull.* **109**, 276-294.

Van der Kloot, W. G. (1960). Neurosecretion in insects. *Ann. Rev. Entomol.* **5**, 35-52.

Vanderzant, E. S. and R. Reiser (1956). Studies of the nutrition of the pink bollworm using purified casein media. *J. Econ. Entomol.* **49**, 454-458.

van Dinther, J. B. M. (1961). The effect of precipitation on the break of diapause in the white rice borer, *Rupela albinella* (Cr.), in Surinam (South America). *Entomol. Exptl. Appl.* **4**, 35-40.

Vinogradova, Y. B. (1960). The influence of photoperiodicity on the induction of the imaginal diapause in blood-sucking mosquitoes. *In* "The Ontogeny of Insects" (I. Hrdý, ed.), pp. 257-259. Academic Press, New York.

Vinogradova, Y. B. (1962). The role of photoperiodism in the seasonal development of *Anopheles plumbeus* Steph. *Dokl. Akad. Nauk SSSR* **142**, 481-483 (transl. for Am. Inst. Biol. Sci.).

Vinogradova, Y. B. (1965). An experimental study of the factors regulating induction of imaginal diapause in the mosquito *Aedes togoi* Theob. *Entomol. Rev.* **44**, 309-315 (transl. for Entomol. Soc. Am.).

von Frisch, K. (1950). "Bees: Their Chemical Sense and Language." Cornell Univ. Press, Ithaca, New York.

Wahl, O. (1932). Neue Untersuchungen über das Zeitgedachtnis der Bienen. *Z. Vergleich. Physiol.* **16**, 529-589.

Wallace, D. R. and C. R. Sullivan (1966). Geographic variation in the photoperiodic reaction of *Neodiprion sertifer* (Geoff.). *Can. J. Zool.* **44**, 147.

Way, M. J. and B. A. Hopkins (1950). The influence of photoperiod and temperature on the induction of diapause in *Diataroxia oleracea* L. *J. Exptl. Biol.* **27**, 365-376.

Way, M. J., B. A. Hopkins, and P. M. Smith (1949). Photoperiodism and diapause in insects. *Nature* **164**, 615.

Wegorek, W. (1960). The influence of the photoperiod on the Colorado beetle (*Leptinotarsa decemlineata* Say). *In* "The Ontogeny of Insects" (I. Hrdý, ed.), pp. 231-236. Academic Press, New York.

Wellso, S. G. and P. L. Adkisson (1964). Photoperiod and moisture as factors involved in the termination of diapause in the pink bollworm, *Pectinophora gossypiella*. *Ann. Entomol. Soc. Am.* **57**, 170-173.

Wellso, S. G. and P. L. Adkisson (1966). A long-day short-day effect in the photoperiodic control of the pupal diapause of the bollworm, *Heliothis zea* (Boddie). *J. Insect Physiol.* **12**, 1455-1465.

Welsh, J. H. (1930). Diurnal rhythm of the distal pigment cells in the eyes of certain crustaceans. *Proc. Natl. Acad. Sci., U. S.* **16**, 386-395.

White, D. (1965). Changes in size of the corpus allatum in a polymorphic insect. *Nature* **208**, 807.

Wigglesworth, V. B. (1934). The physiology of ecdysis in *Rhodnius prolixus* (Hemiptera). II. Factors controlling moulting and "metamorphosis." *Quart. J. Microscop. Sci.* **77**, 191-222.

Wigglesworth, V. B. (1961). Polymorphism—a tentative hypothesis. *Symp. Roy. Entomol. Soc. London* **1**, 103-113.

Wigglesworth, V. B. (1964). The hormonal regulation of growth and reproduction in insects. *Advan. Insect Physiol.* **2**, 247-336.

Wilkins, M. B. (1965). The influence of temperature and temperature changes on biological clocks. *In* "Circadian Clocks" (J. Aschoff, ed.), pp. 146-163. North-Holland Publ., Amsterdam.

Williams, C. M. (1946). Physiology of insect diapause: The role of the brain in the production and termination of pupal dormancy in the giant silkworm, *Platysamia cecropia*. *Biol. Bull.* **90**, 234-243.

Williams, C. M. (1952). Morphogenesis and the metamorphosis of insects. *Harvey Lectures Ser.* **47**, 126-155.

Williams, C. M. and P. L. Adkisson (1964). Physiology of insect diapause. XIV. An endocrine mechanism for the photoperiodic control of pupal diapause in the oak silkworm, *Antheraea pernyi*. *Biol. Bull.* **127**, 511-524.

Williams, C. M., P. L. Adkisson, and C. Walcott (1965). Physiology of insect diapause. XV. The transmission of photoperiod signals to the brain of the oak silkworm, *Anthereae pernyi*. *Biol. Bull.* **128**, 497-507.

Williams, G. (1959). Seasonal and diurnal activity of Carabidae, with particular reference to *Nebria, Notiophilus*, and *Feronia*. *J. Animal Ecol.* **28**, 309-330.

Wilson, F. (1938). Some experiments on the influence of environment upon the forms of *Aphis chloris* Koch. *Trans. Roy. Entomol. Soc., London* **87**, 165-180.

Wohlfahrt, T. (1957). Über den Einfluss von Licht, Futterqualitat und Temperatur auf Puppenruhe und Diapause des mitteleuropaischen Segelfalters *Iphiclides podalirius*. *Tagunsber. Wandervers. Deut. Entomol., Berlin* **2**, 6-14.

Wolfson, A. (1964). Animal photoperiodism. *Photophysiology* **2**, 1-49.

Wright, J. E., K. D. Kappus, and C. E. Venard (1966). Swarming and mating behavior in laboratory colonies of *Aedes triseriatus*. *Ann. Entomol. Soc. Am.* **59**, 1110-1112.

Yamashita, O. and K. Hasegawa (1965). Studies on the mode of action of the diapause hormone in the silkworm, *Bombyx mori* L. V. Effect of diapause hormone on the carbohydrate metabolism during the adult development. *Nippon Sanshigaku Zasshi (J. Sericult. Sci. Japan).* **34**, 235-243.

Zabirov, S. M. (1961). Factors governing the seasonal development cycles of the spinach leafminer *(Pegomyia hyosciami* Panz.) and the cabbage maggot *(Hylemia brassicae* Bouche) (Diptera, Anthomyiidae). *Entomol. Rev.* **40**, 148-151 (transl. for Am. Inst. Biol. Sci.).

Author Index

Numbers in italics refer to pages on which the complete references are listed.

A

Adkisson, P. L., 90, 97, 150, 152, 155, 159, 165, 172, 175, 176, 177, 180, 190, 195, 200, 220, 234, *240, 241, 242, 244, 245, 264, 265*

Albrecht, F., 114, *240*

Alexander, N., 99, 100, 155, 157, 158, 161, 179, 181, 192, *241*

Allard, H. A., 85, 124, *240, 248*

Allen, W., 35, *210*

Anderson, G. B., 128, 186, *255*

Anderson, N. H., 54, 67, *240*

Andrewartha, H. G., 138, 139, 152, 154, 155, *240*

Ankersmit, G. W., 202, 217, 220, 228, 234, *240*

Apple, J. W., 153, 217, 231, 232, 238, *240, 242*

Arbuthnot, K. D., 233, 234, 238, *240*

Aschoff, J., 10, 26, 57, 67, 81, 101, *240*

B

Babcock, K. W., 153, 155, *240*

Baker, F. C., 151, 190, 191, *240*

Bakker, K., 47, *241*

Ball, H. J., 98, 109, *241*

Banerjee, A. C., 34, 37, *241*

Barber, G. W., 238, *241*

Barker, R. J., 173, 198, *241*

Barnum, C. P., 17, *249*

Barry, B. D., 234, *241*

Bateman, M. A., 46, 79, *241*

Bates, M., 55, *241*

Beards, G. W., 142, 152, 202, *241*

Beck, S. D., 28, 83, 84, 89, 94, 98, 99, 100, 109, 142, 144, 147, 148, 152, 153, 155, 156, 157, 158, 159, 161, 170, 173, 174, 178, 179, 181, 183, 190, 192, 193, 194, 196, 197, 217, 219, 231, 232, *240, 241, 242, 244, 245, 250, 255*

Beckel, W. E., 147, 190, 196, 238, *257*

Beling, L., 28, *242*

Bell, R. A., 152, 159, *240, 242*

Belozerov, V. N., 191, 203, *242*

Benjamin, D. M., 91, *253*

Bentley, E. W., 27, *242*

Bier, B. M., 205, *247*

Bilstad, N. M., 192, *242*

Birks, P. R., 126, *252*

Bishop, J. L., 202, 206, *249*

Bittner, J. J., 17, *249*

Blake, G. M., 162, 191, *242*

Bletchly, J. D., 41, *254*

Blickenstaff, C. C., 201, 202, 206, *243, 251*

267

Subject Index

A

Abraxas miranda
  diapause, pupal, 198
    induction, 141
    intensity of, 159
  geographical populations, 217
Acalla fimbriana, diapause, adult, 202
Acheta assimilis, rhythmic activity, 15-17, 37
Acheta commodus, diapause of
  effect of ammonium ions, 157-158
  water uptake during, 155
Acheta domesticus
  feeding activity rhythm, 28, 37
  locomotor activity rhythm, 15-16, 37
  mating activity rhythm, 37
  physiological rhythms
    hemolymph sugar, 86
    sensitivity to anesthetics, 92
Acronycta leporina
  diapause, pupal, 198
  geographical populations, 217
Acronycta megacephala
  diapause, pupal, 198
  geographical populations, 217
Acronycta psi, diapause, pupal, 198
Acronycta rumicis
  diapause, pupal, 198
    induction of, 141
      critical daylength, 144-145, 228-229
      photoperiod, role of, 163, 171
      temperature effects, 144

      thermoperiod, role of, 148
  geographical populations of, 216
    genetic factors, 235-236
    latitudinal effects, 228-229
    temperature requirements of, 230
  seasonal development, 230
Acrydium arenosum, diapause of, 139, 191, 202
Actogram, 19
Actograph, 19-21
Acyrthosiphon pisum
  diapause, embryonic, 186
  photoperiod and polymorphism, 127-128
Adelphocoris linoleatus
  diapause, embryonic 186, 189
  geographical populations, 217
Adult emergence rhythms, 41-54
  characteristics, general, 41-43
  developmental rate, relation to, 109-112
  ecological adaptations, relation to, 50-51
  endogenous circadian rhythms of, 43-46, 50-53
  methods of study, 43
  phase setting factors in, 44, 47-49
  photoperiodic entrainment, 44-49, 51-53, 68, 72-77
    growth stage sensitivity and, 46-47
    skeletal photoperiods, effect of, 74-77
  seasonal changes in, 50-51
  temperature effects, 43-44

polymorphism, 136-139
rates of growth, 108-109
imaginal, *see* Diapause, adult
induction of
dietary effects, 149-151
endogenous rhythms, role of, 178-184
hormonal functions, role of, 167-168
photoperiodic effects, 139-151
duration of phases, 169-172
gradual daylength changes, 161-163
growth stage sensitivity, 200-201
light-breaks, 172-178
light characteristics, 163-166
number of stimuli required, 197
summation effects, 160-161
types of responses, 140-142
temperature effects, 144-149
thermoperiodic effects, 144-149
intensity of, 158-160
photoperiod and thermoperiod,
effects of, 158-160
larval, 189-197
induction of
growth stage sensitivity, 194-197
photoperiodic effects, number of
stimuli required, 197
physiology of, 192-194
nymphal, *see* Diapause, larval
obligatory, 225
parental determination of, 137-138,
187-188
prepupal, 189-197
photoperiodic induction of, 189-192,
194-197
physiology of, 192-194
termination of, 193-194
pupal, 197-201
photoperiodic induction of, 200-201
physiology of, 197, 199-200
termination of, 199-200
reproductive, *see* Diapause, adult
seasonal development, relation to,
218-228
termination of
chemical factors, 157-158
photoperiodic effects, 151-161,
199-200
sensory factors, 153-154

temperature effects, 152-153, 199-200
water balance, effects of, 154-157
time relationships in, 166-184
endogenous rhythms, 178-184
interval timer, 137-138
types of, 135
Diataraxia oleracea, pupal diapause, 168, 171
Diatraea saccharalis, larval diapause, 190
Dichlorovos, rhythmic metabolism of, 90
Dieldrin, toxicity, effect of photoperiod
on, 91
Dimetilan, rhythmic metabolism of, 89-90
Dimorphism, *see* Polymorphism
2,4-Dinitrophenol, rhythmic metabolism
of, 90
ssociation, gonotrophic, *see* Diapause,
adult
sulfoton, metabolism, effect of photoperiod on, 91-92
Dolichopoda linderi, rhythmic cuticle
growth, 108
Drepanosiphum platanoides, adult diapause,
202
Drosophila spp.
adult emergence rhythm, 41, 61-62
flight activity, recording of, 20
Drosophila melanogaster
adult development, stages of, 110
photoperiodic entrainment of,
109-112
adult emergence rhythm
photoperiodic entrainment of, 47-48
rate of development, relation to,
109-112
neurosecretory cells, circadian rhythms
in, 98
prothoracic gland cells, circadian
rhythms in, 99
Drosophila persimilis
adult emergence rhythm, 47
photoperiodism and water balance,
211-212
Drosophila pseudoobscura
adult emergence rhythm,
photoperiodic entrainment, 47-49,
72-77
temperature coefficient of, 60
thermoperiodic entrainment, 78-79

photoperiod, effect of
  gradual daylength changes, 162
  light wavelengths, 164
  phase durations, 169-170
  temperature effects, 146
Growth, insect
  general physiology of, 104-107
  photoperiodic effects, 108-109
Gryllodes sigillatus, photoperiod and wing
  form, 114
Gryllus campestris
  diapause, nymphal, 191
    photoperiodic induction of, 228
  locomotor activity rhythms, 37
  photoperiod and growth rates, 228
Gynopara, 121

H

Haemotobia irritans
  diapause, pupal, 199
    photoperiodic induction of, 200
Halisidota argentata
  flight activity rhythm, 25-26
  larval feeding activity rhythm, 28-30, 38
Haltica saliceti, diapause, adult, 202
Harrisinia brillians, diapause, prepupal,
  190
Heliothis virescens
  diapause, pupal, 198
  rhythmic sex response, 35
Heliothis zea
  adult emergence rhythm, 41
  diapause, pupal, 198
    photoperiodic induction of, 200-201
    seasonal development, relation to,
      220
  metabolism of toxicants, photoperiodic
    effects, 91-92
  photoperiodic effects on wing pigments,
    113
  rhythmic sex response, 37
Heptagenia lateralis, locomotor activity
  rhythm, 36
Hormones
  diapause, 166-167, 188-189
  growth, role in, 104-107
  juvenile, role in adult diapause, 205-206

Hyalophora cecropia
  diapause, pupal, 199
    induction of, 199
    respiration during, 158
    termination of, 152, 199
5-Hydroxytryptamine, rhythmic production of, 99
Hylemya brassicae
  diapause, pupal, 199
    photoperiodic induction of, 145
      critical daylength, 145
Hylophila hongarica, see Hylophila prasinama
Hylophila prasinama
  diapause, pupal, 198
  geographical populations of, 217
  photoperiod and polymorphism, 113
Hypera postica
  diapause, adult, 202
    behavior during, 201
    juvenile hormone, role of, 206
    lipid metabolism during, 203-204
    photoperiodic induction of, 206
Hyphantria cunea, pupal diapause, 198

I

Insecticides, rhythmic metabolism of,
  89-92
Interval timer
  polymorphism, role in, 132-134
  time relationships, 166-168, 177
Iridomyrmex humilis, rhythmic mating flight
  activity, 35, 39
Ischnodemus sabuleti, nymphal diapause,
  191
Ishnura posita, photoperiod and seasonal
  development, 228
Ixodes ricinus, larval diapause, 191

J

JH, *see* Juvenile hormone
Juvenile hormone
  role in diapause, 188, 204-205
    feedback control systems, 104-105
    growth physiology, 104-107
    polymorphism, 106-107, 125-127
    reproduction, 106-107

L

M

seasonal development, relation to,
222-225
temperature, effect on, 222-223
types of, 159
geographical distribution of, 223-225
geographical populations of, 216
photoperiodism in, 222-225
seasonal development of, 222-223
Manduca sexta, diapause, pupal, 198
Mansonia aurites, feeding activity rhythms,
30-31
Mansonia fuscopennata, feeding activity
rhythms, 30-31
Megoura viciae
diapause, embryonic, 186
polymorphism, relation to, 137
photoperiod and polymorphism,
juvenile hormone, effect of, 106-107
light-breaks, effect of, 177-178
neurosecretory system, role of, 97
oviparae, determination of, 125, 128,
129-134
summation of photoperiods, 161
temperature, effects of, 144
virginoparae, determination of,
128-134
wings, determination of, 126
photoperiod receptors, 97
Melanoplus differentialis
diapause, embryonic termination of
chemicals, effects of, 157
water, effect of, 155
metabolic rhythms in, 82
Melicleptria scutosa, diapause, pupal, 198
Metatetranychus ulmi
diapause, embryonic, 186
induction of, 141
diet, effects of, 149-150
photoperiod, effects of,
daylength changes, 162
light characteristics, 164
phase durations, 170-171
temperature effects, 146
time relationships in, 168
seasonal development, relation to,
218-219
geographical populations of, 217
Methyl parathion, rhythmic metabolism
of, 90-91

Metriocnemus knabi
diapause, prepupal, 191
photoperiodic induction of, 164
photoperiodic termination of, 151
Microtendipes pedellus, adult emergence
rhythm, 50
Milliphot, definition of, 10
Monotanytarsus inopertus, adult emergence
rhythm, 50
Moonlight, *see also* Lunar periodism
activity, effect on, 31, 51-54
light intensities of, 10
photoperiodism, effects on, 10
Mosquitoes, *see also* genera and species
photoperiodism and reproduction, 214
and water conservation, 213
Musca domestica, photoperiod and
insecticide action, effect of, 91
Myzus persicae
diapause, embryonic, 186
photoperiod and polymorphism,
127-128

N

Nasonia vitripennis
diapause, prepupal, 191
photoperiodic induction of, 137-138,
195
Nemobius yezoensis
diapause, nymphal, 191
photoperiod and polymorphism, 114
Neodiprion rugifrons, diapause, prepupal,
191
Neodiprion sertifer
diapause, prepupal, 191
geographical populations of, 217
Neotenin, *see* Juvenile hormone
Neotetrum pulchellum
diapause, nymphal, 191
photoperiodic termination of, 152
Nephotettix bipunctatus, geographical
populations of, 217
Nephotettix cincticeps
diapause, nymphal, 191
photoperiodic induction of, 114
photoperiod and polymorphism, 114
Nepytia phantasmaria
flight activity rhythms, 38
larval activity rhythms, 30

283